Born in 1946, Sir John Lister-Kaye is one of Scotland's best-known naturalists and conservationists. He has lectured on wildlife and the environment on three continents and has served prominently in the RSPB, the Nature Conservancy Council, Scottish Natural Heritage and the Scottish Wildlife Trust. His Aigas Field Centre, founded in 1977, has won international acclaim for its environmental education programmes; it continues to welcome study groups from all over the world. In 2003 he was awarded an OBE for services to the Scottish environment. Sir John is a *Times* columnist and the author of six other books. He lives at Aigas with his wife and family.

The Aigas Field Centre website can be found at: www.aigas.co.uk

Song of the Rolling Earth

A HIGHLAND ODYSSEY

John Lister-Kaye

ABACUS

First published in Great Britain in 2003
as a Time Warner Original
Reprinted 2003

This edition published by Abacus in 2004
Reprinted 2006

For permission to quote from their work, or other copyright, the author gratefully
acknowledges as follows: Sir Frank Fraser Darling, *The Way I have Come* and
Wilderness and Plenty; John Gifford, *The Buildings of Scotland – Highlands and
Islands*; Elaine Franks (foreword by John Fowles), *The Undercliff*; John Prebble,
Culloden; Stephen Hawking, *A Brief History of Time*, published by Bantam Press,
used by permission of Transworld Publishers, a division of the Random House
Group Ltd; T.H. White, *The Goshawk*; Stanley Cramp and C.M. Perrins, *The
Handbook of Birds of Europe, the Middle East and North Africa*, reprinted by
permission of Oxford University Press; Rachel Carson, *A Sense of Wonder*;
Gavin Maxwell, foreword to *Ring of Bright Water*; Brian Jackman,
The Countryside in Winter.
Despite every attempt to trace authors or copyright holders, in the following
instances permissions could not be obtained: Thor Heyerdal, *The Ra Expeditions*;
Dr E.G. Neal, *The Badger*; Dr I.F. Grant, *Everyday Life on an Old Highland Farm*. In
these cases the author apologises for this omission and takes this opportunity of
thanking the copyright holders for their understanding.

A CIP catalogue record for this book
is available from the British Library.

ISBN-13: 978-0-349-11761-4
ISBN-10: 0-349-11761-6

Typeset in Century Old Style by M Rules
Printed and bound in Great Britain by
Clays Ltd, St Ives plc

Abacus
An imprint of
Little, Brown Book Group
Brettenham House
Lancaster Place
London WC2E 7EN

A member of the Hachette Livre Group of Companies

www.littlebrown.co.uk

CONTENTS

ILLUSTRATIONS

by Derek Robertson

ACKNOWLEDGEMENTS

The people I really need to thank are those many thousands of visitors to Aigas – schoolchildren and adults – over the last twenty-five years, who have attended our courses and programmes, supported our work and kept us going. Their enthusiasm and interest has been uplifting; it has inspired us, ever broadening our horizons. Without them there would have been no Field Centre, no motivation to get to know and understand this place, no tale to tell. But inevitably I have relied upon a much smaller number of friends and Aigas staff who have helped me gather my thoughts, who have corrected my inaccuracies and hauled me out of the mire whenever I got stuck. To them all I extend my deepest gratitude.

Particularly, I owe much to Andrew Matheson, who surveyed Aigas for me right back at the very beginning; to Sorrel Bentinck, who unstintingly promoted Aigas in the early years; to the late Tommy Wallace, great naturalist, mentor and friend; and the late Clodagh Mackenzie, whose love and wise counsel is sorely missed. To Peter Wortham, Rob Graham and Roland Ascroft, our first professional staff team; to Katherine Stewart, our crofting specialist and longest-serving lecturer; to Robin Noble, our able consultant; and to Billy Horne, our endlessly flexible and accommodating joiner, who, together with Dick and Hugh Bethune, have given us unstinting support at times when we could not have managed without it. To all of these I extend my warmest thanks. Since writing this book Dick Bethune has died; he went quickly and quietly, with no fuss, as in everything he did. He leaves behind him a legacy of blessed memories perpetually sparked by the presence of his handiwork – the hallmark of excellence – constantly renewing our gratitude as we go about our daily work.

For many years I have taken for granted the help and support of my family, Warwick, James, Amelia, Melanie, Emma, Hamish and Hermione. Aigas is their home and as such has been inextricably woven into our work. Their constant interest in what is happening, in who is staying here and how things are going, has been a great buttress to the Field Centre, and their regular participation at many levels, from cooking and washing dishes, fencing and felling trees, building jetties and trails, droving cattle and rescuing sheep from the loch, to piping guests in to dinner and pulling vehicles out of bogs, has been invaluable.

Throughout the writing of this book, my Field Centre colleague Jessica Seal has been my constant and dependable assistant and advisor. At the end, with great enthusiasm, Derek Robertson undertook to illustrate the book with its sensitive woodcuts and drawings. To both I am extremely grateful. Others who have helped include Alan Samson and Catherine Hill of Time Warner Books, Paul and Louise Ramsay, Martha Crewe, Magnus Magnusson, Sebastian Skeaping, Amelia Lister-Kaye and Eleo Gordon, all of whom have generously given of their wisdom and their time to read various drafts of the manuscript. Norman Gillies of Sabhal Mor Ostaig and Paul Ramsay have helped me grapple with the Gaelic language, and Robin Noble has steered my inadequate archaeology. Duncan Macdonald, Sarah Kay and Susan Luurtsema have provided invaluable support by checking out biological and scientific references. Pat and Alastair MacRae of Craigdhu and Finlay MacRae of Oldtown of Aigas helped me with MacRae family history, and Giles Foster and the late Hon. Simon Fraser with references to the Lovat Estate. Duncan Maclean and the late Helen Foucar gave me a valuable insight into the recent history of the Aigas Estate. I am very grateful to Dr Ieuan Evans of the National Institute of Health in Washington DC, for helping me grasp some of the physiological complexities of the human brain. To my daughter Hermione and my wife Lucy, who have borne the day-to-day brunt of my distraction for so long, my thanks and my love.

This book is about my home in a Highland glen and the wildness of the mountains and forests, which frame our daily lives. Yet it is far from being a conventional natural history.

A home is much more than the sum of its parts – its people, the geology, climate, the flora and fauna, however well one may come to know and understand each of those components – and it can take years to see a broader picture. In that long process one becomes a part of the place. It shapes your life and you witness it shaping the lives of those who share it with you: highly personal experiences more to do with the human spirit than with science and history. Slowly one begins to feel a sense of belonging.

I have lived at Aigas for more than twenty-five years. My four children and three stepchildren have grown up here, in and around the field studies centre that has been our home. Every day, my wife Lucy and our youngest daughter Hermione interact with our colleagues and our guests, hundreds of whom pass through our hands each year. Together we set out to explore the Highland landscape, its people and their poignant history, its wildlife and the long saga of the land itself. Our aim is to share this special place with others who care about such things; our reward is to watch it happening. To us all at Aigas, it has become a way of life.

So this book is a journey of discovery; it is an attempt to see some of the bigger picture we call home.

John Lister-Kaye
House of Aigas, January 2003

For Lucy and Hermione, both

A song of the rolling earth, and of words according,
Were you thinking that those were the words, those
    upright lines? those curves, angles, dots?
No, those are not the words, the substantial words are
    in the ground and sea,
They are in the air, they are in you.

WALT WHITMAN, 1819–92

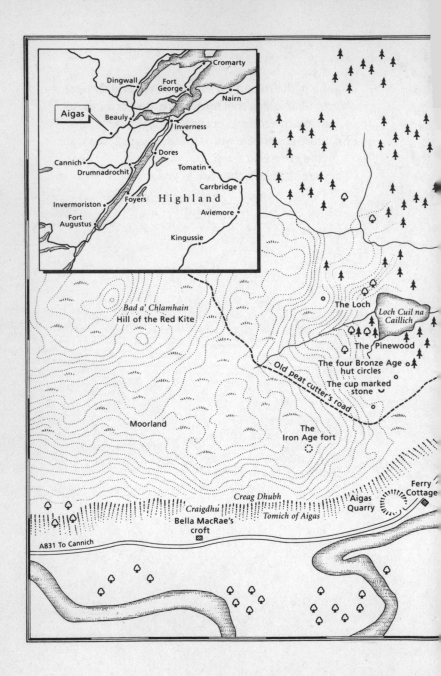

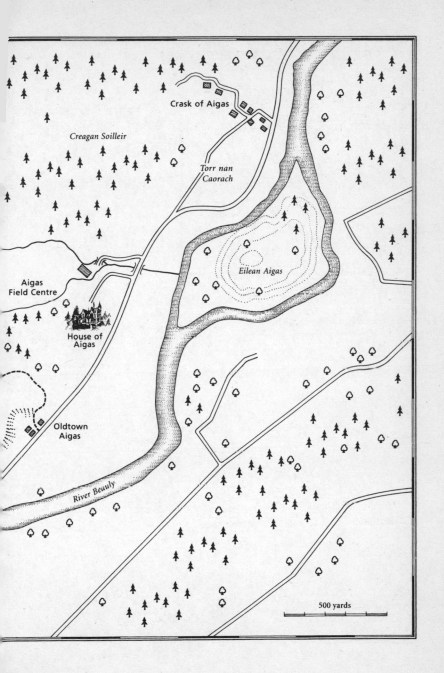

Crask of Aigas

Creagan Soilleir

Torr nan
Caorach

Eilean Aigas

Aigas
Field Centre

House of
Aigas

Oldtown
Aigas

River Beauly

500 yards

ONE

The First Butterfly

The question of all questions for mankind – the problem which underlies all others and which is more deeply interesting than any other – is the ascertainment of the place which man occupies in nature.

THOMAS HENRY HUXLEY, 1825–95

I am slumped in a small green boat on a Highland loch. It's uncomfortable – the seat board snags my back – but it's too much effort to move. Around me, above the lochside trees, mountains and moors jostle to a lost, cloud-churning horizon.

It is summer – such as summer is hereabouts. Birch fronds trail like lace to the watery sky reflected at their feet. Water lilies lap at their own table, glossy green dinner-plates that encircle me; a loitering breeze nudges the surface with the silver ruffles of a silk shawl. Gnats hang in vertical ovals, like mobiles, twenty-five to the cubic foot, nameless – they won't keep still long enough for me to identify them – dancing their peculiar rites to a tune only they can hear. Highland darter dragonflies, with bodies the colour of blood, quarter the lily maze in wing-rattling zigzags, occasionally alighting on my oars, which stick out from the rowlocks like splinted limbs. Their bulging, multifaceted orbs swivel and tilt. Predatory. Every nervy jerk is assessing opportunity. I eye them back. Whatever raw instinct is fired by my fragmented image comes to nothing. They lift off, rattling.

I am supposed to be fishing, but it's too warm. Anyway, I'm a lousy fisherman. The rod idles across my knees. My dry fly is out there on the frowning water, miming. The audience is unresponsive; but I'm never bored. Aigas never dulls. This is a great place to be.

I come up here, to the loch, only ten minutes' walk from the house, to think. The rod is really an excuse. If someone comes along and asks, 'What are you doing?' and I were to say, 'Thinking,' I know I wouldn't get any peace. But around here fishermen command respect. They bask in a distinction of their own fabrication: part mystique, a little know-how, lots of tricky, essential-looking kit, and buckets of hogwash. They catch your eye – a bit like a Rottweiler does. You hang back. You don't rush up and hug a fisherman. You watch and admire. So I take the rod along to fool the world. I come here to let thoughts float in like my fly. Then I cast them out again and see what comes. Sometimes, just every once in a while, I fool a trout, too.

In 1968 I came to live in the Highlands of Scotland. Two years later I had begun to build what was to become the first field-studies centre in this beautiful country – a place where people come to learn about the Highlands. It is beautiful for all its historical grief and contemporary contradictions, beautiful in its soft melancholy and beautiful in its perplexing cragginess. I was enchanted by its mystery and uplifted by its hills. I wanted to breathe its quickening, gulp its tangy air and roll breathless in its wide, whispering tundra – its wildness. I needed to uncover that paradoxical beauty for myself, to embrace it, and to allow myself to be engulfed by it. I wanted to belong to it.

It felt as though I was coming home, familiar and welcoming in its intoxication, but exciting and a little frightening, too, like first love. I was sifting through, picking over its steep forests and clouds and garnering its omnipresent gift of sparkling water like handfuls of gold and silver coins. I was casting about for its purest sensations as though collecting shells on a beach, marvelling and pocketing its treasures with a smile. I needed to be part of the place, to toil here for my survival like the keen-eyed kestrel, shifting from level to level of bright air, searching my way forward, splitting clean wood, breaking rock by my own hand. And I hoped to share my spoils with others. I planned to invite strangers to come and join me, to discover treasure of their own, to reveal something of themselves, as I had.

I knew some natural history, and the Highlands seemed to me to possess it in a way that was essentially different from the heavily manicured pastoral greenness of my English childhood. In the Highlands in the 1960s many people still lived side by side with nature and they were embraced by it within the normal rotation of their everyday lives, as still happens in Africa or other parts of the undeveloped world where interaction with wildlife and wild country is the norm rather than the exception. They seemed to me to be the richer for it, although I am the first to admit that back in those early, heady days of learning I had no insight beyond that of my own direct observation. Much later I was to find that things were almost never what they seemed to be. For now I was a youth in love with wildness and what I perceived to be the natural world, yet still struggling to reconcile a handful of uncomfortable, fundamental truths that had coloured my life and my vision up to that moment. All I really knew was that I was here, I wanted to stay and that I had to find a way of making that possible. But that, of course, wasn't the beginning.

I have such trouble with beginnings. I like to be able to place my finger on a particular moment when a thing starts – touch the spot – but I never can. The deeper the insight I achieve, the fewer answers I seem to own. After years of blundering about I have come to call it 'the insight conundrum'. Nature does it to me all the time. It seems that whatever I explore, whatever I select for scrutiny and study – a badger, a hermit crab, an insectivorous sundew or a wood wasp, even a brown trout – I always end up with the same problem. More questions arise than I can possibly answer. I can't seem to tie down anything. You think you know the beast or the plant, you stalk it, watch it, plot its ways, trap it on film, write it down, begin to think like it, fancy you've got its measure and – *whoops!* – up pop the unanswerable bubbles, like the marsh gas rising around me in the loch, glistening orbs of surprise loaded with the unknown, bursting unexpectedly. Where did they come from? Why now? What chemistry vented them, belching out of unmeasured depths of black ooze? Decomposing plants – yes, we all know that. But which species and for how long have they been rotting there? How deep . . .?

And what about our feelings? The emotional responses that guide our actions, colour our days. Keats's revelation that 'beauty is truth, truth beauty' rocks uneasily on the surface of this loch, like the lilies all round me. Science, in its perpetual search for truth, often seems to me to be too tightly focused, too quick to deny the spirit. In the chilly process of analysis beauty is cast aside, discarded. It is a process with which I have always been ill at ease. And all too frequently my own clumsy attempts at research have seemed to be irrelevant, leading me nowhere so that I wish I had just accepted my instincts and left it at that.

I think about Bushmen and Aborigines, the Sami or the Inuit – any native people living in direct association with their natural environment. They all manage to possess an enviable intuition, a depth of comprehension and appreciation, even pre-science, of the natural world without a scrap of data or any objective control over their observations. A private magic all their own – intuitive, individual and precious – encompassing what to us are fact, religion, art and culture, to them is just life, round and full. Perhaps, after all, the insight conundrum is a yearning, a backward glance.

In a few weeks' time a late summer moon will sink these lilies overnight, exploding their turbidity, leaving only an untidy scatter of frost-browned stems still to waterlog and sink. I have no answers. A million blind alleys of unknowledge drift me ever further away from the bank, out into darker water, away from the comfort of fishermen's yarns and the surety of knowing what's really what, where I'm headed, what I am. We like to think we're in deep, but we're really just dabbling in the marsh.

Thinking helps me accept a little, helps me abandon a few alleys, lets peace slide over me like the bulging, rolling cumuli high above, troubled and restless, but serene from this distance. The clouds become a philosophical currency with no beginning, no end. They are dependable, absorbent, forgiving. When I want them they're always there, spinning eternity, rolling on like Churchill's Mississippi, 'inexorable, irresistible, benignant'. You can give to them and they always accept. You're never alone. They thrive on diffidence: no fear of rejection there. 'Not a cloud in the sky' doesn't happen much round here. Too much ocean squeezes us. Clouds are to the Highlands as canals are to Venice. They belong here. Clouds reeling and rotating with the hills, taking and handing back: constants, ever-present. Fat, life-giving constants. Great sky-rollers crashing soundlessly ashore, thundering on to ice-shattered rocks polished smooth by the rain-wave of millions of rolling centuries. Long ago I came to the conclusion that this is one hell of a place to live.

Whereas moving to the Highlands, by any measure the wildest and grandest scenery in Britain, and determining what to do when I got here were both conscious decisions, they were not, in themselves, a beginning. Nor did it suddenly come to me one day while sitting in the bath that I wanted to run a field centre, or that I wanted to be a naturalist – or an anything, for that matter.

Nor can I honestly say at what stage in my childhood I fell in love with nature. I know only that early on something began to haul me magnetically towards a lifelong fascination with the natural world. The insight conundrum writ deep: personal.

So, to come up with a beginning and something of an answer, for myself as much as for anyone else, I have chosen the small tortoiseshell butterfly, *Aglais urticae* – the stinging nettle butterfly. This is a common little insect belonging to the order *Lepidoptera* – 'the scaly winged' (an accurate, if prosaic, classification for the wondrous riot of inspired design recurrent throughout this group of insects). By whatever accident of creation, this butterfly unwittingly infiltrated some of my earliest sequential memories.

I was in a large, ancient, rambling Warwickshire manor house with very long corridors and unused bedrooms which had been mothballed throughout the war years. Elegant rooms full of glazed cotton chintz and fine porcelain, which had witnessed centuries of upstairs–downstairs nocturnal high-jinks, were, by 1950, fusty and gloomy behind permanently pulled, faded sun-blinds; rooms loved but unfulfilled, money present but unspent. But to small tortoiseshell butterflies and to an inquisitive child they were a delight; places of apparently secure hibernation for the butterflies and of constant discovery for a small boy. Some of them were alive. Catching them in clumsy fingers crumpled the exquisite symmetry of their wings. Then I condemned them to early death by thrusting them into the frosty sunshine to see them fly. Others were clenched in winter torpor, and I prised their wings apart to reveal the kaleidoscopic treasury of colour inside, permanently damaging them in the process. Yet others were truly dead, succumbed, perhaps, to mothballs – in those days omnipresent naphthalene incense seeped insidiously from every drawer and wardrobe. These were dry and brittle, so that their wings snapped off in my fingers. Oblivious to the pathos of their plight, the very existence and ready availability of these butterflies – every room concealed half a dozen – in my childhood home aroused in me a fascination that is with me to this day. I thirsted to know more about them then, and I do so yet.

Those bungling first encounters with nature were narcotic. At night I dreamed of a world of gyrating, hovering butterflies of ever greater and more fantastic colours. Whatever alchemy the small tortoiseshell brewed inside my childhood skull stuck. I have one on the desk before me as I write, stiff and ragged in death, brought to me yesterday by my ten-year-old daughter Hermione who, for the present at least, is my co-conspirator in a shared passion. She found it behind the curtains in my study, desiccated against the window by late summer sunshine, or just one of the fallen that are thankfully allowed for by nature's habitual extravagance. If I raise it to my face and explore one scaly wing – the scales are invisible without a good lens – I no longer see an insect. I see an arc of the planet, wild, bright and sunlit, as from a porthole high in space. Simultaneously subtle and startling, the blended hues merge along the convoluted edge of a nameless continent. I see golden-orange strands dotted with dark volcanic islands and deep bays with kelp-strewn inlets and reefs fringed with henna and gold, all rimmed by occasional flashes of bright shell-sand that encircle tiny, shimmering lagoons of jay-wing blue. Beside its abdomen dark forests cascade to the orange shore, hair-rivers bleeding burnt sienna silt into the ocean's edge. When I flip it over to the underwing, the sun has gone. Night envelops the earth. The same shoreline merges and folds, but dimly etched in charcoal and sepia, lit with the strange, amber glow of an African moon. When I place it on the desk again only its immaculate symmetry hands back its name.

The daytime delight I found back then in the small tortoise-shell did not let go. At night I imagined jungles and forests through which I was led on a journey of discovery by a fearless, invisible and ownerless hand. Slowly I was hatching the notion that there was something far greater out there to be explored, some immeasurable Aladdin's cave to be discovered, mysterious and forbidden and nothing to do with the daily round of humans such as my parents. I began to view the world as a conspiracy of decorum perpetrated by adults, a world of propriety – manners and teacups and a desire to keep me clean and neat and tidy and well away from anything really interesting. They didn't seem to understand that there were secrets to expose and riddles to unravel, stones to roll back, chilling labyrinths to explore.

By the time I was ten I had poked my nose into the private lives of most things that ran, slithered, flew or grew in the English post-war countryside. Collections expanded around my bedroom in order of childish appeal: birds' eggs, moths and butterflies, bones and feathers, as well as such less appealing items as little boxes of roe deer droppings, sprouting hairy mould; owl pellets with their mysteries painstakingly picked out from the fur wad – mouse incisors, shards of bone and claw; and, my prize collected on a river bank, a pike's jaw – sinister and snapping even in cartilaginous death.

From time to time my mother remonstrated, pulling a face and saying, 'Surely you don't want *this*?' Between forefinger and thumb she held well away from her the dried husk of a great crested newt, as flat as a bookmark, carefully peeled from the road. I had to guard my treasures. What she couldn't comprehend, what was wholly beyond her genteel domestic ken, was that these shells of once-pulsating life, these fragments of truth, were the clues with which I planned to crack the riddle. They were keys to the dark tunnels down which I had begun to grope my way, the first tentative tesserae of a vast and noble mosaic, epic and inspirational, the scope of which I had barely glimpsed.

Outside, meanwhile, a menagerie of patient and long-suffering, ill-tamed wildlife consumed my every waking hour, their plaintive cries sinking with me into my private jungle at night. Mostly these were tragic creatures, injured or orphaned, rescued or donated, which came and went all too rapidly in my eager care. Weasels, badger and fox cubs, roe deer fawns, baby grey squirrels of shot parentage, road-casualty hedgehogs, wind-blown rooks, magpies filched from the nest, a one-winged raven, turtle dove squabs, tawny owlets like tennis balls, kestrels, and tanks of newts, toads, frogs, lizards, slow worms and grass snakes. I discovered the pathos of the common finale of all keepers of wild creatures – mornings of death, stark in the cage. Many would have died anyway, slowly and doubtless in great suffering, of starvation or eaten alive by predators, maggots or scavengers. I learned early that nature gives no quarter. Even now I like to fancy that my intervention, although frequently unsuccessful, achieved something nobler than just adding the stress of captivity to their woes. These were not pets. Guinea pigs, budgerigars and tortoises did not interest me in the least. What drew me to these broken shards of nature was their very wildness, the gleaming cye, the defiant hiss, the snapping jaw. Through them I was able to imagine what it might be like to be wild and free – to be a weasel hunting a wood mouse, a kestrel surfing fine air. My reputation seemed to draw them in until finally education caused my remarkably tolerant parents to call a halt. 'We must help him to grow out of all this' was an aside I overheard and which I could not comprehend. I lay awake at night, as the Bible says, 'pondering these things privily in my heart'.

The fishing has served its purpose. It's going to rain. I may as well pack it in. I begin to reel in. The eared willows rimming the loch come alive. A troop of long-tailed tits weaves tapestry into each thicket. Their thin cries are barely audible as a simpering wind flutters in the silver-green weft. I watch them shuttling from bough to bush, seeming to lead each other forward so that they progress in a jerky, undulating stream as though pulled on threads. I take up the oars to follow them. Rain spots stipple the water and ricochet from the waxen lily leaves. Clouds are thronging now, dark nimbostratuses bowed with mood, stumbling forward as if forced by a snowplough. Darkness spreads over the water like a plague. They say if you don't like the Highland weather, wait five minutes. They're right. The loch sizzles, gently frying for a moment or two. Water runs to the end of my nose. I begin to wish I'd brought a coat. A bitter eddy skirts the boat like a shiver and rattles in the willows. I can feel the nudge of it on the bows. And then it's gone. I reel in.

When I look up again backlit cumulonimbuses, jubilant with whiteness, come roaring in from the high moors, swirling wildly. They shout and jockey, shouldering up to the departing darkness, like the stags in these hills see off contenders in the rut, swamping them in power and authority. I reel in. Yellow light bursts through. Patches of brilliant cornflower blue – just enough to patch a sailor's trousers with, so they say – startle me as they diffuse across the water beside me, burnishing the lily leaves to a patina too bright to look at.

The sun is hot on my face. I screw up my eyes, still idly reeling in. Suddenly my arm jerks. The rod is almost snatched from my hand. I snatch back. Adrenaline surges at both ends of the line, muscles screaming like sirens. It is a shared truth: the trout and me. Both hearts alarming, both shocked into red alert. I am scrambling to my feet. Damn it all! Two and a half hours of fruitless casting and just when you're not trying, wallowing in neutral, mind on clouds and long-tailed tits – anywhere but on fishing. I'm all set to go home and *wham!*

Something in the tuggy trail of the fly has fired this trout to strike. Behind the inscrutable eye something snapped. In a surge of predatory reflex he has curved up to the clouds and mouthed his fate to the sky. Instantly he knows his mistake. Chitin's crunchy tang and the sweet abdominal juices of nature are replaced with pure artifice: feather, bristle, fuse wire and steel. Trout can't spit. Away he goes, reel rasping like a corncrake, line taut as a blade, and I'm struggling to balance with the tip of the rod arcing down, bucking from side to side. Oh, yes! This *is* a trout.

By another trick of fate, for a few years before I was sent off to school, I had fallen in with a countryman; a man so old that he didn't mind talking to a small boy. For fifty-nine years he had been a gamekeeper, a paid killer of all that I held dear. I first met him plucking Brussels sprouts sugared with morning frost; his leather fingers tossed them in twos and threes into a trug of leeks, just pulled. I stood watching him, not afraid to be there, just to speak first.

Bob wore his age in a way that entirely denied his youth. It seemed to me that there could never have been a spring in his step, never a skip or a jump, no flush of excitement warming that ancient, grizzled pallor. Slow and stoical, he was serving out his days as a gardener. A lifetime of wandering the woods on his own had left Bob at odds with his fellow men. If he had ever smiled he had long forgotten the trick. In its place was a grimaced gesture, a token showing of tar-stained teeth; a scowl which belied the kindness he showed to Snap, his arthritic mongrel, and to me. He had an old black bicycle with a wicker basket at the front where Snap sat tied by a length of binder twine, and always a thick hessian sack neatly folded over the crossbar. For weeks I wondered what the sack was for. One day I found him sitting under a thorn hedge in the pouring rain. The sack was over his shoulders, a corner held up to shelter the dog under his arm. His pipe down-turned, he told me: 'Why d' y' think, lad? To keep off the bloody rain!'

He smelled of tobacco and leaf-mould, earth-rich and friendly, the same as the potting shed where he sat drinking sweet tea from an enamel mug, breaking bits of his biscuits for Snap. I never saw him without his greasy tweed cap. His old tweed jacket had holes at the elbows where the lining poked through, frayed and pinstriped. His trousers were navy serge such as postmen and railway porters wore in those days; below them scratched leather gaiters were buckled on to bulky, once-black army boots with hobnails and steel heel plates that clicked on stone and cobbles – free issue to the Home Guard. His once-white flannel shirt had no collar, just a studless opening at his prominent Adam's apple over which the skin sagged in tidy, parallel terraces. His face was at once fascinating and repugnant. The outdoor life had tanned him to leather, but to a leather ill-kept and weary with abuse, like some old item of harness. His face was expressionless yet suffused with anger and madness, neither of which had ever quite surfaced. There was a double gap in his bottom teeth, just left of centre, through which his pipe protruded as though those teeth had been plucked out for the purpose. His lower eyelids fascinated me; they hung away from the hazy opacity of his eyeballs, allowing bloodshot lagoons to lie there, waiting to spill. But those eyes, dimmed now, had watched and seen and learned all down those long pipe-sucking years of manic destruction, saying little, forgetting nothing.

Bob Bryson was ripe pickings for a boy entranced by nature. From Bob I was to learn fast – and shockingly, for there was no grain of compassion left in his soul. He never hesitated to stab his fork into a twitching molehill, plucking the impaled mole into the light, swimming tragically on a prong, bright blood oozing on to black velvet like a murder in a club smoking-room. 'He'll not miss that one,' he would mutter. (I never dared ask who He was.) Or to poke out magpies' nests with a long stick so that the hatchlings, naked and reptilian, with blind, bulging eyeballs the colour of plums, snagged floppily through the thorns to the ground. Killer he was, but he was also a natural historian of great perception with none of the benefits of education or even literacy – I only once saw him write his name in a slow, looping pencil script, stopping in the middle, laboured and unsure. If killing was his trade it was so in a world of far greater abundance of wildlife and habitat than we know now. Yet he was wise enough to know that what was happening elsewhere, beyond the swing of his life's scythe, was not good. 'Look 'ere, boy,' he confided, jabbing his pipe stem at a dark, blotchy moth on a sooty tree trunk, 'this 'ere is the peppered moth, leastways it bloody should be. When I were a lad it were all silver and speckles, like its name, but then so were the oak and elm bark it sits on so that y' couldn't see the bugger. But now, because of bloody Birmingham belching smoke at us all bloody day, the bark is black and to survive the moth has to match, else some bloody bird'll come by and pick it off. Shows it's not daft! Eh, boy? What d' you think?'

What old Bob, thought by clods to be a clod, didn't know in his pipe-pointing, laconically eloquent, hessian-and-hedgerow sagacity, was that the peppered moth was already a biological phenomenon enjoying distinction. To this day it is one of the classic examples of industrial adaptation. He was not alone in giving it credit. It had been first recorded around Manchester in 1848, sporadically spreading or spontaneously occurring in other heavily carbon-polluted areas across the country. When, several years later, I met it in biology textbooks as a case study in polymorphism, I relived our sharp moments of discovery. I glowed with pride that, long before, we had discovered these things for ourselves.

Thank you, Bob; wherever you are now. Not one minute of all those hours' peering and pondering with you was wasted. 'Don't ask so many bloody daft questions, boy. Look for yourself and you'll see soon enough. There's little you can't discover biding your time and watching.' Bob has never made it to the past. He is with me now as then.

Later, other truths began to close in on me. The wide-eyed boyhood idyll was waning. The dream-jungle now held fear, pools of blackness where unimagined dangers lurked. The guiding hand was gone and loneliness descended, fog-like, chill and cloying. Something harder-edged was creeping in, unease gradually dawning: the awful genesis of an understanding of man's relentless and universal impact on wild nature. It was the beginning of an ecological awareness that, a few years earlier, far away on another continent, Aldo Leopold had paradoxically labelled 'a life of wounds'.

As I reflect upon how my early interest in nature bears down on this tale, I become increasingly aware that my school years and their values – the values I was sent there to receive – are a part of me still. The block of early years from when a child ceases simply to receive impressions without question until he or she emerges at the other end questioning virtually everything is a period of great psychological absorbency. It is not so much the knowledge one is fed that sticks – I never did manage to learn the dates of kings and queens or my nine times table – as the manner in which that knowledge is presented. I find it remarkable forty years later that I can recall in intricate detail the interiors of rooms, the clothes individuals wore, the petty rules and the singular expressions used by my peers, and yet much of the substance I was there to learn quickly evaporated. It is a signal lesson in natural history and in animal behaviour. The most vital information to retain is the way to react to testing situations; acquiring fitness for survival other than that already present in our complement of genes. In human terms, how to behave. For all the application of analysis and critical faculty and for all my professed independence of spirit I cannot block out those early imprinted values, nor can I erase their presence at the very core of my perception.

When I was sent away to a prep school to board with scores of apparently similar boys from apparently similar backgrounds I was astonished to discover that I was unusual – even abnormal. At the age of nine nobody else had a working understanding of British natural history; most were profoundly bored by it and others found it repulsive or a cause for ridicule and scorn. At thirteen I progressed to a much larger school. My life was to change entirely. Now there were hundreds of boys, of whom many seemed at first to be grown men. I had not mixed with eighteen-year-olds before. They were tall with growly voices, they shaved and all wore tweed suits with waistcoats and long trousers. Most alarming of all, some of them strode about with the air of gods in flowing black academic gowns, as, bewilderingly, did the teaching staff, some of whom looked every bit as youthful, if not more so.

As if this were not enough, the very first initiation (or was it intim-
idation?), on day one, was chapel.

In an awkward gaggle, struggling uncomfortably with our new
uniforms and stiff, separate starch collars fumblingly attached
with studs, some seventy of us new boys (Plebs, we were called)
were led to our pews allocated in 'houses'. I was in Stanton;
branded, as it were, for life, although what arbitrary process
planted me there I never discovered. Three hundred and eighty
males briskly and silently filed in and took their places around us
with military familiarity, all wearing expressions of mildly bored
sufferance; their compulsory presence accepted without any hint
of enthusiasm. We were at the front. I remember wondering if I
dared look round. A flurry of gowned and hooded masters swept
in to their pews and finally the headmaster stalked solemnly to his
place at the front. The chaplain uttered some comfortable words.
Then the organ swelled into the prelude to 'Jerusalem'.

This was baptism not just by fire, but by thunder and lightning.
Nowhere else in my fifty years on this earth have I ever been
trapped in the midst of almost four hundred either potential or
actual lusty rugger players packed tightly into a confined space all
trying to out-yell one another in the rousing words of that all-
defining hymn. It was like the whole of Cardiff Arms Park with
the Welsh twenty points ahead in the last five minutes of the
game, all crammed into a small parish church. '. . . *Bring me my
arrows of des-ire.*' What in the name of God's breakfast were they?
'*O clouds unfold!*' My whole world was unfolding, right there. Was
this a call to arms? What was coming next – a crusade? Were we
all to rush out and crush some hapless tribe, to return in triumph,
their heads on spears? Nothing in my love of England's green
and pleasant land had prepared me for this.

Chapel was to happen every day of every term, twice on
Sundays. This was the stuff of Empire; bags of nationalistic moral
roughage being rammed home so that we came to live on it.
Morning Prayer: the *Venite*, the *Te Deum*, the *Jubilate Deo* – all

word-perfect in a few weeks, navy-blue Psalters lying untouched, and then the roar of nine hundred identical leather soles and heels shuffling to sit down as a gowned god flowed to the lectern. '. . . *Here endeth the lesson.*' Oh, no, it didn't! It was not to end for another five years, by which time it was data: conditioning, given like medicine, taken religiously by us all. *Amen*.

What I did not know, and had certainly not been a considera- tion in sending me to that school, was that it lay in the midst of an eight-hundred-acre coastal National Nature Reserve. I am sure that at the age of thirteen I had no idea what such a thing was, but to my delight and astonishment I quickly found that we were released into entirely unsupervised freedom in our free time. On Saturday afternoons and evenings and all day on Sundays after chapel I was free to explore its damp, ferny woods and wild, lonely headlands.

The Axmouth–Lyme Regis Landslip on the south Devon coast is one of the most remarkable geological phenomena in Britain. In his exhaustive tome *A Textbook of Geology*, published in 1882, that irrepressible Victorian Sir Archibald Geikie FRS, whose stark evi- dence appears later in my Highland story, records the Landslip:

> In the year 1839, after a season of wet weather, a mass of chalk . . . slipped over a bed of clay into the sea, leaving a rent three quarters of a mile long, 150 feet deep and 240 feet wide. The shifted mass, bearing with it houses, roads and fields, was cracked, broken and tilted in various directions.

That Christmas Eve at around midnight a vast chunk of clifftop farmland broke free and slid quietly and gently towards the sea, coming to rest as an islet known as Goat Island, separated from the new chalk cliff by a deep chasm. A whole southern English estate had effectively parted company with the world of agriculture and human influence and slipped away in the night to do its own thing. It was a geological splinter group. A scion of prehistoric England, breaking free. Part of the slipped land comprised wheat fields, already sown. The following summer they were harvested by hand in front of crowds of, some say, ten thousand onlookers. It became a great Victorian spectacle drawing tourists from all over Britain and a Mecca for fossil enthusiasts who crawled over the ammonite-decorated lias beds and chipped gleaming sharks' teeth out of virgin chalk terraces.

Slowly, as tourist interest in the land receded and it was abandoned because of its inaccessibility, nature reasserted its authority. Dominant ash woods began to cover the lost fields and exposed rocks and soils. A riot of undergrowth and wildlife invaded its cracks and fissures. It scrolled back ten thousand years, sloughing off the now-forgotten relics of man's activities. The cottages fell to rubble and disappeared beneath nettles and fireweed. Bramble jungles closed over the stranded farm tracks and the wheat fields sprouted unkempt crops of their own. It went gloriously wild – for a hundred and twenty years nature romped unimpeded across its abandoned terraces.

It was into this extraordinary Robinson Crusoe wilderness that I strode, wide-eyed, flushed with excitement, in 1959. In Elaine Franks's exquisitely illustrated sketchbook *The Undercliff* (1989), a moving foreword by John Fowles precisely mirrors my own experience:

> on a fine summer's day the Undercliff is . . . a triumphant denial of contemporary reality, an apparently sub-tropical paradise . . . not a roof to be seen, not a road, not a sign of man. It looks almost as the world might have been if man had not evolved, so pure, so unspoilt, so untouched it is scarcely credible, so unaccustomed that at times its solitudes may feel faintly eerie.

For five unfettered years I was to be given the run of this remarkable woodland. I was eventually to depart that place with the

Greek alphabet more or less intact but persistently in the wrong order, with mathematics a wholly impregnable fortress, and with a well-honed facility to duck and weave to the ruthless jungle-lore of a boys' public school.

In their beneficent wisdom my parents could not have chosen a school more appropriately suited to a child of the backwoods. That they had no idea the Landslip existed, nor of its potential relevance to their son, smacks of fate. What they could never have guessed and almost certainly did not want was that it would finally concrete in place a passion for nature that was already strong. Sometimes these things just happen. As Bob was always telling me, 'That's the way of it, lad, and there's nowt y' can do about it.'

My inheritance was not propitious. My father was an engineer busy expanding a quarrying empire, my grandfather the co-founder of a multinational cement manufacturing company and my family heritage throughout the eighteenth and nineteenth centuries was one of mining the West Yorkshire coalfield. Industry's messy trail ran thickly in my blood. If I am guilty of fighting away from it, it was not premeditated. As a young adult I accepted family inducements and pitched in – euphemistically labelled a 'management trainee'. To gain experience I was sent to Swansea, or rather to work in Port Talbot on the South Wales coast: steel town. One did not live in Port Talbot, one lived in Swansea, in sight of, but set apart from, the mess.

Sir Henry Bessemer (1813–98) was the grand old man of steel smelting (although the invention of the Bessemer process was not his – it had been worked out in the USA a decade before it was introduced to Britain in 1856), but he was *not* an environmentalist. No such thing existed throughout the heady century and a half of British industrial expansion. Environmental considerations were not included in life's equation. It was of no concern at all that the system for producing low-carbon steel by using coke as the reducing agent and blasting it with oxygen was pure poison to the atmosphere. The sea was big and the sky was bigger. 'Moab is my washpot and out over Edom do I cast my shoes' was what we had all been taught. Rivers and streams were simply drains for the disposal of any waste.

From my bedroom in Swansea, safely tucked away on the other side of Swansea Bay, the broad night sky flickered with vermilion fire as the blast furnaces erupted their toxic oxides into the atmosphere. Every day when the coke ovens opened and spewed their molten contents to be doused with cooling water, vast steam clouds billowed upwards, laced with their invisible cocktail of sulphur and nitrogen. For miles around Port Talbot the skeletons of trees groped at the poisoned sky: 'bare ruined choirs where late the sweet bird sang'. Margam Marshes, the salt marsh that surrounded Europe's largest steel hot mill, had once been one of the great wetlands of Britain. For thousands of years Margam had been a marshalling ground for tens of thousands of wildfowl and wading birds – ducks, geese, dunlin, curlew, snipe and many more – for breeding, feeding, dabbling, diving, roosting, moulting, displaying and for haggling, whistling, piping and crying the rare and singular music of wild mudflats and marshes. For overwintering it was a natural haven of tidal runs and cuts, salt marsh and brackish ponds, rushes, sedges, *salicornia* and *zostera* grass beds and invertebrate-rich ooze stretching as far as the eye could see. 'The sea is his and he made it: and his hands prepared the dry land.'

When I arrived in the mid-sixties all I found was ochre scum on stagnant pools stretching for miles, rank, muddy and senile, right out to the Bristol Channel. Nothing moved. No insects hummed in the dead straw-like rushes, even sparrows and starlings kept well clear of the spreading murk. Solitary carrion crows hurried across an empty sky. It rankled. It was 'bloody Birmingham belching bloody smoke' all over again, but on a scale the like of which neither Bob nor I had ever dreamed. Happily, Bob would never know.

The task was interesting, the company often stimulating, but the spirit was choking. I was eclipsed by industry's stark images, its armour of unreasoned priority over every other consideration, its single-minded despoliation. It was like an act of war, waged ceaselessly, day after day, decade upon decade, against entirely benign forces of nature of which I had come to see myself as an inseparable part. I was not experiencing the present. As awful awareness passed over me like the rank clouds of sulphur dioxide above, I began to see that I had arrived in an inevitable future. The process was unstoppable: progress equals profit equals industry equals pollution, so help me God. This is what Bob had glimpsed and I had been too young to understand. Lifeless Margam and the yellow scum were where we were all heading. For the first time I think I began to understand the ways of the white man.

This is some fish. I have played him for ten minutes now. He has hauled me clear of the lilies, towed the boat out into open water. But there's no sight of him yet, just a line slicing the water like an incision. Now closer, then panicking and ripping away again towards the deepest hollow of the loch, perhaps where he will have harboured below the long winter ice, a safe sepulchral darkness lurking in his memory like a familiar church.

The rush is over. I am steady again. I begin to feel sorry for him. The challenge now is to get him into the boat without harming him and to set him free. I'm a hopeless predator as well as a lousy fisherman. It isn't that I *can't* kill, simply that I don't want to any more. I did once, aplenty, and never found it a contradiction to my love of nature, but gradually the fervour waned, like colour seeping out of an old photograph. You get too close; think too deep. There are predators enough out there, thinking and unthinking. Nature doesn't need me any more. I can be excused. I'm better with clouds.

He tires now and I can reel in again, gently, so that I don't panic him. He comes easily and I rest him as he approaches the boat. I can see his mouth breaking the surface, agape, as if he's gulping air, although he's probably just easing the strain on his aching jaw. I lower the net into the water – gently, gently . . . slowly . . . mustn't splash – and tease the rod tip over towards the submerged net. I can see him now, on his side, exhausted and bewildered. Then he rallies. He arcs downward out of sight again, line snarling out. I let him go. It won't be for long. He can't fight the constant tug of the line tipping him skyward. I have stolen his neutral buoyancy. He's like a ship now, bows up, always heading back to the surface, away from his friendly deeps. Here he comes again, slower this time. He's near the end. I can see his eye-bead, fixed and glassy, and the olive sheen of his back – and he's in. Without knowing it he has swum over the landing net gripped in my left hand and he's mine. He surges again, flicking wildly in mid-air, but it's too late. First his buoyancy and now his leverage, both gone.

On the bottom of the boat he flaps and gapes for a second or two before I grasp him firmly and twist the barb from his upper jaw. Luckily it hasn't torn. He is undamaged. The puncture will close as quickly as a snag on your finger. I lie him on one hand, praying he won't flip again. I pick the nylon mesh away from his two dorsal and three ventral fins and then a pectoral on either side, always the last to free. The boat bows to the water as I lean over. He'll be fine, although the incident is twice logged. He is a wiser fish, the harder to take again, and one I shall not forget. I take a last look, sliding him into the loch with both hands and holding him steady as he readjusts his swim bladder and reassembles his cold, fishy wits. He is beautiful, plain lovely, about three and a half pounds. Not huge, but good and chunky, living treasure, as satisfying as a cash reward – a fish to be proud of. I'm reluctant to part with him just yet. I eye him like a brain scanner, grasping the moment and sealing him in. I'm gem-struck. This muscular thong of slippery genes I am holding is three hundred and fifty million years old. This fish has swum to my loch all the way from the Devonian, two hundred million years before the first dinosaurs set a ponderous reptilian foot ashore. This fish is old, old, old. God rewards success with neglect. Trout have been trout for most of that time because they are so damnably good at being trout. The same DNA pulling my image into that dark pool of an eye, the loch within a loch, got caught, speared or netted,

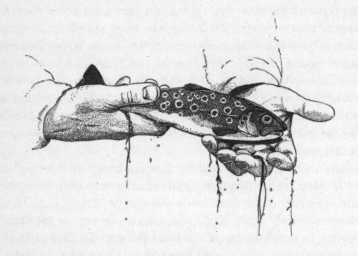

was held and eaten by Australopithecus, Neanderthal and Cro-Magnon fishers in their time. He is a gaping, flexing, quivering triumph of evolution. A prize for any man. *Salmonids*, his family, only got to be where they are by being experts, exquisitely honed to the finest tolerances for survival. I feast my eyes over his glossy side and full, curving belly. He is an orange pip, my trout, ergonomically designed to shoot forward just as the pip does, squeezed between your fingers. This means he can lie in a current and the forces of the stream hold him static with minimal energy spent. His fins and his tail keep him right. They are his steerage, trim and weave. His tail, as tall at the tip as his body depth, is the power. The whole ventral musculature is laid down in the vertical plane to charge that tail with extravagant flip. But his art lies as much in his colour as his unthinking hydrodynamics. He is, after all, a predator too, not just of flies on the surface, but of just about every swimming and floating organism, animal or vegetable, which happens across his vision – including his own small fry. Cannibal. (Ferox is the word fishermen use to describe big old cannibal trout, snag-toothed and much bigger than this one.) Nature gives no quarter. If tiny trout fry are foolish enough to venture away from cover, out of the weed and lilies, to expose themselves to the lurking dangers of the deeper water, they will be taken.

His back is dark olive, as dark as my khaki shirt, but with an underglow of amber and as smooth as a bottle. From above he is a slip of shadow, a quivering stick, a wave of slender weed. But on his flanks he wears an array of finery irregularly sprinkled on in stipples and stabs of colour stolen from a Seurat canvas. As his slippery skin warps around the orange-pip curvature of his flanks, so it diffuses quickly to the patina of old silver pitted along his whole length with spots of red as striking as a robin's breast, or marsh-marigold ochre, gin-bottle green and tropical aquamarine. His eye is a golden ring with a bead of jet set darkly and knowingly at its absorbent, unblinking core. Does it ever sleep, I wonder, that lidless eye? And what about mid-winter, in the numbing cold trapped far below a lid of ice ten inches thick? Is it still watching in torpor, with that saturnine, limpid stare? It's the insight conundrum again. The insides of his gills flare the colour of rowan berries.

My fingers sense a quickening in the soft of his belly and before I know it, he is gone. A ripple of gentle power rings the surface as the tip of his tail glides slowly, almost disbelievingly, down and away. Leverage and buoyancy fully restored. He is wild and free.

TWO

The Torrey Canyon

A selfish and blind preoccupation with material interests
has caused us to reduce this cosmos, so marvellous to him
with eyes to see it, to a hard, matter-of-fact place.

ABBÉ DAVID, 1826–1900

At 2.30 a.m. on Saturday, 18 March 1967 fifty-nine-year-old Captain
Pastrengo Rugiati turned in for bed. His ship was making good
time across the Bay of Biscay in weather that was uncomfortable
but not threatening. He scribbled a message to his chief officer,
Silvano Bonfiglia, to call him when the Scilly Isles came into radar
range. He slept soundly.

His ship was called the *Torrey Canyon*, laden with one hundred
and twenty thousand tons of crude oil from Mena al Ahmadi in
the Persian Gulf, bound for the BP refinery at Milford Haven on
the Pembrokeshire coast. She was one of the largest ships in the

world, only sixty feet shorter than the great liner *Queen Elizabeth*, and one of a new breed of super-tanker whose capacity had been almost doubled in size by the insertion of a new middle section in Japan only two years before.

At 5 a.m. Bonfiglia turned on the scanner. The Scillies came into range at 6.30 a.m., about twenty-five miles ahead on the port bow. He thought they should pass the islands to the west, on the seaward side, so he altered course placing them dead ahead. It was not his job to take major navigational decisions, so he telephoned the captain's cabin and reported the position. To Bonfiglia's surprise Captain Rugiati instructed him to resume the original course because he planned to pass the Scillies to the east. He did as he was told. Captain Rugiati had only once sailed inside the islands, between the Scillies and the Cornish coast, seventeen years previously and in a much smaller ship.

At 6.55 a.m. the captain appeared on the bridge. He confirmed his instructions and ordered his helmsman to steer the ship to the east. He was in a hurry to get his tanker into Milford Haven to catch the evening tide. By passing the Scillies to the east he could save half an hour. At 8.18 a.m., knowing it was too late to alter course to the west, the captain took a second decision to pass between the Scillies and their outlying, notorious Seven Stones rocks. They are clearly marked by a light-ship, which lies seven miles north-east of St Martin's Head in the Scillies and fifteen miles to the west of Land's End.

At 8.46 a.m. the duty watch on board the Seven Stones light-ship could scarcely believe his eyes. A huge ship was steaming up from the south, heading straight for the rocks. He raised the alarm, and warning rockets were fired immediately. At 8.48 a.m. the captain shouted to his helmsman to 'Come hard left'. At 8.50 a.m. she struck. The vast tanker had run aground on Seven Stones at full steam ahead, just fifteen miles west of Land's End, the toe of Cornwall.

I was thankful I didn't have to go to work that day. I stayed in bed until after nine o'clock. I was playing rugby in Llanelli that afternoon and I was in no hurry. The radio blurted inconsequentially until, at about 9.30 a.m., the music was interrupted by a news flash that a ship had gone aground off Land's End. I remember thinking how close that was out across the grey waters of the Bristol Channel. As I drove to Llanelli it was no more to me than another blustery day.

The wind, running from the north-west, freshened all day, rising to twenty-five miles an hour, gusting to gale force eight on the Beaufort scale. It was to blow itself out within the next twenty-four hours, but for the *Torrey Canyon* and her cargo of oil that was too late. She was firmly aground and badly holed; the huge slick that slid from her fractured hull was eight miles long by nightfall that Saturday. That night the radio coverage told of a major drama beginning to unfold.

On Sunday fourteen members of her crew were taken off by the St Mary's lifeboat, another nine by helicopter winch and a further nine in a courageous last-ditch attempt by the lifeboat before conditions became so hazardous that they were forced to withdraw. This left only the captain and his four principal officers on board. By Monday the storm had passed; the sea was calmer with only a moderate swell and no wind. It began to look as though the ship could be hauled off the rocks and a major disaster averted. Salvage experts and tugs assembled and there was positive talk about a successful rescue. But it was short-lived. As preparations for a big tow progressed, gas evaporating off the crude oil was building up below decks. The ship's generators had to be turned off to avoid an electrically sparked explosion. A salvage engineer went to the engine-room to make an inspection and when he opened the door it blew. The violent blast injured seven men, two were blown overboard into the sea. It ripped a hole eighteen feet square right through the three steel decks above the engine-room. The salvage engineer, although recovered from the sea, was dead. It was the beginning of the end. On Tuesday, 21 March the *Torrey Canyon* was abandoned, although the salvage saga was to run for a further eight days before she was declared a total loss. By then the action of the increasingly heavy seas and the tugs pulling at her stern had broken her in two, releasing a further thirty thousand tons of oil into the sea. At its worst, once the ship had broken into three, the slick measured thirty-five miles long by twenty miles wide – eight hundred and seventy-five square miles of oil.

It was Britain's first major oil spill. The country was ill prepared and inexperienced. The Royal Navy cleared the area of all shipping. Attempts were made to set fire to the slick offshore by bombing raids from eight RAF Buccaneer jets. Dense black smoke rose eight thousand feet into the air. To keep the fires burning, twenty-six Hunter fighter jets roared in, two at a time, dumping their under-wing fuel tanks containing a hundred gallons of jet fuel on to the wreck and the slick. This was only partially successful, the fires lasting for only about four and a half hours. The next day, bombing was resumed, this time napalm. Rockets were used to open up the wreck. The bombing continued for three days. Altogether 161 1000-pound bombs, 11,000 gallons of aviation fuel, 3000 gallons of napalm and 16 rockets were dumped, loosed off or fired at the wreck. The *Torrey Canyon* had been destroyed. She finally sank from view a month later. Those tactics have never been deployed since.

By now the saga gripped the whole nation. For me, perhaps just because it was so close – or perhaps not – it was much more than a front-page drama. It felt curiously prescient in a way that nagged and persisted, like a cold coming on. I kept the radio permanently tuned, anxious not to miss a report, almost as if I were expecting to hear my name mentioned. I viewed the television coverage with chilling, tingling dismay. Nothing I had seen or heard in the news reports told me that we were facing a major environmental disaster. I just knew it. It seems obvious now, but back then we had no direct experience; such terms were not in common use.

The spillage of crude oil is a post-war problem, but by the mid-sixties, although marine pollution was being widely discussed by scientists, there had been very few major spills, and as far as the general public was concerned, it was not a big threat. We all knew about tar cropping up on beaches, but most people, if they ever thought much about it at all, passed it off as an inevitable consequence of the war years, like concrete and barbed wire, which would eventually, somehow, go away.

I was no stranger to death. Old Bob had shown me most things dead so that I came to know their anatomy intimately. Wandering along beaches, I had often found oiled bird corpses and shaken my head with complicit acceptance. Margam Marshes had hardened me, forcing me to accept that there was a price attached to progress. I enjoyed a car and the mobility which enabled me to escape up country to the hills at weekends. I had accepted that some losses were inevitable. Besides, a few individual seabirds here and there from the tens of thousands that come surface-skimming across the waves to breed every spring did not seem to be a pressing concern – losses allowed for like the small tortoiseshells and Bob's moles. But there were others more experienced who had seen the emergent dangers and were worried.

Even as the *Torrey Canyon* was heading for the rocks, the Norwegian explorer Thor Heyerdahl was constructing a reed boat in which to try for an Atlantic crossing. In *The Ra Expeditions* he does not mention the *Torrey Canyon*, but that book, published in 1969, is exceptional for its day for the public stand it makes against marine pollution. Well out in the South Atlantic, after several weeks at sea, he and his crew come across

> drifting lumps of black asphalt as far as the eye could see. The Atlantic was no longer blue but grey-green and opaque, covered with clots of oil ranging from pin-head size to the dimensions of an average sandwich. We might have been in

a squalid city port. It became clear to all of us that mankind really was in the process of polluting its most vital well-spring, our planet's indispensable filtration plant, the ocean. We must make an outcry about this to everyone who would listen. What was the good of ... fighting over social reforms ... as long as every nation allowed our common artery, the ocean, to become a common sewer for oil slush and chemical waste? Did we still cling to the medieval idea that the sea was infinite?

Yes, Thor, we did.

My love of natural history had set me up for some level of elementary awareness. When in childhood you learn to play a musical instrument, and you love it, you learn to appreciate and understand music in its component parts rather than just its compound effect, a different dimension and a very personal level of involvement – a sense of belonging. 'What *are* you doing?' my friends at school would enquire incredulously as I pored over some insect crawling across my desk, as if looking closely at insects was obscene. But it was endemic, a part of who I was: no going back, no good denying it or fighting it off. I was a hopeless case.

We had not foreseen what could or would be the wider impact if a super-tanker lost its cargo at sea, just as now we have yet to experience what man-induced global warming will bring. But back then I had no doubt. I had never been surer of anything in my life. It wasn't just in my bones, it was in the pit of my stomach; an empty trembling, a strength-sapping void. It was in the dryness of my mouth, in the stinging of my eyes. I wanted to drop what I was doing there and then, and go there, not to perform any particular function – I never imagined I could do anything to prevent it or lessen its impact. It was as though I had been told that someone dear and important to me had died – that it had happened – but that I refused to believe it until I had seen the corpse for myself, clutched the cold hand and then forced myself to face the awful truth. It was as if a hundred years of what we had done to Margam Marshes were being crammed into a few hours. It was the awfulness of the inevitable future arriving, out there, almost within sight, right now.

Land's End seemed to split the oil slick in two, its blackness threatening some of Cornwall's most famous beaches and some of her most majestic coastal scenery. At sea there were now nineteen ships employed spraying detergent on the oil. Burning it had failed and our inexperience led us to seek to disperse it by any means we could. It assumed top government priority. Prime Minister Harold Wilson, who had a holiday home in the Scilly Isles, came down to inspect the damage for himself. Troops were deployed on land and the navy at sea, and there was a huge effort from local authorities and the public. Thirty thousand gallons of detergent were being poured on to the sea every day. On Easter Sunday morning at 1.27 a.m. the first oil hit the first beach at St Just and Sennen Cove. An almost continuous tide of foul black oil was engulfing the toe of Cornwall for over sixty miles from St Ives in the north round to St Michael's Mount in the south.

The story ran and ran. The column of smoke rising from the bombed wreck was visible from my window as a dark smudge along the western horizon, obscenely beautiful, like an unmapped mountain range melting in the setting sun. I could taste its rancour on the wind, like Brasso, metallic and sour. But the national dailies and television coverage gave frustratingly inadequate information to someone who urgently needed to know fact and detail. No one seemed to be interested in the huge threat to marine life, especially the birds, so vulnerable on the surface of the sea. I wanted answers – hard numbers. Which bird species? How many of each? Nobody seemed to understand that at this moment in the year tens of thousands, possibly hundreds of thousands, of seabirds were mustering, bobbing, diving and feeding and displaying in huge rafts on the surface of the sea just to the west of us. Out there, off Cornwall, feeding on the colossal balls of sand eels in the shallow waters of the continental shelf, was their habitual collecting ground before dispersing to their breeding cliffs up and down the length of Britain. No one seemed to realise that it would be decades before this incident was over.

It isn't really surprising. In 1967 there was no such thing as an environmental correspondent. Regular staff reporters and newscasters barely seemed to know a swan from a seal and somehow always managed to get them both wrong. Desperate for a good story, some even invented birds that didn't exist. When at last the emphasis did shift, one Sunday paper was to report that penguins were dying in their thousands and another that nearly 90 per cent of the rare Macaroni bird had been wiped out. (The French for razorbill is *petit pingouin* and for puffin is *macareux moine*.) The nearest penguin was the other end of the globe and, if he meant puffins, there were mercifully few present in those waters.

I was close, only a few miles across the water. I had to go. It was important to me in a way I couldn't explain or deny. I gave up trying to discuss it with my work colleagues. Not to have gone would have shut me off, forced me to deny old Bob and shrug off all the years of prying, exploring, observing and learning as though they had never happened. I felt severed from my own origins, my alter ego pretending to colleagues that I was unconcerned, abstract and indifferent like them – that it was unfortunate, of course, but that maybe in the grand scheme of things it didn't really matter. Nothing could have been further from the truth. I was mesmerised by it, almost afraid to go and look because I knew that it was bigger than my work. In the pit of my stomach I sensed that my brief courtship with industry was over. What I would find was irresistible and it would prove to be cathartic.

Easter provided a brief holiday. I took three days' leave and drove to Cornwall. As the oil came ashore on more and more beaches and in harbours, coves and estuaries all round Cornwall, so the extent of the environmental tragedy gradually revealed itself. I drove first to the tiny, picturesque harbour of Porthleven on the south coast where I had holidayed as a child. Thick black scum swirled in and out on every wave. The harbour was massed with people running, people shouting, getting in one another's way, women in tears, old fishermen open-mouthed in disbelief. Drums of detergent were being tipped into the sea willy nilly, without any real sense of co-operation or co-ordination, turning the black crust into a frothy, cappuccino mess. I saw no dead birds, only people traumatised, frantic and helpless.

Next I drove across to St Ives Bay on the north coast. I walked among lines of soldiers who were spraying the magnificent sandy beaches between the Hayle Estuary and Godrevy Point. It seemed hopeless. Each morning was like war without declaration. The air was thick with the pungent smell of crude oil, stinging and nauseous, and with every swirl of the tide a new rim of oil curved on to the shore. Here, in the sludgy sand, I followed the sickening trails of birds that had been washed ashore and had struggled up the beach to die. Out towards the point I found large numbers of guillemots clogging the viscous rock pools, bunched in tens and twenties, alive but clearly doomed. I walked the tide line in a trance. I had never imagined the sheer numbers of guillemots, razorbills and shags, arranged by the falling tide in long, greasy furrows along mile after mile of black, treacly beach. Most were dead, but some clung on, shuffling nowhere on black reptilian wings, bills weakly gaping, and shining eyes staring helplessly out of trauma and the surreal.

The trance was short-lived. At Perranporth I found a grey seal cow heaving and moaning in mortal enteritis. A red-throated diver lay like a stained rag with ruby eyes obscured beneath vile glue. A puffin, clogged in black batter, scarcely recognisable except for the size of its normally comical bill, lay among the grim hordes of guillemots. With the toe of my boot I turned over an oyster-catcher, usually so vibrant and rowdy, now a silent black blob only discernible by its orange bill, blotched and dull, limp and tangled among the glutinous bladder-wrack. I felt angry, choked. Limpets had let go of their rocks and lay about in shallow puddles iridescent with detergent. Some remained clinging to the rock, but had shed their shells: knots of dying tissue hanging on. Mussels gaped open; scarlet sea anemones lay floppily dead on the tide line, lifeless gobs of fading colour; sea urchins were like rusting cannon balls caked in chocolate scum.

I wanted to stay and help, but I was in the way. I drove to the bird hospital run by the RSPCA at Mousehole, near Penzance, and offered to help there, but was turned away again, staying only long enough to see why. They were overwhelmed. They had no time or spare staff even to tell volunteers what to do. Birds,

mostly guillemots and razorbills, were arriving at the rate of dozens an hour. By Easter Monday they had over six hundred birds alive, and many more already dead. At the height of the seabird disaster, emergency cleaning stations had been set up at Sennen, St Ives, Mevagissey, St Keverne, Veryan, Ruan Monor, Newquay, Perranporth, Hayle, St Day and Stithians. Eventually they were to have to cope with some eight thousand birds. A far greater number than this died at sea and on the beaches, uncounted and uncollected like the dead of some ghastly medieval war. A million gallons of toxic detergent were tipped and sprayed on to the coast of Cornwall during the following two weeks, probably far more poisonous to the marine life than the oil itself. And that was only half the story.

The winds had shifted and the vast slicks of oil at sea trailing back to the still oozing wreck now drifted towards the coast of France. In the days ahead the Channel Isles and Brittany were to suffer just as badly, if not worse, decimating their seabirds and virtually wiping out their precious oyster beds. But by then I had seen enough.

On that last day I turned away from the sea and drove back over Bodmin. The stark heights of granite moorland echoed my blackening mood. I stopped on the moor and walked into the bitter wind, breathing oil-free air like a miner returning to the surface after failing to rescue his colleagues. The sun's wild wheel rolled out the low hills like black loaves. Beyond rage and indignation something was tugging me away. Some inner conditioning seemed to be challenging my presence there, hauling me back to the small tortoiseshell butterfly so that I could expiate this trauma and start again. I did not want to be a part of this. I wanted to reject it, hurl it back, tell them it was unacceptable. Where was Aladdin's cave now? What was this to do with the ascent of man? If this was progress it was sordid, shameful: a price too high. 'O Lord in thee have I trusted: let me never be confounded.'

It did the trick, though. My industrial days were done. That was it. Escape to a new role was all I wanted now: a swerve away from the abyss. Somewhere out there, over the hills and far away, lay an atonement that would assuage the collective guilt of consumer association – help me wash the blood from my hands.

THREE

The Loftier Ash

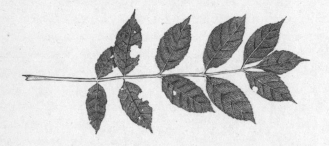

Man is not himself only, he is all that he sees;
All that flows to him from a thousand sources,
He is the land, the lift of its mountain lines,
The reach of its valleys.

MARY AUSTIN, 1868–1934,

I am sitting in my study. The ceiling is high, some twelve feet or more, with a broad, fluted cornice which draws the eye into a wide south-east facing bay of three sash and casement windows. Darkly grained pine-panelling and huge shutters frame the view out across the river valley to the forest beyond. The bay window occupies the whole of that side of the room. It begs the summer morning in from when the sun first tops the Reelig Moors until it turns laggard and begins the long slide towards what we used to call the children's mountain, Beinn a' Bha'ach Ard (pronounced *Ben of Eye-khart*), the hill of the high byre, misty and dependable above the moors. Its shadowy-blue corrie harbours mystery in summer and its winter snows are like candyfloss spun by the slanting sun.

Even on a dull day the room is bright. Light reflecting from the polished panelling laughs off its symmetrical formality. The view across the glen and the sunlight ensnared by these windows must have been important to the Victorians when they commissioned their design to the peculiar requirements of their day. Long before such arbitrary constraints as planning controls imposed themselves upon our landscape, the well-to-do had a well-practised knack of filching the best positions for grand houses, framing uplifting views for themselves and thrusting their image upon the world from the other end.

There were dwellings here long before the Victorians came, and had been just about for ever. By that I mean that once, long ago, this place was pristine, like an upland Eden before God parked Adam in its midst. It was a place where nature laid down her cryptic rites of succession after the glacier and its meltwater finally slid away down the river. Nature reclaimed this place from the ice and planted out her garden in her own unhurried way with an unfolding patchwork of bog, open field and climax forest of pine, birch and oak. Wild boar wallowed in its bogs and red deer harboured beneath its spreading shade. In its lush greens of riverine meadow wild cattle grazed and roe deer delicately pruned the yellow-flowered broom. It spread its woodland cloak high into the heather hills where brown bears plucked berries from blaeberry lawns nursing the dry clearings, and whelping she-wolves lay up in its hidden caves. Bright flushes of rank grasses and flowers striped the wet slopes and birch scrub and juniper tangle filled the high gullies. Out on the arctic snowfields of the hilltops the velvet muzzles of reindeer teased mosses from among lichen-covered stones.

How many millennia ticked by before man arrived we do not know for sure, but it could easily have been five or six. Time aplenty for nature to perfect her Eden by creating a nameless valley forest of great abundance and beauty. Nor do we know whether Middle Stone Age or Mesolithic men came here at all. Almost all Mesolithic hearths and caves have been found on the west coast of the Highlands where there is a reliable year-round supply of protein in fish, shellfish and crabs, as well as seals and birds. If they did come here, they passed through, perhaps hunting a deer or clearing a small patch of forest with fire, leaving no clues, no middens, no bone-strewn caves and, alas, no evocative artwork on smoky walls.

We do know that the next wave of human settlement pitched here about five thousand years ago, walking like Christopher Columbus into this now scarcely imaginable Xanadu. They were what we have come to call Bronze Age people. What they found they liked, and some of them stayed. It pleases me to imagine a gaggle of them, rugged and sunburned, chattering excitedly about their adventure, paddling up the river from the coast in their coracles and dugouts. When they reached the rapids at the Aigas Gorge they would have had to haul out at the Druim Falls and clamber up the steep rocky walls to see what lay ahead. If landscape impinged upon their lives at all, the view must surely have stopped them in their tracks, snatching their wind as they met head-on the rainbow hills, the tender, bluish mists and the luminous radiance of the broad, green-wooded valley with its dark, snaking river, lush meadows on either side. It was Coleridge's 'and here were forests ancient as the hills, enfolding sunny spots of greenery'. In whatever long-abandoned tongue, somebody must have said: 'What a hell of a place to live!'

Those people had a list of essential requirements for survival. The view would not have been enough for them, however uplifting. Aigas measured up and they began the long, laborious process of man-taming the land and forest.

Yet the part of the house in which I write is Victorian and the view I survey from my wide bay window is long past imagining as a primeval forest, or for that matter a settlement of Bronze Age farmers. For the Victorian builders, arriving afresh, almost as fresh as our early settlers, the site criteria changed utterly. No longer crucial were water, soil and shelter, all here in good measure. Nor was defence, or a lookout from which nervously to eye the surrounding landscape, as I am sure it had been throughout the many troubled centuries of internecine tribal feuding in these glens. Suddenly, in the nineteenth century, propped up by industrial wealth and power, appearance was everything. They wanted their building to be strikingly different from every other house in the glen.

From the road that winds up the edge of the flood plain unreliably emulating the river, the house appears to be a castle commanding the valley. But it shares nothing else with the defensive strongholds for which the Highlands of Scotland are famous. It is a carefully premeditated deception – plain trickery. It's a *trompe l'oeil* arising more from a rush of blood to the purse than from any genteel manifestation of art and sophistication. It bows before the giddy blast of an ephemeral fashion, little guessing that the moment would pass so soon; a lily gilded in perpetuity.

In his gazetteer *The Buildings of Scotland*, John Gifford describes Aigas as:

> Superbly sited on a hillside, it is an inflated neo-Jacobean villa . . . [with] a tall tower, its height increased to dotty [*sic*] proportions by a candle-snuffered corner turret; huge cannon spouts poking out of battlemented rounds add to the martial effect.

For all its huff and puff, its tower, the balustered balcony straddling the façade, its crenellations, crow-steps and elaborate ornamentation, 'dotty' is right. The result is a tangle of architectural influences swept together in a whirlwind of extravagant nineteenth-century competition, mostly to prop up the spiralling self-importance of the wealthy Victorian gentry who built it. They came and went from this place, transforming it in their own unstoppable way for only sixty-seven years from completion in 1877 until 1944 when their insubstantial dynasty fizzled out altogether. They seem to have done so without much of a thought for the future nor a care for the past.

Their legacy is now the fabric of our daily lives, but what they did and why they did it is also never far from our consciousness. Like wind-blown seed, human destiny cannot determine its own haphazard path. They would never have guessed that, contrary to design or plan, their imperialist ideals and the long consequences of their actions would become our own justification – part of our reason for being here at all. The heyday of the Highland Victorian sporting estate is past but their dramatic modification of the landscape, like a mini-glaciation, lives on.

It is only a hundred and twenty-five years since a procession of horse-drawn carts delivered to bearded and leather-aproned masons the first finely cut and fluted, meticulously numbered sandstone blocks. Only one good life and a half have elapsed since they were manhandled from their straw beds to be eased into precisely ordered position on the foundations. It is a labour barely acknowledged: scarcely a finger-snap of time in the ponderous history of this place. Yet here I sit and their unwitting bequest is now my home and my work.

I did not come to Aigas straight from those dark days of industry; far from it. I came to the Highlands chasing another, quite different dream. I had been encouraged to write by the naturalist, geographer and author Gavin Maxwell, with whom I worked for a brief spell at the very premature end of his life. He asked me to write the story of the last of his famous otters, Teko, which was to die in my care in 1969. I buried Teko on Eilean Ban, the tiny Hebridean island in the straits between the Isle of Skye and the mainland at Kyle of Lochalsh, which had been Maxwell's last home. That story became my first book, *The White Island* (the literal translation of Eilean Ban). Natural history and writing about it have been the essence of my life for forty years, the entwined themes around which my whole existence now seems to have spun. But writing, and in particular natural history writing, is about as precarious a career as one could choose. It equates with acting, but acting restricted to one refined genre, such as performing only in medieval tragedies, or an artist insisting upon woodcuts as his only medium. If I were to survive, natural history had to deliver up other harvests, other ways of swimming against the tugging tide that threatened to drag me back to industry.

The notion of a field studies centre – or initially a natural history guiding service – was not long coming. A tiny, persistent nucleus of Maxwell's readers was not content with the written page. It is an inevitability of literature that the reader is drawn to discover more. Those who write lyrically about a place, especially a place so beautiful, remote and hauntingly evocative as the west coast of the Highlands in the late 1950s, can and often do create local mini-industries around their focus. In the summers of 1970 and 1971 I hired myself out, trading under the name of Highland Wildlife Enterprises, to meet the aspirations of those few besotted enthusiasts who had written to me after Maxwell's death. The timely publication of *The White Island*, finishing the Maxwell story, fuelled this embryonic interest. By 1972 I had a viable, seasonal business about which I wrote in *The Seeing Eye*. I could tramp my beloved hills and glens all summer and retire to my lonely cottage to write all winter.

But we had done too good a job. Word spread; the next four years witnessed a dramatic expansion. A constant trickle of visitors from all over the globe was now making its way to the high, secluded valley of Guisachan, at the far west end of this glen, where I had settled and created a base. By 1976 we had outgrown that place. It was too remote, the property too small, we had an infant son and twin daughters on the way, and the opportunity for further expansion was very limited. We had to move. In the closing pages of *The Seeing Eye* I wrote:

I relived the dream of a large country house in its own grounds: a vision of space and rooms specially designed for library, laboratory and workshop, dining-room and sitting-room, in which we could house our groups in comfort and build up an atmosphere unhindered by our own living space and the restrictions of a young family.

That evening, against the setting sun, I drove down the valley to look at it ... Its turrets and towers stood out against the flaming sky in a fairy-tale silhouette of Gothic architecture. A young roe deer watched us attentively from a laurel shrubbery and swifts hawked and screamed round the tower above.

As I write, more than a year later, after a long and desperate campaign to persuade the owners to sell it before neglect took too great a toll, we have won through. The place is ours. Aigas it is called, and its pink sandstone silhouette gives little indication of the urgent work to be done.

Back in those early days the type of business venture Aigas Field Centre represented was unheard of. Most observers perceived it to be a mildly dotty distortion of normal commercial practices by a not-so-mildly dotty eccentric who had little or no idea of where the norm lay. Officials of the Highlands and Islands Development Board, the government agency established in 1969 to help the Highland region extricate itself from the backwater of dependency mentality it had become, stared back at me in uncomprehending indifference. The notion that people might pay to come and look at nature in any way other than from inside a coach or a car – the scenic-drive approach – was entirely alien to them. After a month of studying my ideas they politely wrote to decline their help and to suggest that I would do better to create a caravan park or a campsite.

Others thought I was mad. 'Why don't you get a job with the Nature Conservancy,' my father suggested benignly, 'if it is nature you are really interested in?' The whole tone of the question seemed to indicate that he still thought (or hoped) I would grow out of it. It was with ill-concealed anxiety that he eyed his son, yet never quite revealed that he really thought I was hell-bent upon ruin. By 1977 my mother was gravely ill. She accepted the inevitability of her early death with great fortitude. She allowed her romantic and artistic nature to hide any private doubts she may have had about me. Whether by then she was fully able to comprehend exactly what it was I hoped to achieve is questionable. Her faith lay in the all-forgiving premise of where there's a will there's a way, and a mother's love. She knew that I was determined, that along with her romantic nature I had also inherited her gritty resolve. For all the miles and the yawning chasm of idealism that separated the substance of our lives, I never once perceived anything but honest, open-hearted encouragement from her: that if you believe in what you are doing then that is what you must do. By the time we were properly up and running she was dead.

Contemporaries and friends would listen to my ideas and simply fail to understand what it was we were up to. 'A sort of hotel with a lecture,' we were later told someone had said. Yet others, old friends with whom we stayed, would listen enthusiastically as we outlined our future. After a while eyes would glaze over and we became aware that we had lost them somewhere along the way, passed out of their vision and into a murk too dense for them to explore, so that next day they would enquire again: 'What is it exactly you are starting up?' Or, 'A field centre, did you say? Just what is in this field that is so interesting?' Another asked ingenuously, 'Is it some sort of religious movement you're involved in?' Yet another thought we were founding an agricultural college.

There seemed to be a double block operating. The one was just *what* it was we were up to, and the second why on earth it had to be in the Highlands of Scotland. No one, after all, *lived* in the Highlands of Scotland, did they, except perhaps a few crofters?

Weren't there icebergs in Loch Ness all winter? What would we do then? We were to learn that friends and family to whom we had meticulously described our plans had wrapped them around with their own sanitised interpretation so that it came back to us like a game of Chinese whispers. 'They're starting a wildlife park up there, or a zoo or something,' or even 'a green retreat for wealthy, stressed-out city folk – all birds and flowers and that kind of thing'. The hippy flower power of the sixties was still too close. In the minds of many we were part of some sort of alternative culture, not quite drop-outs, but not a million miles from them either.

It was a problem we were to have to cope with for many years; it still exists in some quarters. It is to do with the remarkable denial by our materialist Western culture of our origins and the environment that surrounds us, from which we all glean our existence, whatever our profession. Nature is a God-given resource, plain and simple, there for man to use or abuse at his pleasure and for his exclusive profit. The concept of respecting nature, working with it instead of simply exploiting it, of learning about it, admiring it and enjoying it in any way other than as entertainment, remained deeply and powerfully alien to the vast majority of my fellow men. Even now, thirty years on, I still meet those whose facial expressions reveal a profound malaise: who still believe that jobs in the environment are not *proper* jobs. Accountants and salesmen, welders and lorry drivers are proper jobs. Those who dabble with nature are somehow fanciful, airy-fairy, even wacky; a slightly unwholesome, not altogether welcome splinter group closer to Zen Buddhism than to reality. Like Henry David Thoreau and John Muir a century before us, we were to face ridicule long before we would meet with approval. It would be decades before our friends and neighbours in Strathglass really understood what it is we do.

In this big, valley-lit room I have squandered thousands of hours at my desk, staring out at the River Beauly straggling along the strath. It glides between dark alders that crowd the banks on either side as though they are lining up to see something important go by, the water like black marble as they lean to get a better view. This room is a lookout, an eyrie. It is from here that I have scooped up the seasons, letting them slide through my fingers like sand; counted down the years and pondered the ever-shifting warp of this Highland scene. I share my days with a broad diorama of living forest, water, mountain, rock and cloud. It weaves, unpicks and weaves again its own perpetual, dizzy frieze. I watch it expand and contract to the rhythmic systole and diastole of the mountains. It wouldn't surprise me if, one day, Tolkien's great dragon, Smaug, came smoking and flaming into view from his cave high in the Affric Hills to the west. The pulsating clouds and snow squalls rampaging like Friday-night hell-raisers come funnelling through so fast that you have to dive for cover. And rain descends, sharp and angry as a cornered cat, or sometimes so brutal and all-smothering in its persistence that the cattle in the river fields turn away, heads down, eyes shut, to stand grimly sodden for whole days at a stretch. And then comes the light, spilling over the valley brim.

One of the great glories of living among hills above the 57th Parallel, north of Moscow and north of Churchill on Hudson Bay, is the benison of low-angled light. Dawn doesn't flood serenely in, as in low country or on a great plain; here it gathers behind the mountain like the clans themselves, building force and energy, a presence luminous and kinetic, waiting to happen like a war. Then it comes tipping in, molten and clean, as a lake overflows its dam. It arrives streaming, dancing, slicing, shafting, piercing, embracing, or trailing across the fields like a lapwing feigns a broken wing. All day the sun prods and fools with cloud and mountain like a child with a torch, spotlighting fragments of the frieze for fun. If I could orchestrate it, along with woodwind and strings I would need whole ranks of trumpets, cymbals and kettledrums, all mixed in. I am drawn back to it over and over again. It nags at my brain's core, barging in like a child and dragging me from my work, imploring me to stand and applaud its every whim. Now subtle as a flute, it wraps warmth and comfort around me like a lullaby; or it comes crashing down, a great cathedral organ exploding, open diapason, tumultuous and vibrant so that I am forced to the window, and held there. Later it can be tragic and yearning, like so many of the folk songs of the Gaels, echoing the historical misery this glen has known, poignant as a weeping violin.

Across my vision runs the glen road. People zoom past, sealed into their cars, coaches and vans. They are strangely apart from the view, and, for the most part I fancy, unaware of its existence or their impact upon it. They hurry by, a-throb with personal and impersonal stereos, about their business in Beauly or Inverness to the east, or Glen Affric, some twenty-five winding miles to the south-west, where, high above them in the snowy womb of the mountains, our river, the River Beauly, is born. The road is a perpetual reminder of the fundamental paradox of our life and work at Aigas. For every visitor to the field centre there are tens of thousands of others out there who have neither the time nor the inclination to ponder their creation. And yet it is their endeavour that provides the wealth and stability that allows us to exist. Like the *Torrey Canyon* bringing the oil that made the petrol that enables us all to enjoy mobility, idealism has to achieve a balance or it founders altogether.

Sometimes I think Western man strives to exist in a separate world from the real one that surrounds us. We seem to spin in a dull orbit of our own invention, denying the inspirational ellipse of our creation. Modernity forces us to live in ever-deeper isolation from our origins. We build our houses, our towns and our cities as temples of separation from our deep belongings, further and further away from the source of our being. We live a lie. It is as though there is a truth out there we are afraid of and need to hide from. I have come to think of it as a collective betrayal of something bigger than the sum of all of us. It seems as though we are ashamed of our long association with nature, hiding away and preoccupying ourselves with trivia – doilies, frippery and perpetual entertainment and fun, ever more banal.

For all its benefits, science has dumped materialism in our back yard and we have welcomed it in with arms flung wide. We are fooled by its novelty and its deceptively endless solutions; our naivety overlooks that it gives us no insight into wildness, holiness, happiness, the sacred, art, dreams, fortune, hope, love, joy, magic or the spirit. Yet, when I sit among my neighbours and friends at the back of the local kirk, heartily we sing: 'Ponder anew, at what the Almighty can do.'

It is from these windows that I see lissom otters, shiny as a twist of current, leave the river on bright June mornings long before the rowdy human world is up. They skirt the edge of the fields and scour the ditch for frogs and elvers, past us on their way up the burn to the loch. One day recently an otter was passing where the burn runs down the side of the one-acre paddock where we keep our few hens and ducks and Hermione's pony. A white farmyard duck, looking for all the world a living replica of Jemima Puddleduck, and every bit as naive, had wandered away from her friends in the paddock's muddy pond where they habitually dabble away their days, slipped (ducked) under the fence and down into the burn, which babbled seductively to her under the midday sun. I don't believe the otter was duck hunting. He must have passed the paddock dozens of times, slinking from pool to pool, unseen beneath the ferns of its shady bank, on up to the loch from which the burn issues half a mile further up the hill. I hope she never had time to realise her mistake. To the otter she was no more than a wild duck that didn't fly away – his lucky day; a duck, not sitting, but innocently rediscovering her beginnings, just doing what ducks always do in water. Just as her genetic predisposition had enticed her to the stream, so the otter's genes snapped it into lethal mode. No more duck. A few white feathers drifted downstream. Otter and duck disappeared into a drain.

From these windows I see the herons stalk the sedgy river shallows, stabbing at salmon parr as they flit downstream, and often an osprey wheels over and crashes into the flow, rising untidily to row away across the forest with a trout twisting grimly in its talons. I see the broad-winged goshawk spiralling high above his hen nesting in the tight spruces below. Spindle-legged roe deer delicately swim the river, dark noses and white-spotted chins tilting above the flow, and, stepping free from the shaken rainbow, they tiptoe ashore to the sweeter browse on this side. From here I have watched the gentle evolution of the birch woods. They are a private pageant. 'Dancing ladies,' someone said to me once. The rich plum of their winter twiggery bursts into a soft, pastel cloud when the first tiny leaves open for my birthday in May, and then slowly they darken to the universal summer stain. Later, in the cool of late October nights the chlorophyll drains away and for a few brief, exultant weeks, my view is all gold. I see the fiery red of the autumn sun creep into the wild cherries – geans, they are called here – and the brilliant silver-gilding of the aspens that are dotted about among the birches. For sheer glitz both of them

challenge the blowsy scarlet of the rowanberries, which, any day now, will bring a harlot's glamour to this luxuriant wash of August green. It is a transformation that never ceases to make me smile and shake my head in awe as the wind comes rippling across their bunched crowns like a bow wave. After the first moonlit frosts have spilled down the slope of the glacial valley wall during the night, I come into my study in the mornings and I can trace their umber trail across the bracken in the misty river fields.

It is from my armchair in the window here, too, that I have watched people come and go: Americans, Canadians, Australians, New Zealanders, Japanese and the Brits with their unmistakable Britishness flying high; discreet adults and boisterous children, and the many others who have coloured our lives for these past twenty-five years. And it is from this window seat, in part, that I have watched my own children play beneath the slanting Highland sun and the humbling shade of the old ash tree – certainly the oldest tree in our wooded grounds and older than any of the present buildings here. It is to the ash tree that I often look when things turn awry. It has stood over the waxing and waning of many human lives in this place. It's thought to be three hundred years old now, and looks to be in its prime yet. It's also a native: *Fraxinus excelsior*. Not only does it belong here, like the Highland clansmen it has known, but the eighteenth-century botanical boffins who named it were right. 'The loftier ash' is descriptive as much of its grand proportions as of its superiority over the other native trees, Scots pines, birches, alders, aspens, rowans, geans and sessile oaks of this glen. I can only stand and stare up into its whispering canopy and wonder about the joys that have passed through and the tragedy it has stoically witnessed here at its foot all down those turbulent centuries.

The first time I entered Aigas House was a discouraging overture. I knew that it was empty, and that it had been locked and deserted for several years. I knew, too, that for the previous unhappy thirty years or so it had been used by Inverness-shire County Council as an old people's home. The ravages of two world wars had left a whole generation of Highland womenfolk without husbands or sons, brothers or grandsons to care for them in old age.

The Highland glens and islands of the Gaidhealtachd were a prime recruiting ground for the crack regiments of the British Empire. In this remote and mountainous land every lad knew by the age of ten how to filch a trout from the burn, snare a rabbit and stalk a roe deer, and they possessed the unavoidable reputation of centuries of fearless clansmen. Young men and boys flocked to wear a regimental tartan. The result stands starkly among the hills in the dozens of war memorials that list the names of those who never returned. Village after village was shorn of its youth. By 1955 there was a desperate need for institutional accommodation for the lonely relics of these whole communities whose manhood and future had been mown like thistles. Aigas was empty and available. After crude conversion it was big enough to dormitory a succession of up to forty of these lonely souls. For nearly twenty years they eked out their final days here, seeking solace in smuggled whisky and the pathos of their common plight. Legislation governing the conditions of such homes closed it down in 1972. The key finally turned on this sad era and the house's uncertain future. The council official who walked away from the iron-studded oak front doors of what had once been a proud, if never elegant, country residence closed behind him a desolate shell. It had been reduced by ever-constricting council budgets and shoddy maintenance to a shabby mausoleum, dated and obsolete, inhabited only by the ghosts of sorrow. It stood gaunt and disdainful above ragged lawns and an advancing jungle of laurel and rhododendron shrubbery. That was almost the beginning of the end.

By 1972 the old Inverness-shire County Council itself was doomed. A new political bud was stirring. Regionalisation was in the air, a gathering movement to reorganise local government, expand boundaries and broaden responsibilities, sweeping up the old county councils like so many dead leaves. It arrived in April 1974 with driving sleet squalls that rattled against these plate-glass windows staring darkly out across the valley. Ownership of all county council assets was formally transferred to the brave new Rionn na Gaidhealtachd – Highland Regional Council – the local government authority for the vast and substantially empty mountain fastness of the Gaelic Highlands and Inner Hebrides.

Brave and new it may well have been, but the last thing anyone was worrying about was a decaying mansion tucked away behind rampant rhododendrons in a lonely glen. Just as there had been no maintenance money available in the dying days of the old council, so there was none now for anything so self-evidently redundant. My enquiries about it were met with prevarication and, later, irritation and bad grace when I pressed my suit. No one seemed interested, far less keen to discuss it or admit responsibility for it. I knew it was empty – one could see that from the road. I had wandered round the outside, fighting my way through thick shrubbery and across rank lawns uncut for years. Aigas House was an unwelcome entry on the new authority's books; it belonged to the past, the icon of an era now dispensed with and frowned upon. For the moment it was not only out of sight but firmly banished from mind.

Not so to a handful of opportunistic locals. There were, inevitably, pickings to be had. There was lead on the roof and miles of copper pipe inside. Ornamental urns graced the terrace steps and there were elegant Victorian pig-ironwork gates and railings. The laurels and rhododendrons seemed to conspire with these night raiders who struggled away with their weighty spoils, as they did with small boys playing in the labyrinthine tangle whose throwing arms could not resist the huge windows. The air of neglect and decay that time would eventually have achieved on its own was greatly advanced by the unwelcome energies of others.

By the time I first set foot inside, reluctantly escorted here by an official of the new regional council that had finally given in to my pestering – perhaps in the hope that having had a look I would go away – there was snow on the hall floor and an elegant drift across the foot of the stairs. The valuable lead flashings on the pyramid-shaped glass skylights had been torn free – 'lifted' is the euphemism old men mutter in this glen, shaking their heads and declaring that 'the weather was in it'. Heavy triangular panes had crashed forty feet to the hall floor and shattered into a thousand shards. Large yellow stains were spreading across the domed plaster ceiling where the sun-melted snow or the driving rain had leached into the fabric of the roof. A large patch of plaster had fallen and left the shape of Africa in exposed lath. The missing piece lay curiously intact in the snowdrift at the bottom of the stairs.

The ash tree has witnessed it all. I stand at its foot. Great roots have corrugated the ground around it with broad woody thongs undulating outwards in a circular plate of tangle and deep grip, roots that trail far across the lawns in every direction. It is solid, purposeful, locked in. Its trunk writhes with power. It is all heart. My fullest reach, both arms stretched, extends to less than a third of its circumference; an inconsequential hug leaving me in awe of its rigid grandeur. Its bark is deeply grooved with long vertical ripples of hardness like a throng of ribbed buttresses all heading upward, shoring up its might, shedding veils of green dust at my touch. Pleurococcus lurk there: colonies of unicellular lime-green algae cowering along its knuckly edges, avoiding the sun. The bark fissures draw in treecreepers: those tiny mouse-like birds that dash upwards in little jerky pulses, defying gravity to pry their impertinent bills into crannies that open and close like folding mountains. Then, giving in to the earth's pull, they flick down again, back to Start, like a game of snakes and ladders never won.

I am enthralled by this tree, rapt. Every time I stand here I shrink; it grows. I age; it shrugs off such foibles, and just goes on expanding into a thousand shaded alleys. What is ten minutes or a week when you're three hundred years old? It has more than three million leaves flickering up there. Three million solar panels arranged in five pairs and one at the tip of each set of eleven. Every single one is awake and working, churning out green power. When it needs a rest it dumps the whole lot – all three million – in the space of a day and a night. They spiral downwards, issuing their last solar gasps. They bear their final shreds of precious energy like legacies to charity, back to the earth. Last November a night of crystal stars yawned its sign. In the crisp

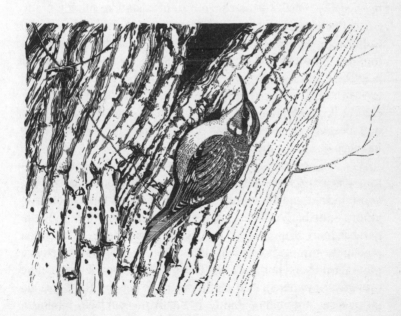

morning the whisper of streaming leaves drew in my eye from a long way off. It was like a pale green curtain rippling a hundred feet high. I ran to be in its midst. It was having an Armistice Day all of its own. I held out my arms as they fell and fell; they fell until my head and my shoulders were laden. They heaped on my upturned hands and shrouded my arms in living gravity. Still they kept coming, sheafing down in palmed fronds until I was dizzy with them. My cup runneth over. I was in a wild but soothing dream, endlessly floating downwards, my whole vision in every direction a blur of green and grace, elegant and ethereal, like a ballet performed in the vertical plane. After a while I was weight-less, floating in green pastures, the earth rising to meet each gentle wave of verdure, swallowing me up.

Once shed – glory be! – within just a few weeks, sucked under by sleepless earthworms churning out casts like muddy tooth-paste, the leaves become pure soil feeding the very roots whence they came. No wonder it can afford to daydream for six cold months. Why can't we invent something so damnably smart? I just love it. This tree is funnelling water up in a towering column, tons of it, and transpiring it invisibly into the sky. It's exhaling clouds. It runs on rain and the air you and I don't want. I breathe out, feverishly, as deep as I can. I fancy I have more carbon diox-ide deep down. It's the least I can do.

The ash is a high-rise conurbation in wood. Sixty-eight sepa-rate species of leaf-devouring insect munch around its canopy; two hundred and twenty-five epiphytic lichens have chosen to infiltrate the bark cells for a safe perch and a free ride. Only the oak has more. Dusky thorn moth caterpillars jostle multi-legged among the throng, hooked on chlorophyll, unable to stomach any other flavour, and nothing else occurs to the ash-bark beetle. If he ever goes anywhere it is to another ash tree near by. His whole life is a secret, tunnelling darkly beneath the surface, mining a labyrinth of intricacy that I only get to see when I throw an ash log on the fire. If the bark sheds in my hand, coming away in an arc

like a limpet finally letting go of its rock, on the revealed surface
of the wood I find a secret inscription engraved as finely as fili-
gree, whispering in riotous hieroglyphics over every inch of the
log.

High up there, latticing the winter sky, drinking it all summer
long, trapping sunlight deep into its soft, chartreuse maze, is a
tracery flecked with jubilant chaffinches and bickering jackdaws,
lustily singing robins and trilling titmice. If it is three hundred
years old, as John Miller, our local dendrologist, assures me it is,
then it has known three hundred generations of these residents
and heard their timeless, word-perfect syllables swelling air.
Every year robins nest somewhere within the dry-stone ha-ha
under the ash tree's long evening shadow: six peppery eggs
tucked up in moss, horsehair and somebody else's feathers; one
thousand eight hundred eggs within the web of ever-broadening
shadow; eighteen hundred specks of opportunity. Many will have
addled, most tiny stabs at life will have expired somewhere
between shell and feather, or soon after, but a vital few, the chosen
ones, year after year, made it up to the crown to bellow out grace
all over again.

But it is the human story that grips me most. It tingles my
spine and claws at my guts if I try to think it through, my hands
caressing ridges of the crinkly bark, eyes shut, struggling with
the insight conundrum, fingering the Braille backwards down
three centuries of incomprehensible grief and sorrow. Yet long
before that, long before the ash tree even germinated, not centuries but thousands of years ago men and women came and
settled here and began to shape the place we now know as Aigas.

FOUR

The Iron Age Fort

Even God cannot change the past.

AGATHON 447–401 BC

My horse can remember the sabre-toothed tiger.

His name is Grand Canyon, although that never really stuck. We know him as Barney. Big Barney. He is huge, but made like a race-horse. His parentage is thoroughbred and Irish draught, bringing forward the stature and bone from his Irish mother and disguising it within a sleek and elegant racer Stubbs would have paid to paint. He stands over eighteen hands high: liver chestnut with a finely sculpted neck and silky woollen skin as refined as his father's genes. I bought him because I had never seen a horse like him in my life. His previous owner steeplechased him with modest success. He was fast and very bold, but far too big. At twelve he was slowing up (or is it slowing down?) and that suited me fine. His owner said to me that day, 'Every horse you've had until now is a Ford. This is a Ferrari!' I drove home wondering just what I had got in the trailer.

Barney is far from ideal for this rough country. Tough and stocky Highland garrons do better, but they lack grace. I have to be careful he doesn't put his long legs into holes or bogs, but for me his height is a pure joy. I ride to see the country, to pick my way through hills and glens, over tracks and forests. I am ten feet off the ground, wafting over the heather like thistledown, although if I'm careless enough to fall off I have to find a wall or a boulder to get back into the saddle. Opening gates is theatrical: jump off, open the gate, lead him through, close the gate and then climb the hinge post until I'm standing on top of it, posing like Artemis on a plinth. He and I have been rehearsing it for ten years now so he knows the routine backwards. He steps close in so that I can swing back into the saddle from my perch. He's like that, obliging and gentle. (A rope ladder would be good, rolled up and tied on behind the saddle.) And going through forests can be testing. More than once I have been busy scouring the ground, tracking a deer, and failed to see a branch coming. I find myself perched, clinging on like a koala, and Barney looking back at my dangling boots, eyeing me as if to say, 'What's so interesting up there?'

Today we're headed uphill. There is a hump on the horizon four hundred feet above the house. It dominates, looking down over the glen and the property as though God plonked it there as an afterthought, just for that purpose. When you arrive here, rounding the corner at the gorge, it grabs the eye like a beacon up there on the skyline, standing out against the softer hues of the moors and the quilted woods. There is even the suggestion by one of the Gaelic speakers in the strath that the Aigas notch (*eigg-ais* – the notch waterfall), which we choose to believe is the river gorge, is not the gorge at all, but the bump I'm heading for. If you were coming upriver from the south-east, emerging from the gorge, it is a large lumpy outcrop on the skyline with a steep escarpment falling away to the moorland to the west. It has an almost artificial-looking face, cut and distinctly cliffy. When you get there, beneath it lies a jumble of huge boulders that have crumbled off it like sultanas from a cake. It is such an unusual feature that it unquestionably landmarks the place beneath. So the amalgam word *Aigas* (from the Gaelic *eigg-ais*, pronounced *ay-gish* by the locals and *ay-gas* by the uninitiated), the suggestion goes, could be the waterfall beneath the notch on the skyline, just as well as the notch of the gorge. Supporting evidence for this theory is the island of Eigg, one of the Small Isles in the Inner Hebrides, which derives its name from a similar escarpment. But no one knows. Such is the mystery of this craggy, sparsely peopled land that we must weave these imponderables into the fabric of our daily lives. They are embellishments like cloud shadows painting the face of the mountain – there one minute full of power and suggestion, thrusting the very rock into your day, alive with promise, and then gone again, as passing as a mood.

At the loch I can just reach the wicket gate without having to dismount. Barney turns routinely on to the forest path into the pinewood. He has done it many times. Prickly juniper bushes scrape my leather boots and tickle his flanks so that he twitches. I duck under low branches as we climb steeply up through the dark trees. I lie forward on to his neck to ease my weight off his back, allowing him to push from behind with his great shining rump. After a few minutes we emerge on to the moor and into hard sunlight, the clumps of bell heather beside the path as bright as a bishop's cassock. I ponder the forest's silent march out into the moor. Even against the prevailing wind pine seed is germinating far out among the heather so that little trees of dark bottle-green are dotted about in clumps and clusters in every direction. It heartens me to see nature at work on its own, without the help of man. It is reassembling its order after centuries of rough justice, mostly grazing and burning, which created these moors from the original climax forest human beings first walked into at Aigas some five or six thousand years ago.

I am searching for those nameless, long-lost men and women today. Archaeology is a growing interest among our adult visitors to the field centre. I need to go and look at what there is out there on the land to get my thoughts straight. You read round a subject, find the relics and ruins and inspect them on the ground, and come up with an image of what might have happened and why; but it leaves huge gaps. I like to inject some practical thinking: try to figure out what I would have done had I been around at the time. It's a purely speculative process, and one which rarely produces conclusions or even great enlightenment, but it helps. It feels good. I try to think the landscape. The bump *is* an Iron Age fort – at least, there is an incomplete ring of ancient stones on the top of it. They don't belong there geologically and you would have to have the inspiration of God to lug them all the way up there if there wasn't a good practical reason. Even the most unpractised eye can tell that someone has been messin' with the skyline. The Ordnance Survey map says *Dun* – a fortified mound – which is a good start. Local archaeology records yield scant assistance, but their mere acknowledgement, a sprinkle of symbols among waves of contours, like shells cast upon ribbed sand, quickens my imagination. That's where we're headed.

The broad south-facing moorland slopes that stretch ahead of us have probably been farmed continuously for centuries. Twenty-five years ago, when my crofter neighbour and friend Dunc MacRae died and his son Finlay took over the Oldtown of Aigas croft, the hill ground ceased to be worked except for a few sheep in summer. The pastures slowly reverted to heather. Rabbits grazed the better greens, keeping them open and free from the encroaching moor until myxomatosis arrived in the glen in the late 1970s and wiped them out. Seizing a chance, as nature always does, two leguminous shrubs blew in and took over: broom and gorse – in that order. Ever since then the oases of old pasture on the better free-draining soils have been a tangle of these two yellow-flowering, coconut-scented weeds.

Why is it that weeds are often so beautiful? On a June day under a pitiless sun the yellow pea-flower blooms are a crescendo of heady, pollen-clouding jungle that bombards my skull with imperceptible shocks of beauty. They cluster in huge, undulating blocks as if a mad painter like Van Gogh has gone berserk with his brush, stabbing clots of brilliant sun, vibrant with heat, right across the landscape as far as the eye can see. Their heady scent diffuses piercingly on the motionless air. They are ten feet high. They spill over each other, tangling their trailing stems through years of previous dead growth so that you have to hack your way through with a billhook or a chainsaw.

A few meagre paths, nibbled open by sheep and deer in winter, bisect this jungle. I have to ride through these to cross the half-mile of thicket separating us from the bump on the hill. As we begin to wade into the tangle, I sense Barney's anxiety. He is shoulder high in the broom. Wisps of blossom flick over his face and he twitches nervously, nostrils flaring. He stops. I have to ease him on, patting his neck and talking softly and reassuringly. I am sure he remembers the sabre-toothed tiger. Today is particularly bad. Perhaps the coconuts are smothering his sense of smell as well as his general nervousness about being ambushed in such thick country. Horses are plains animals, like zebra. They are a species designed to live in wide-ranging herds on open grasslands and in broad canyons. Their security lies in numbers and the collective ears and noses of many individuals working together for the protection of the herd. Instinctively they give thick cover a wide berth, knowing by millions of years of successfully surviving as a prey species that lions and tigers lurk in such places. It is vital knowledge. They hand it down. I know he will be happier if I lead him; I slide off and take him through on foot. He follows without hesitation. Being led is pure instinct, too. I see acquiescence gleaming in the pond of his eye. I may not be the herd, but in a fix like this I'll do. Any port in a storm.

I wonder why it is that we accept the genetic heritage of most things except ourselves? Most people understand that dogs piddle on lamp-posts because deep programming is telling them they have to; they are scent-marking a territory – something domestic dogs have not *needed* to do for millennia. No one really believes that a canary in a cage sings its little heart out to please us; it is because it's programmed to do that. It wouldn't be a canary if it didn't sing. Out-singing each other is what has made canaries a success for millions of years. As horses have speed and eat grass, and dogs have a bark and a set of carnivorous teeth, they are what they are, dictated by their genes, whatever else humans may require of them or whatever funny shape we may distort them into by selective breeding. The genes are the same genes, just assembled in a different order: a Pekinese or a greyhound; a huge half-thoroughbred like Barney or a diminutive Shetland pony. All dogs bury bones and all horses can remember the sabre-toothed tiger. Some just show it more. Why, then, do we limit the common acknowledgement of our genetic heritage to the colour of our hair or our blue eyes? For all our doctrinaire notions we are the product of our genes shaped and moulded by the environment in which we live. The plain fact remains that there exists not one shred of evidence that our children can inherit even one tiny jot of learned information.

You wouldn't know it in this glen. Judging by the way traditions die hard in the Highlands one could be forgiven for imagining that they are in the blood. 'Ach, well, what d'you expect?' they say. 'He's a Macdonald' (or a Macgregor or a Fraser or . . .). 'Never trust a Campbell,' say the Macdonalds. (I have often wondered what the Campbells say about the Macdonalds behind *their* backs.)

When I came to live here in the late sixties I met the widow of a doctor who had been in practice, father to son, for three consecutive generations in Glenurquhart, a glen running parallel to ours a few miles over the hill. He was called Willie-Frank Macdonald. Joycie (pronounced *Choicey*) Macdonald told me many remarkable stories about doctoring in remote glens between the world wars and since. Many seemed to relate to the astonishing ability of the doctors, Willie-Frank or his father or grandfather, accurately to diagnose illness and disease from a preliminary consultation and without any of the technical back-up we need today. I quizzed her on this: 'How can he possibly have known that at one glance?' Or, 'Surely he would have had to have done blood tests to determine that?' To which her reply was 'Not if you or your father or grandfather had attended the birth of, treated throughout life and buried every member of every family in the glen for the best part of three generations.'

The great authority of those remote Highland medical practices was that they had cross-generational records detailing everyone in the community back for the best part of a century. If only nowadays our medical records contained that hard information pieced together over a similarly long period; if only they could be collated by a doctor who knew you personally, occupationally and socially, from childhood to maturity and beyond! And if your condition and your genetic heritage had been discussed in the long winter nights, beside the fire, with a former generation of doctors, even his own father, then diagnosis might not be the quasi-scientific lottery it is in today's helter-skelter medicine. Oh to be able to inherit that inspired intuition and insight supported by time-won information! Oh to possess a gene loaded with the knowledge that oozed from the soil and echoed from the rock of these land-locked communities in their far-flung mountain fastnesses!

The sabre-toothed tiger, *Smilodon*, disappeared as recently as ten thousand years ago. It was widespread in Europe and America where fossil records and whole peat-preserved skeletons are relatively common. They and their prey were hunted out, it is now thought, by the advancing tide of Stone Age men who colonised tiger territory for the first time. Poor old *Smilodon* had no image of man the awful predator in his genetic memory-bank, man the gang-killer who respected neither sabre tooth nor tusk. *Smilodon* possessed no instinct to run and hide. Why would he? He had never run from anything. The same fate awaited the colossus of the steppes, the woolly mammoth in its lumbering herds, benignly munching reeds while skin-clad Cro-Magnons pierced their huge flanks with flint-tipped spears. It seems probable that, aided by climate change, post-Ice Age man, man the incomer, man the invader, the perpetual coloniser of new lands, man the fire-raiser and destroyer of his own habitat, also brought about the downfall of the European bison, the woolly rhinoceros and the cave bear.

Today, if you visit the Galapagos, the islands that Darwin plucked from anonymity for ever, you can sit with his dull but celebrated finches at your elbow. Giant tortoises will lumber up to have their throats scratched and fur seals will haul out to snore beside you on your rock – all this despite the merciless ravages of early European settlers and whaling boats calling in to replenish their stocks of fresh meat. The long memory just isn't there. Man is too recent an arrival to have permitted natural selection – there of all places – to have worked its singular and perpetual way. It is, frankly, a miracle that any indigenous Galapagos wildlife has survived at all.

By the time these ancient European species had logged on to reality and wound up their experience-banks by that mysterious leap of flesh and the spirit from learning to inheritance, from Lamarck to Darwin, it was too late. Their numbers were too low; man had fragmented their habitat, perfected the killing techniques, broken the food chains and condemned them to immortality on a cave wall. All we can do is finger the bones and fossils and plug in the imagination. And, for a frisson of aura, for a moment of dazzling beauty and truth, we must visit Altamira, Lascaux and the Kesslerloch, where, to many art historians, the Cro-Magnon cave paintings remain among the greatest and most unforgettable works of art known to man.

The horse was with us then in Europe, as now. Like the zebra in Africa today, herds of wild *Equus*, the prehistoric progenitor of the modern horse, roamed the plains and wild grasslands of Europe, including Britain, before the land bridge with the Low Countries disappeared at the end of the last Ice Age. Barney's forebears were there at the time. They knew all about the throat-ripping ambush tactics of *Smilodon*, who, the size of a modern lion, but bulkier and slower, lacked the speed and agility to give chase and pull down its herbivore prey. Instead it lurked crouching in the undergrowth, needing just one chance to deliver a lunging, mortal slash. Once the unhappy *Equus* was bleeding to death, following it up was easy.

Equus has gone, too. The last truly wild horses of the world are the zebras and wild asses of Africa and the Mongolian wild horse, Przewalski's horse, named after the Russian explorer Nikolai Przewalski in 1879, although dilution by domesticated stock makes it doubtful whether any pure-bred herds still exist. Yet while Barney's wild ancestors shared the fate of *Smilodon* and the woolly mammoth, their domesticated descendants are assembled from precisely the same genetic chips. The memory may be a little misted over by domestication and schooling, but it is still there: a dark hereditary fear surfacing like a shark, clouding his brain with panic. Barney is having an attack of vivid primeval recall. Training and heredity have clashed inside his big, gentle head and left him trembling: adrenaline coming in little quickening rushes. I lead him on. He follows willingly, almost too fast, so that I stumble. While I'm in front he thinks I'll get my throat torn out first. He's happier now. He can rely on me as he would rely on the herd of his long memory. I'll lead him clear and he can relax again.

We come out on to a band of smooth rock high above the loch. It is called Luncheon Rock, a fine picnic place framed by mountain and forest and a view across the glen. In a circle of stones the ashes of a fire mark the last occupation, not by Iron Age raiders but by something similar: Aigas Field Centre staff celebrating the summer solstice a few weeks ago. At this latitude our night recedes to a flicker of darkness at midsummer, and returns in anger in winter. It's an old tradition here. At 11 p.m. on 21 June they gather to watch the sun slide behind the glowering stump of Bad a' Chlamhain – the hill of the red kite – to the north-west. It skims low behind the pinewood, spreading its purpling afterglow round us in an arc of cold fire, to emerge again by 1.30 a.m. as a steely lunge at the heart of the turning year. On such a metaphysical night and with the help of a bottle of wine and a song it is perfectly possible to rekindle the shadowy spirits of the Bronze Age men who built their village here three thousand years ago.

Slightly below us, in cleared rings of broom and gorse, there are three distinct Bronze Age hut circles and a further one lost in a tangle of growth. There are others further up the hill. Some are about twenty-five feet in diameter and the others much larger at fifty feet. Their perimeter walls are now no more than two feet high; the deposition of three millennia of soil and peat has filled them in. Back then they would have been five feet high for certain, possibly more, and they once had roofs. These were either huge conical thatched roofs pitched from a central pole for the smaller ones, or the bigger circles may have been only partially roofed from an inner ring of poles with the centre open to the sky. One day we'll get round to excavating one of them so that we know.

They have entrances at the south-east, facing the morning sun. Archaeologists refer to them rather prosaically as 'hut circles'. The smaller roofed ones were probably just homes; the larger ones seem likely to have been livestock enclosures for sheep and goats, partially roofed round the walls for shelter. All the circles are contained within a walled field system of about twenty acres in size, with smaller walled divisions inside. There was a sturdy band of stone-hauliers here once upon a time. Ten good houses could have been a community of fifty to seventy people. Aigas was a busy place all those centuries ago.

Our own resident archaeologist, Robin Noble, who has worked closely with us for nearly twenty years, admits we know very little about these people. We place them in the middle of the Bronze Age, which dates approximately to three and a half thousand years ago. The Highlands is rich in such sites, some very well preserved, especially chambered burial cairns. Others, like these, lie unexcavated and unspectacular to the eye. They are faint scribblings on the face of the moor. They tell us that people lived here and worked their short lives away breaking the soil to grow food and tending their livestock. When the climate was kind they expanded their number and extended their range, and when it dipped into the worst the Highlands can offer they suffered accordingly. Just as surely as drought decimates primitive peoples in desert countries today, so wind, rain and the long, cold winter drove these people into retreat. All their energy was consumed in survival. No time for frills: art and creativity submerged in toil. We know that when these Bronze Age communities first established, the climate was mild and productive. Settlements moved up the hill on to higher ground. Later, when the climate failed again, they were driven back to these medium heights, ultimately even lower still, to the very edge of the flood plain of the glacial valley, where they remain to this day.

As we leave the circles we pass an earth-locked boulder beside the path. It has been cleared of broom and bracken by our rangers so that it stands out. On it is a pattern of 'cup marks' – curiously smooth indentations as on a chequerboard, but asymmetrically set, of varying sizes and depths, but about teacup diameter. They look as though they have been ground out with a fist-sized pebble, a task of some endurance in hard metamorphic schist. This is no idle graffito. Whoever did it spent many hours at it and had a clear purpose in mind. These markings commonly adorn sites of this period, almost as if they are a cryptic signature by the architects of the day. No one has any real idea what they mean. They could be signposts, way markers, territorial flags, even sacred stones of mysterious religious or ritual significance, for touching, kissing, bowing to, or at which you mutter incantations as you pass. Could they be crude calendars counting decades or centuries, or a log of sacrifices perhaps, or family records, marking births or deaths of great leaders? This one has twelve 'cups', some more clearly legible than others, their mystery invaded by rings of algae and lichen in ochre and silver-black arcs. When I run my fingers over the grainy surface of the rock, curving the hollow edges, I pray for the message to reveal itself. Nothing comes.

We brush our way along the trail through surging bracken, leaving the circles and their little broom-filled fields behind us. I pause. The day is rare, anodyne. I can't pass by. I have to stop to take it in, sip its warm intoxication like mead. It's compulsive, tugging at my conscience, as though if I don't I shall be letting someone down. High above me wisps of cirrus stretch and feather to nothing. Coconut scent floods up at us in crescents of hot fragrance, climbing Barney's long legs and smiting me under the chin. The air hums and the far hills waver and blur: out of the picture, muted. Bumble-bees struggle past my face like thieves with pollen baskets so laden with golden plunder that they can barely fly. A cock chaffinch is bellowing the same refrain over and over again from high in a little birch tree, his cinnamon breast rising and falling to the task like a virtuoso soprano. From deep in the jungle willow warblers' descending scales merge and overlap like piccolo students practising in a conservatoire.

The day seems to cast a new light on the whole intricate texture of the world, shattering familiarity, starting anew, making me look

all over again – think it through. Beneath Barney's shod hooves
flecks of silver mica shine out of the hard grey rock worn smooth
by the ice. It withdrew from this land between ten and twelve
thousand years ago. Ever since, life has blown, crept, slithered,
crawled, flown, tiptoed, plodded, galloped, walked, clambered and

run in here to make its pitch for survival. Even as the glacier was
ponderously departing, clawing its way back up its glen like some
mortally wounded dragon returning to the mountains, nature was
stealing its march. As it was flushing out its icy hollows, littering
its copious entrails across its path, so every dumped boulder and
alluvial fan, every drumlin and esker, every outwashed morainic
excrescence was baring its soul to the dreams of opportunity.
Nature never pauses. Colonisation and succession are ruthless

purges: first-come-first-served rushes for exposed nutrients like bargain-hunters fighting over jumble at a sale.

The first to claim territory are there anyway. They never went away. They are the unseen bacterial and microbial legions that encircle and bombard our world like mould around a loaf. In every crevice, between every grain of sand and in every stagnant pool, this microscopic locust horde is devouring nutrients and establishing life. Blowing in with this aeolian life-dust were the spores of fungi, algae and lichens. Primitive plants such as mosses and liverworts wove their tundra carpets here and laid down the first gritty soils. Glossy-leafed ferns spilled from the rocks. Along came vascular plants with enzyme-secreting roots to tap in and build more soils by their own hallowed processes of cyclical decay. Trees germinated and flooded the colonisation process with depth and yet more opportunity. Invertebrates: bugs, beetles and winged insects of myriad colours and forms streamed relentlessly into anonymous niches. Reptiles: lizards, slow worms and adders poked and writhed in dark crannies. Frogs, newts and toads tirelessly plodded along their damp corridors northwards. Birds and mammals expanded their range to load the spreading forest with drama and song. The eagle soared overhead and the wren trilled deliciously in its thicket. The wood mouse quivered in its grassy nest and the wild boar rootled through the woodland glades. Man arrived and etched his inscrutable pockmarks on the rock. Man, microbe, bug, plant, beast and bird together struggled, fought and died for this little patch of wonder. They came and they went, some species gracing the millennia with their long presence, others fading away without a trace, vanishing into eternity's great, mysterious maelstrom.

I don't know which sense to concentrate on. I'm beating off salvoes of giddy impression, rushing me, coming at me on all sides like Apaches, out of nowhere. Here I am now, with Barney's blood surging beneath my creaking saddle and the dark sweat of a million trembling years staining his silky neck. Here are the remains of these ancient houses, the homes of people who also breathed this same gilded moment, laughed in the crushed coconut sunshine, lugged stones across this unrepentant land. Here are these chaffinches and warblers reaping their little harvest of history, reciting the creed, doing what they do best for all they are worth, loading each vibrating gene with perfection. I mop my brow. Barney plucks at a broom shoot with a jingling snatch of the head. He munches frothily, pale green gobbets dribbling from the rings of the bit.

I pick these moments like ripe fruit. I close my eyes and try to commit them to memory so that I can return to them later. Sometimes it works. This is a day to revisit when winter lays siege to the house and consumes all thought, when sleet clots the windowpanes and rushes of arctic fury rattle the slates. Like the image of *Smilodon*, I want this shred of living to be pinned to a gene so that ten thousand years from now some light-headed youth passing this spot will pause involuntarily, sense the faint tug of an unidentified, poignant nostalgia and mop his brow, too. Surely that is the great burden of mankind: that we cannot automatically pass on our golden trove of information. Each generation has to relearn it. Barney never had to learn to be a horse. It came to him with a skip and a jump in a spring meadow when he first saw his own curved image in his mother's dark, limpid eye. It never occurred to him that he was anything else, then or now. If I carry a gene or two from these Bronze Age folk, why aren't they speaking to me? Why can't I sweat a little at the neck?

What is clear is that this vibrant little village needed somewhere to run to when harvests failed, when neighbours turned nasty and survival became difficult. We aren't exactly short of evidence that humans behave like that when the going gets tough. This was good land. Here at Aigas were freshets of bubbling spring water and precious *Festuca* grassland on the free-draining soils of a south-facing slope. The animals met the winter snows sleek and well fed, and the crops gave up their bounty in surplus to see them through the long, dark days. Elsewhere might not have been so favoured. They possessed the seeds of envy. If a raiding party of starving neighbours came, they needed refuge, fast.

The Iron Age fort is a short haul away now. We have to cross a patch of bog – leap off, lead Barney carefully round it, reading the vegetation for firmness – and on up through the heather. This is it. After a struggle up the steep rocky incline, we have arrived on the top of the bump. It would have taken them only twenty minutes to run here; to shout to each other in the little fields, to snatch up babes and yell at the children, then to scurry up the steep cliff to the walled stronghold on the top. Perhaps the men stayed longer to defend their livestock, meet the raiders face to face and try to beat them off. Strong words flying in the wind, dark threats of reprisals if they persisted; fierce scowls on angry faces and hair free-flowing. Tense fingering of weapons. If they failed, perhaps they fought their way back up the slope, finally turning and scrambling up the rocks while their families launched a barrage of rocks, arrows and spears over their heads at the aggressors.

Once here their lives should have been safe. This is a real fortress. It is a ruin now, nothing but a jumble of stones where the walls stood, but you can see that it was a real structure. Perhaps it was even roofed, although you wouldn't need a roof unless besieged for days on end, and the winter gales would have plucked it off for certain. A good band of fit men and women could have defended this position well. There is only one vulnerable side, to the south-west, where a determined raiding party could rush the fort, and it is on this side that the strongest wall seems to have stood. It would have been a persistent aggressor who risked the inevitable casualties of such an attack.

But their lives are all they might have saved. Standing here looking down on the little fields and the hut circles I can sense the rising anger, the mounting grief of seeing their homesteads burned, flames licking through the heather thatch of their huts, yellow smoke clouding the forest and the moor. My pulse quickens at the thought of their helplessness as they stood here watching their sheep, cows, pigs and goats driven off or spitefully slaughtered in their pens. What if it was the dead of winter? What if the raiders took all the stored grain and burned the haystacks? Did they stand here knowing that survival for another four or five months would be well-nigh impossible on wild game alone? Did the men swear revenge and counter-raid to snatch back what their families had to have?

I have dismounted and tied Barney to a broom bush. He is busy eating it. Today the view is brain-emptying, absorbent. It hollows me out. To the east I can see the distant shimmer of the Beauly Firth fifteen miles away at Inverness, and the cat's cradle of the Kessock Bridge, which links the Highland capital to the Black Isle. I can see the route the glacier took to the North Sea. Its long channel cuts deeply into the rock to the valley floor some six hundred feet below me. I can see where its creaking arm elbowed the fault line at Aigas and headed off to the firth. And I can see how it melted its way back again, a thousand feet of ice half a mile wide; and where zillions of tons of green meltwater washed out the rock crevices, sculpting terraces and laying trails of morainic jumble behind it like some colossal mining machine.

Down there the river rules now. The valley was harnessed for hydro-power in the 1950s, so some of its former might is locked away behind the dams. But it can still surprise us. Every few years when a very wet winter spell coincides with a warm wind from the Gulf Stream, the snowfields in the mountains are stripped off like blankets from a bed. The meltwater crashes and surges down the steep ravines, building unstoppable rage and power. When it hits the already full river it bursts out across the flood plain, sweeping away the bank-side trees and levelling the fields with its scummy silt. But Highlanders are canny. They build their valley houses and farms just above the flood line, carving out shelves in the glacial wall just big enough for a cottage and a byre. I have never seen a flooded house in this glen.

Barney and I are turning for home. I gather the reins and prepare to lead him down the steep path to the moor. He stands his ground, eyeing me warily. Something is wrong. 'Come on, old boy,' I say reassuringly, rubbing his velvet nose. He snorts and throws his head. Something *is* wrong. I know him well enough to know he's not fooling. Perhaps I frightened him by coming up so steeply? I turn to look at the path. Yet we've done it many times before and it has never bothered him. I look back at his legs and run my hand over his soft flanks. His feet are fine; hooves like dinner plates and tummy rumbling with indigestible broom. I can't see anything amiss. I try again. Up goes his head and I get that wide-eyed look, rimmed with white, the frame of fear. If he could shout he would be doing so now. I look round again, puzzled.

I walk the three or four feet to the tumbled wall of the fort, to the breach where we came in half an hour ago. As I do so a little rising hiss, edgy and sharp, breaks the air. I stop dead. There, a yard away, coiled like a rope on a large flat boulder, soaking up the afternoon sun, is an adder. She is magnificent, fully two and a half feet long (I estimate later – she's impossible to gauge coiled up). Only females get this big. Barney is standing in the broom like a moose in a willow thicket, peering out at me with a look that says: 'If you think I'm walking past that, forget it!' I back off the adder, quietly. I unhitch him and lead him gently in the opposite direction, to the far end of the fort, twenty yards away, where I tie him to another bush. 'What a clever boy,' I murmur, patting his neck. He is happier now. I return to the adder, tiptoeing in.

The adder or common viper, *Vipera berus*, is the only true snake we have in the Highlands and it is poisonous. I have seen a spaniel keel over and die on the moors. It's not aggressive, but it's no good telling Barney that; he's digging up genetic nightmares again. 'A snake is a snake and that's that! Horses don't mess with snakes!' But if you anger it, or corner it, or tread on it, especially if you have feet like Barney's, it will strike and hurt. The hiss means just that: 'Don't push your luck!' I don't plan to, but I do want a good look.

I see adders every year, usually up on the moors, and almost always basking in the sun. Like crocodiles, they need to raise their body temperature before they can hunt – a sort of solar loosen-up. But usually they slide off into the heather and one rarely gets a chance to examine them properly. This lady is different: she's out and exposed in all her scaly splendour – 'a serpent more subtle than any beast of the field which the Lord God hath made'. She's clearly not keen to abandon her sunbed. I creep up. She hasn't moved, but as I approach she turns her head to face me, her forked black tongue stabbing air. I creep closer, down now on all fours because I don't want to threaten her. I am back where I was, a yard away. Her head is poised, resting on air; the length of her sleek, fat body is coiled into a bun like the knot in a postmistress's hair. I can't see the short, pointed tail: it's tied in, lost.

The eye of an adder is lidless and unblinking. It's a tiny jet bead as cold as bronze. Two black stripes paired like eyebrows flow back from behind her eyes towards her body, highlighting the focus of her hard, angled little face, like a wedge prising open the afternoon air. I ease closer. I am impaled on that gleaming dot of menace. Perhaps she is measuring me up with that stare, thinking of dislocating her jaw and swallowing me whole so that my boots stick out and I bulge ludicrously inside her scaly stocking. Her face is implacable, inscrutable, no hint of a smile or a sneer. She just coldly looks, utterly still, like Moses' brass serpent, a moment cast in the fiery properties of magic. They say you can't stare down a snake; snakes always win. Whoever said it is right. I can tell I'm not going to win this one. It's like championship chess, the atmosphere redolent with tension and suspicion. I've forgotten whose move it is.

She probably lives on lizards. They are common here. And newts and frogs, and the occasional small mammal like a vole or a wood mouse. When she comes out of hibernation, where she has been underground for almost half the year, she is hungry. She will nose out the convenient glut of meadow pipits' nests in the deer grass and the heather, gorging on eggs or tiny fledglings, bare and blind, building her strength for mating and producing her young in high summer. This lady looks fat; she has fed well. I can breathe more easily now.

I had never paid much attention to snakes until a few years ago when I was sitting under a dry-stone wall eating sandwiches with a few field-centre guests. It was June and the day was bright and high. We had been up in the hills searching for the little moorland falcon, the merlin. We had found a pair nesting in an old hooded crow's nest in a low birch tree, so we were pleased. We sat down to eat and doze in the warm spring sunshine. In front of us lay a grassy patch of delicate little flowers, the yellow tormentil, clusters of eyebright and the vivid blue of the sky reflected in the tiny petals of milkwort. Clots of buttercups sprinkled sunshine across the sheep-cropped quilt. A rustling movement in the long grass to one side attracted our attention. It persisted as though something vital was going on in there, life beavering away, purposeful and repetitive. I pressed my finger to my lips to urge the others not to make a sound. I had no idea what could be so busy in there. A shrew, perhaps? An adder emerged. He didn't slide, or slither, as one might expect of a snake, he whirled. He was a dashing wisp of cord, like a whiplash flicked across the grass. We were all startled by this rush of reptile, but we kept our silence. In a moment he had spun around and flashed back into the long grass. More thrashing about. He was unquestionably male. The zigzag pattern down his spine was strident: bright zig and brighter zag, attention-snatching like an alarm signal. He was sandy yellow and hard-edged black, a contrast of sharp, waspish elegance. After a few more moments of waving grass he emerged again, to repeat the same looping circuit of excitement. Something was up, of that we were certain. He was entirely oblivious that five people were keenly observing this wild dance. But this time, instead of returning to the long grass, he took off across the sward and disappeared into a heathery clump. Almost immediately another, smaller, just as brightly patterned adder appeared from the same grass and seemed to be pursuing the first. In seconds they were back, one chasing the other, whipping through and turning to face one another down with powerful up-and-down jerkings of the head and neck. I guessed these were two males contending for a female.

While all this was going on, to one side of the clearing a third, much larger, adder arrived, lazily and apparently unconcerned. Her darker colouring and larger size gave away her gender. She coiled quietly in a corner and appeared to watch with that coldly dispassionate viper stare. Several times the males came back towards her. Each time the larger of the two saw the other one off, fencing and feinting, weaving and whipping, barring his way and jabbing his angled little head constantly into his opponent's face. Finally the smaller male seemed to give up and headed off into the undergrowth, chased by the larger male until out of sight. Then the victor quickly returned on his own.

We were witnessing an ageless courtship rite – the tale of inex-orable telling, the dance of two suitors to an irresistible melody as old as the rock itself. It was mesmeric. We dared not move. We were as transfixed as if caught up in an Oriental carnival pageant of dragons and gods. In all my years of wandering the hills and meeting adders I had not guessed such speed and agility were possible, such power of suggestion, such aboriginal posturing. But we had seen nothing yet.

Our male came swishing back to his love. He pranced around her victoriously for a moment or two and then pressed his suit with fervour and passion. To begin with she ignored him (as females will), so he slithered urgently all over her, from the flatness of her delicate head to the tip of her coiled tail. He mouthed her entire length, flicking his black tongue over the whole surface of her back, whipping round and facing her head to begin again, tonguing his way over her eyes and neck in the most affectionate and persuasive courtship I have ever had the privilege to

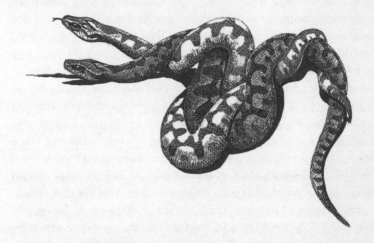

witness. Slowly she began to respond, to ease the hinges of her scaly armour, loosening her coils, beginning to writhe herself in time to the constant rippling of her lover. At this slightest gesture, this merest hint of reptilian acquiescence, he flew into ecstasies of ardour, redoubling his efforts to cover her entirety, pushing his sharp little head into her coils and oozing unstoppably through the knot like mercury through your fingers. He seemed to be literally prising her apart. This success drove him wilder still. He hopped and he skipped, he tapped her head with

his own in a tattoo of urgency; he tied himself in knots that unravelled themselves in a slither of silken sensuality. He became a
flowing figure of eight, the rampant weaving border to a love
poem. He was Eden's diabolical serpent having disposed of
Adam, inventing the original sin in all its aching, raw and desperate sexuality.

At last she was impressed. Her sinuosity arose from its
lethargy and rippled down the length of her voluptuousness. She
loosed her stretching roundness and flowed with him in a
writhing continuum of mounting passion. They swirled together
in a confluence of wild streams, twisting and turning before us,
only a few feet away, over a love quilt of bright starry flowers. He
never ceased his fervent kisses with that flickering tongue, bifid
and black. He never eased the dance, only settling the pace to a
rhythmic, winding duet in the tempo of a Viennese waltz. Finally,
after many minutes of this fertility rite, the male succeeded in
entwining his lover like a vine, spiralling around her in a frenzy of
excitement. He angled his tail beneath her, upside down, and
their lower lengths met in a clinching cloacal embrace. Once
locked together they became one. For a while we sat mesmerised
by this earthly undertaking, unable quite to believe what we had
seen. The word 'snake' had rewritten itself in coils of exquisite cal-
ligraphy, never to be read quite the same again. Very slowly, still
harmoniously writhing and convulsing, they crossed the little
clearing and disappeared into the heather on the other side. We
tiptoed away, unspeaking, in case the spell might break. It was
like coming out into the sunshine after a wild and disturbing film,
a slightly shivery return to a human world that had no language
for what we felt.

It's my move. Since this adder is guarding our exit from the
fort, I have to do something. I pluck a heather twig and gently –
oh so gently – tease it scrapily across the rock towards her head.
She faces it immediately in a jerky little angle. I pull back. She
hisses crossly. I try again. It's too much for her. She's not going to

be mocked: nobody's fool. In a surprisingly rapid turn she flicks round and flows away from me, across the top of the boulder towards the pile of stones from which she undoubtedly emerged. Her body glides after her in one long, sinuous ripple of scaly zigzag. The pattern on her back is stark and clear, a rippling black line like a fern leaf, long and lobed, against the bronze of her flanks and belly. The air seems to split open to let her through. Perhaps the rock will, too.

FIVE

Fraser Country

None but a mad fool would have fought that day.

SIMON THE FOX, 1667–1747

This is Fraser country. Our ash tree germinated in about 1700, source unknown; its progenitors long since atomised in the great whirlpool of nutrients. The Frasers came to prominence as a clan in the power struggle that followed the collapse of the Lordship of the Isles. This last great principality of Gaelic Alba met its end in the dying days of the fifteenth century. They were to become a powerful clan dominating a broad swath of the northern central Highlands and extending down the Great Glen into Lochaber for the last five hundred years. The greater part of our glen was, and to a lesser extent still is, Clan Fraser heartland, home to the ancestral chiefs beside the River Beauly. Here they mixed freely with the Chisholms just upstream, above the laughing confluence of the Farrar and the Glass, the two rivers that combine to become the Beauly. The Chisholm chiefs' fortress, Erchless Castle, stands among the soft river meadows guarding their lands stretching far up into the wild Affric Mountains at the head of the glen. Mackenzie territory is to the north and the MacRae lands lie to the west, beyond Affric, in the rugged mountains of Kintail. The Grants perpetually jostled with Frasers for southern hills surrounding Loch Ness.

I find it intriguing to speculate that the seed from which our tree sprouted undoubtedly spiralled down from the lofty lights of another landmark ash tree close by, which could also have lived for over three hundred years. The two trees together, parent and scion, taking us right back six hundred and fifty years to the golden age of Gaeldom, rich in art, language, religion and education – back even to the reign of Somerled, the greatest leader born to the Gaels of Alba, whose Gaelic revival diluted the Viking influence over the Highlands, the echoes of which resound to this day. However tenuous the link, the notion of such antiquity takes us to the very core of Celtic history – Somerled, whose ancestry leads directly back to Con of the Hundred Battles, the most famous of the High Kings of Erin.

Life is a chain. All the time we forge our own hot links on to its sizzling end. I find it reassuring to haul myself back up the chain from time to time to get a clearer feel for where we all came from, what we are. This place and what we do here have changed my view of history from a scatter of dates and events with little or no relevance to me and my time into a broader understanding of where I live and work. It imposes itself, whether we seek it or not, into every facet of our daily actions. At Aigas we walk with our history, sleep through its troubling dreams, wake to its poignant song in the cry of the curlew, breathe its travail in the soft Highland air. We live our history over and over again.

In the years following our tree's germination life here was tribal, remote, secluded and cut off from the rest of Scotland and the world by high mountain passes, choked by winter snows, at best an arduous four-day ride from Edinburgh. Life could also be grim. The land is poor, made poorer in those days by too many people struggling to eke a living from its acid soils in a slow, reluctant climate.

Most Highlanders lived in abject poverty described at its pitiful nadir in Dr Isabel Grant's remarkable work *Everyday Life on an Old Highland Farm, 1769–1782*:

> The greater part of the population of the Highlands were living under conditions that would now be considered to be incompatible with civilised existence . . . often on the verge of starvation . . . a half-naked hungry people living in mud-floored hovels, peat smoke blackening their faces, before it drifted out through a hole in the dripping roof, the sole room shared all winter through with starving cattle.

Our ash tree witnessed their toil, although its happy position (and probably the cause of its survival) was beside a house quite different from *tigh dubh*, the black houses Dr Grant describes, blackened throughout their interiors by peat smoke from the permanently glowing fire. Aigas, or, as it was then and is again now, Tigh an Aigas, the House of Aigas (reverted by us in 1996 to acknowledge the two hundred and fiftieth anniversary of the fall of Gaeldom at the Battle of Culloden), was a tacksman's house. Tacksmen were the middle class of the clan. They were often relatives of the chief who were given authority and responsibility in the collectivist administration of a tribal people in what had started out as a largely subsistence economy. In a land of minimal natural capital the only means the chiefs had by which to reward their loyal tacksmen was land. The land was a tack (from the Old Norse, *taka*, a taking of income from the land) – a rented holding of better land, fertile fields and grazings, upon which the tacksman could build a house that reflected his status, and which bound him to support his chief in bad times and to fight for him to resolve his quarrels.

Aigas is a favoured site. It is blessed by a quirk of geology deep underground and by the subsequent somewhat untidy legacy of the departing glacier. Its meltwater flushed out the south-facing bowl in which we cosily nestle, depositing terraces and gravelly subsoils that serve us well. Tacksmen who lived at Aigas fared far better than the hovel-bound unfortunates whom Dr Grant depicts. That tacksman's house has gone. We don't even know when the tack was first granted or the first house built – only its demise. We sit on its foundations, so we know that it was roughly square, and probably symmetrical with a central front door and windows on either side, probably three-front facing windows on the floor above. Rooms would have been small and with low ceilings, a fireplace in every room: Highland winters are long and cold. Cutting firewood and peat is pure toil. Documentary records are few, but we believe our tacksman to have been called Hugh Fraser, or Eoghan to his family, the Gaelic form of the name in a land that spoke virtually no English. He was born here, presumably a surviving son of the previous Aigas tenant of the barony of Lovat, the chiefs of Fraser. Hugh was to die among his fellow Jacobite clansmen on the battlefield of Culloden on 16 April 1746 along with one thousand five hundred others.

Our tree and Hugh grew up together. He must have played beside the sapling. Some years ago I germinated seeds from the ash and brought the seedlings on in pots. A year later I selected the best three and planted them out in prominent positions in the grounds. The best of these, a brave stalwart of a sapling, sporting a leader and four shiny laterals that stole a march on all the others, I ceremoniously planted on the south-east corner of the house in a directly corresponding position to its parent at the south-west. I was perpetuating history in ash. I dressed it in a spiral tree-guard to deter the hares and roe deer that tiptoe through in the night, and I scattered a handful of bonemeal at its feet to see it on its historical way. The tree is now doing well, some sixteen feet high with a clean, straight stem and twenty-five laterals clutching a pastel haze.

One June evening this year I noticed that as the sun freewheeled slowly towards the western horizon the parent tree extended a long blueing shadow across the lawn, like an arm reaching out. As the sun pivoted around the ash, so its shadow seemed to be trying to touch its child. Slowly I realised that, entirely by chance, I had planted the sapling at the furthest point of the shadow's reach on the longest day of the year – the stuff of ancients. They met briefly in the tenderest embrace, seeming to linger for a moment before spreading on across the darkening grass.

Hugh grew to be a fine young boy. Too fine. There were forces at work not so far away that were to rebound upon the lives of Highlanders right across the mountains and glens for miles around. The history our tree was wrapping into its ligneous folds was also heading for young Hugh. As yellowing leaves carpeted the grass and its branches rattled in the scurrying winds of incoming winter, our tree heard the urgently whispered news in soft-spoken Gaelic that swept through the glens like flu. Its darkening shadow was reaching out for Hugh, too.

The Earl of Mar's Jacobite uprising had come to nothing when it faced the Duke of Argyll's Redcoat militia at the Battle of Sheriffmuir in November 1715, as did the follow-up by the Duke of Ormonde in 1719. As a Catholic clan, the Frasers were always likely supporters of the exiled King James's bid to recover the Scottish Crown from the Elector of Hanover, the uncharismatic and unwelcome King George I, recently arrived from Germany. No doubt they saw Sheriffmuir as a brave attempt. Although the battle had been inconclusive, the fighting men of Clan MacRae, Catholic neighbours of the Frasers over the mountains to the west, had fallen almost to a man, routed by Argyll's superior cavalry. MacRaes, Frasers and Chisholms are much intermarried in these glens, evidenced by the many existing local gravestones traditionally bearing the maiden names of wives. There must have been much weeping in the glens. It would not be the last. As a tacksman's son, young Hugh would have listened agog at this talk of rebellion and lain awake long into the night churning over in his young head what was meant by a return to the good old days of Jacobite Gaeldom.

By the summer of 1745 Hugh was a grown man in charge of the Aigas tack of small farms and fields and its community of families living around him. His cattle and ponies grazed the parks beside the house, and the goats, sheep and house-cows of his workers who lived around him freely browsed and foraged in the birchwoods and far out across the purpling moors. His barns were filling with sacked oats and barley for the long winter ahead and a dry-sweet fragrance of the meadows hung over the hay sheaves laid in tall ricks. The warm breezes of summer had hardened the herringbone rows of peat cut from a mile into the moors and his clansmen and their womenfolk had toiled to bring them down in creels and build them into dykes in the lee of the byre. Small children sang and made daisy chains beside the ash tree while their older brothers and sisters vied with each other to dam up the chuckling burn with mud, stones and twigs.

When Bonnie Prince Charlie stepped ashore in Glenfinnan on Monday, 12 August that year and again raised the Jacobite standard for his father, the last great clan upheaval was under way. It was a disaster from the start. The Highland chiefs were disunited, uncertain in their loyalty, deceiving the Bonnie Prince and sitting on their hands. But up and down the length of the glen Fraser men and boys were talking of gathering to the cause. Hugh Fraser was bound to follow. Clan loyalty, then as now, is tangible, irrational and real.

The Prince's bold assumption that the clans of the west would automatically rally to him was wildly optimistic. The two powerful chiefs on the Isle of Skye, the MacLeod of Macleod and Alexander Macdonald of Sleat, dismissed the idea bluntly, telling him to abandon the whole plan and go home to France. But he would have none of it; ignoring all the signs of early warning, he relied upon his youthful good looks, his enthusiasm and his charisma to win through. The Jacobite army was never large or constant. Without clear leadership and training, Highlanders, of whatever clan, were always likely to be equivocal soldiery. Although they were to take Edinburgh and much of Scotland in the exciting weeks that followed, the uncertainty not just of the chiefs but most importantly of the clansmen themselves never went away. These were tribal people living by a fragile cattle economy and a subsistence arable agriculture that was absolutely dependent upon the men of the family being there to help work the land and tend the livestock. An adventure that took them away for two or three weeks, and particularly which promised spoil from the hapless victims they looted along the way, must have been attractive – indeed, that had been part of their feuding heritage for centuries past. But the notion of a long campaign, months of marching south with the Prince, as they did, all the way to Derby with the siege of London its aim, was not only alien to them, but also threatened their families back at home. From the start, the loyalty of some clansmen, never very robust, was failing. Men had turned for home all along the way.

The bitter truth was that Bonnie Prince Charlie lacked the military expertise, the manpower, the cash, the reinforcements from France and the will of his men to push on to the capital. Reluctantly he turned back – always a deeply demoralising tactic. At last, after an ignominious, messy withdrawal back up most of the length of Britain, tired, dispirited and hungry, chased by the English troops, the ragged Highland army turned to face its organised, disciplined and well-equipped Hanoverian enemy. Under the command of the corpulent Duke of Cumberland, King George's second son, they had lost no time in drawing in Lowland clans loyal to the Hanoverian cause as they marched north. Most notable were the Campbells under the Duke of Argyll, who had notoriously served the government in the dastardly Glencoe massacre fifty-five years before. Soon other Highland clans who saw the inevitability of failure and wanted no truck with the old Jacobite ways joined them.

Like so many civil conflicts, the Battle of Culloden stands as the tragic epilogue to many different causes. It was inspired as much by the loss of the Scottish and English crowns to William of Orange as by the religious differences that had split the whole of Europe, and the long history of territorial feuding between Gaelic tribes. English fought alongside Lowland Scot and Highlander, Scot pitched against Scot, Catholic against Presbyterian, Highlander against Highlander. More Scots fought against Bonnie Prince Charlie than for him, because many clans had seen and knew in their bones the impending doom that accompanied the young Prince's campaign.

It was all over in less than an hour, the Jacobite Highlanders' brave charges barely reaching the Hanoverian ranks as they were mown down by grapeshot from well-practised cannon and systematic volley firing, rank after rank, from the professional Redcoat infantry. Fifteen hundred men, mostly Jacobites, were to die that day. The rest fled. But it was not to end there. The fat Duke immediately set about earning his nickname 'Butcher' Cumberland for the carnage that followed. The wounded Highlanders were mercilessly slain where they lay groaning, or rounded up and summarily shot. He was determined to crush the cause for good. Worse was to follow over many weeks. He and his militia travelled out into the glens to stamp out the Jacobite enclaves so readily identifiable by their clan names. Twice they came to Aigas. We do not know the order of events, the names or the numbers of the dead, nor the torture or suffering they inflicted upon any lucky enough to escape with their lives. But we do know enough precise details of their methods elsewhere to build powerful images of the actions they took not just here but throughout the glens repeatedly over the ensuing weeks and months.

Close neighbours in Strathglass, the Frasers and the Chisholms were then and are now thoroughly intermarried. They were, and largely still are, Catholics: papists, bound to the Jacobite cause in spirit as well as seen to be allies of France and Spain, who had long been the antagonists of Hanoverian Protestantism. They were a close and ripe target upon which to vent the wrath of King George and provide the opportunity for looting, rape and pillage so keenly sought by rank-and-file soldiery of the day.

Lord Lovat, Chief of Fraser, known as Simon the Fox for his lifelong reputation of devious duplicity, had attempted treachery once too often. Faced with the dilemma of loyalty at the beginning of the campaign, he had decided to hedge his bets, sending his son, the Master of Lovat, and a band of Frasers to join the Prince and the mustering Jacobite clans, and simultaneously pledging his personal loyalty to the Hanoverian cause. Ultimately, against his better judgement, and knowing it – 'None but a mad fool would have fought that day,' he was later to reflect – he had reluctantly brought out some three hundred Fraser clansmen to their defeat at Culloden. The penalty was the forfeit of his lands and his head. Execution was a privilege of his rank, an alternative to being hanged, drawn and quartered like a commoner. His was the last public execution of a peer of the realm, intended to deter other Highland chiefs from dabbling in treason. First, though, was the visitation of fearful retribution; the bitterest price for his defeated people to pay. Lovat was publicly declared the King's enemy and he scuttled for cover as fast as his obese and aged body would carry him.

Under the command of Brigadier John Maudant, four hundred government foot soldiers of the Cholmondeley and Royal Scots regiments marched the fifteen miles from Inverness to the Fraser lands on the River Beauly. Their orders were to carry off all that was movable plunder and to burn that which was not, and 'to lay the glen waste from the sea to the hills'. After looting and pillaging the rich pickings of the chief's houses and estates with tragic inevitability they came to Aigas. The better land tacks were always likely to deliver up spoils worth having to a soldier. The menfolk were gone from here, Hugh dead on the battlefield, and what was left of the others had fled to the hills – anywhere but home. But the women and children, the aged, the halt and the lame stayed on, consumed in their grief and desolation at the awful news from Culloden. They can never have dreamed that Cumberland's revenge would bother with them now. They were wrong. Redcoats came at nightfall and dragged the women from their beds. Small children clutched their skirts. They were raped, shot, bayoneted or clubbed where they lay huddled in the damp cold. Their possessions were hauled out on to the grass beneath the ash tree and squabbled over by the excited troops. The house was set ablaze. That night the blood and beliefs of generations who had lived in this glen since the Bronze Age soaked away into the soils of Aigas.

All the buildings at Aigas were torched, the tacksman's house and the surrounding black houses of Hugh Fraser's workmen and their byres, wood and peat stacks, all blazing in the dark, cold night. The ash tree stood only ninety feet from the old house. Surely the tree must have been scorched by that awful blaze. Perhaps the buds on that side failed to open that year.

In his moving account of the battle, *Culloden*, John Prebble wryly observes:

Nobody has ever succeeded in preventing a victorious army from looting. Victory under arms gives a man the stature of a giant, and occupation the temptations to match it. Licence to kill cheapens the value of life, and respect for property falls in proportion. The less a soldier is paid for the killing (and the dying) the more indifferent society is to his hardships, then the greater will be his greed.

At the end of that sad night our tree stood as a lonely sentinel over the smoking rubble of Aigas. A few weeks later a Major Lockhart of Cholmondeley's was despatched from the garrison at Fort Augustus with one hundred and eighty volunteers to make further bitter raids into the glens. This was a hard man already infamous for his cold brutality. He knew well that the Fraser lands had already been raided, but his was a mission of destruction, a bloody mopping-up of anybody in his way. His progress of murder and rape is well recorded as he systematically raided through Glenmoriston and Glen Cluanie, thence to Strathglass, camping in Struy, only three miles away from here. In Glen Cannich a platoon of his men came across a family of Chisholms out working their land. At the sight of the Redcoats they ran to the woods for cover. They watched in horror as the soldiers set fire to their house and one emerged from the door with a baby impaled upon a sword. Whatever or whoever was left at Aigas and the surrounding settlements would have received no mercy from these raiders.

It is said that one crude dwelling did survive; indeed, the ruins remain to this day of a black house hidden in a hollow behind the wooded rise that conceals the loch. It was missed. A woman widowed by the battle continued to live there as a recluse into old age. She is said to have gone mad with grief at the loss of all her men and the brutal destruction of her community. She gave her name to the stretch of water beside her hovel: Loch Cuil na Caillich, loch of the old woman's hideaway.

Years of confusion followed. The tree grew on, ever stronger, ever higher above the stinging nettles and the gay rosebay willow herb that adorned the ruins beneath its spreading limbs. It took many years for the politics of the Highlands to settle down under Hanoverian rule. Yet despite the prohibition of Gaelic culture, song, dance and verse, tartan and the pipes, and especially the language itself, the community slowly began to recover and a new tacksman took over. He answered this time not to a chief but to crown commissioners for the forfeited estates of the barony of Lovat. With chastening irony they needed a Highlander to run the tack.

Captain James Fraser, an army officer now serving King George, who was an honourable and prominent local, seen to be reliable and industrious, was their man. He rebuilt the house, incorporating a few contemporary ideas and techniques. Although the well remained out of doors, where it is to this day, it fed a sump in the cellars, enabling water to be drawn under cover. But the new house was still square and small with modest rooms and a plain face, unpretentious and expressionless, as if still burdened by memories of the past. By 1760 it was complete under a roof of grey Ballachulish slate. But, presumably because of James's military absence in America, it was his brother Robert who became the tenant, living in the house and managing the land for him. He styled himself Robert Fraser of Aigas. Life was returning to the Aigas estate, a new beginning, even if the old ways of Gaeldom and the clan system had gone for ever.

Our tree saw Robert's children grow up fit and strong, playing hide and seek around its broadening trunk. Perhaps they tried to carve their initials in its bark when it was young and smooth. Or love hearts, as my twin daughters, Amelia and Melanie, used to call them. If they did they are long subsumed, folded in by the tectonic crinkling of the tree's aged crust. We do not even know their names or how many there were in the last decades of the eighteenth century. All we know for certain is that our tree, now approaching a hundred years old, was *excelsior* – loftier than any other ash in the vicinity. Ash wood was valuable, even precious. It is excellent firewood, cleaving straight to the axe and bright in the fire without a spark. It was sought after for its clean, close grain, long ago for spear shafts, now for implement handles and frames for furniture. How many Highlanders desperate for good wood eyed up its girth and fingered its dense, pale bole, erect and true? Many must have done so.

Someone must have fought its corner, must have valued its shady presence and said firmly: 'No! It's too close to the house, we love it. It breaks the wind and the rain from the south-west and spreads welcome shade from the high summer sun.' Or maybe by then it was just too lovely, too graceful, too special, too ancient, too sacred for the dark secrets they knew it held. By now it was one of the noblest trees in the glen. Most others fell to the predatory axes of men struggling to survive. Few ash trees ever celebrated their centenary in these parts. Yet save it they did, passing it on down the years to us, way beyond their most prophetic imaginings, right through the nineteenth and twentieth centuries.

Our tree was to witness all those who had protected it being carried away, one by one, whoever they were and for whatever the cause, borne aloft on young men's shoulders along the old coffin paths, eastwards over the hill to Kilmorack and the clan graveyard. Beneath its bright summer canopy it saw the Highland folk drift away. Many left of their own volition to emigrate to Ireland and on to the United States or Canada. It was happening up and down the length of Europe. A surge of migrating humanity was voting with their feet, away from feudalism, poverty and misery to what they had been told would be freedom and a new life.

Robert died here in 1819. His grainy pink headstone, cut from the same Tarradale quarry sandstone as graces many a house hereabouts, is dusty and indistinct, with lichen and algae in stippled stars of green and black. Few headstones are legible now in the old graveyard below the road. If you scrub away the lichen you can see that his widow is buried beside him, bearing her own clan name, Mairi Macrae, as is the way here. She lived on a few years, but their children had all gone, perhaps drawn south to the Lowlands, Glasgow or Edinburgh, to find work in the rapidly expanding cities, or married away, or, like their eldest boy, to America.

By 1825 Aigas was going wild again, unworked and unloved. It had fallen into the ownership of absentee Chisholms as the new

Fraser chiefs (who, in 1775, had won back their forfeited estates in return for effective military service for King George in the Raid of Quebec) began to sell off land for much needed cash. Chiefs who had traditionally relied upon their clansmen as a fighting force now became remote from their kinsfolk. Fighting men were no longer needed and money and a regular income became far more important. Inevitably rents rose, accelerating the process of emigration. Highlanders all over the north were selling their possessions and leaving, particularly for North Carolina, New York and Nova Scotia, later to Australia. By 1840 it was described as 'emigration mania'. At Aigas the house began to fall into disrepair.

Ash keys spiralling down from our tree now germinated and took root. A throng of its seedlings sprung up around it. But they were to be short-lived. New people and a new activity had arrived on the better lands at Aigas, to make use of the rank deserted pastures and to produce a profit. Sheep were the fashion of the moment. The chiefs were desperate to find income for themselves and industry for the Highlanders. Now they sought to establish ever-larger sheep farms for the production of wool for profit. It was a commercial success that swept through the impoverished hills and glens. Whole families of shepherds and whole flocks of Linton black-faced sheep and later Cheviot ewes and rams were imported from the Southern Uplands of Scotland to the Highlands to cash in on this new market opportunity. They were English-speaking Lowlanders with names like Elliot, Mitchell, Clark, Mundell, Boa and Wetherspune, names still found scattered up and down the length of these glens. 'Ach, what d'ye expect from that lot?' say the old cynics in the glen. 'They came wi' the sheep.' Even to this day they tut and shake their heads. Our tree, less cynical, watched it all.

To begin with, the sheep presented such a rare opportunity that the remaining clansfolk, now collectively called crofters after the Gaelic word *coirtean* (an enclosure), were seen by landowners, governments and their own chiefs to be a problem, even a nuisance. By 1825, large-scale sheep ranching and production farming by Lowland methods were widespread throughout the Highlands. Wool returned good profits to both farmers and landowners. Expansion was inevitable. It was called 'improvement'. Land was being cleared of its people to make way for the new enterprise. In some areas this was done forcibly – the infamous Highland Clearances – shifting whole townships off the better land of the glens to the periphery, the edge of a flood plain, the high rim of a glacial valley, often to the rocky coast to harvest the sea – almost always to the poorest land. On the Isle of Skye in 1851 the factor of Lord Macdonald of Sleat's estates described the 'numerous small tenantry' as 'a scourge'. They were in the way, especially with their small sheep and black Highland cattle ranging widely over an unfenced land: too many people, too many grazing mouths, too little rent. Emigration accelerated.

Some landlords acted sympathetically, genuinely believing they were strengthening their own and the Highland economy by helping folk to move, and thereby ultimately improving the lot of the Highlanders. Others didn't care, pushing them aside, anywhere, encouraging them to emigrate, out of the way; a planned diaspora. Aigas was not cleared. As a tack, it had long been an improved farm, rather than land held in common by its people. Instead its folk probably drifted away, leaving only a few to work as shepherds. But Urchany, the vanished township behind us, up the hill only two miles into the moors, a village of thirty-one families, perhaps up to a hundred and fifty souls, was cleared completely by 1862: rubbed out.

One stark snippet of hard evidence from an independent observer is recorded by the famous Scottish geologist Sir Archibald Geikie, who was busy tapping his rocks on the coast of south Skye beneath the Cuillin Mountains in the late summer of 1853. What he witnessed was the forced removal of the tenants of Boreraig and Suisnish.

I had heard some rumours of these intentions but did not realise they were in process of being carried into effect, until one afternoon, as I was returning from my ramble, a strange wailing sound reached my ears at intervals on the breeze from the west. On gaining the top of one of these hills ... I could see a long and motley procession winding along the road that led north from Suisnish. It halted at the point of the road opposite Kilbride, and there the lamentation became loud and long. As I drew nearer I could see that the minister with his wife and daughters had come out to meet the people and bid them all farewell. It was a miscellaneous gathering of at least three generations of crofters. There were old men and women too feeble to walk, who were placed in carts; the younger members of the community on foot were carrying their bundles of clothes and household effects, while the children, with looks of alarm, walked alongside. Everyone was in tears ... When they set forth once more, a cry of grief went up to heaven, the long plaintive wail, like a funeral coronach, was resumed ... and the sound seemed to re-echo through the whole wide valley ... in one prolonged note of desolation.

The roofless ruins of these townships remain poignantly intact to this day.

Yet by 1840 the new sheep economy itself was in trouble. The price of wool was falling and, more seriously, the land itself was in decline. No longer sustained by centuries of Highlanders toiling to wind back compost from any source, and their gentler regime of cattle grazing, the fertility of the land was slipping away. Intensive sheep grazing is highly selective. It snips off all the good grasses and creates niches for the untouched coarser and woodier plants to fill. The Highlands were turning to heather, rushes, sedges and unpalatable grasses. An accelerating process of degradation was spiralling downwards, out of control. A Lowland farmer who moved north with the sheep wrote in his diary in 1838: 'There is no profit left in this land.'

When humans withdraw from land – any land – nature takes over. Its healing processes are slow, tentative and successive, often taking one small step at a time. Seeds have to arrive and pitch on to exposed soils, fungus and microbes have to blow in and fester new colonies underground, mosses and liverworts weave their delicate cushions. Invertebrates and bugs have to creak and slither into their niches and crannies, nudging, probing, seething, competing for their own special place. Processes have to revolve, ageless, ponderous and good. After the sheep, nature had plenty of scope. Birchwoods returned, lifting from empty fields like a soft morning mist. Heather bloomed triumphant over the moors, and little knots of Scots pines crowned the high, dry knolls. A consequence of this gentle restoration was a rapid re-emergence of wildlife. Red grouse, enjoying unlimited heather, exploded across every moor. Salmon surged up the rivers unsnared and red deer, which by 1811 had been hunted down to only six small mountain areas (called forests – a relic from the days of real forests) of the Highlands, expanded unchased across broad, deserted hills. Like an ancient benediction, the ash tree prevailed over this tidal ebb and flow of people and animals, fungus and lichen, grasses and heather, bugs and beasts. They passed by, weeping and departing, arriving and labouring, creeping in the night or blown through like thistledown. Our tree stood braced among it all, partaking, sharing and belonging, never still and never silent, but a constant, issuing presence. Its papery lights drank the summer sun; its tracery rattled against the rage of winter.

Queen Victoria and Prince Albert toured the Highlands for the first time in 1842. On his return south Prince Albert wrote, 'Scotland has made a highly favourable impression on us both. The country is really very beautiful, although severe and grand, perfect for sports of all kinds.' By 1848 they had acquired Balmoral estate. The foundation stone of their new castle was laid on 28 September 1853 – on the same day that, far away, on the other side of the Highlands, Sir Archibald Geikie was witnessing the evictions from Boreraig on Skye. Our ash tree was now one hundred and fifty years old.

Without knowing it, the royals had endorsed a fashion that was changing the face of the Highlands almost as much as the Battle of Culloden. The abundant salmon in the mighty rivers of the north, the red grouse that rose in clucking flurries from tree-less purple moors and the rapidly expanding red deer herds, when added to the soulful drama of the empty glens, did, indeed, make it perfect for sports of all kinds. It has come to be known as the Balmorality Epoch, a sardonic sobriquet that stuck, coined in 1932 by the barbed political commentator George Scott Moncrieff. 'The association of high Victorian style with the dedication of huge areas of upland exclusively for field sports, awarded the seal of approval by Her Britannic Majesty Queen Victoria, Empress of India, upon whose empire the sun never set' was an irresistible force. By now everybody who was anybody wanted a Highland sporting estate. There were plenty of enthusiastic takers in the world of burgeoning industrial capitalism that was sweeping across Europe and America. A class of nouveaux riches emerged, redolent with competitive snobbery, desperate to emulate a traditional land-owning aristocracy. They were another new economy for the Highlands, land prices soaring higher than ever known before, and a bonanza for land-rich chiefs and lairds who were again desperate for income after the collapse of the wool price. Aigas had much to offer: the Druim Falls flashed with leaping salmon; the hazy moors above us were clotted with coveys of grouse; and every autumn the mountain corries echoed the challenge of roaring stags. It was only a matter of time before somebody wealthy came along and bought the Aigas tack to convert it into a sporting estate.

He was named Oswald. John William Haldane Gordon-Oswald, to be as precise as he would have wished, was the head of the family. In a long frock coat, a fine bronze statue of James Oswald MP – 1865, John William's father, merchant and politician, stands proudly at the north-east corner of George Square in Glasgow's city centre. The Gordon-Oswalds were a respected and much vaunted Glasgow shipping family who had, with crying irony, made money from shipping Highlanders (among other disposable goods) to the New World. They had also shipped back to Scotland the cheapest timber cargo they could find for the return journey: pitch pine from the Pine Barrens of New Jersey. There was a good market for construction timber in Scotland, which by the nineteenth century had no usable native timber of its own left. Over several centuries our forests had been cleared for agriculture, firewood, charcoal for iron smelting, or simply grazed and burned out of existence. It is a well-tested truism that the closer you are to starvation the less you plan for your future.

But something important had changed. These new owners were not workers of the land; they were not dependent upon Aigas or its local workforce at all. They lived off industrial profits and came here for pleasure, to be seen to be indulging the highest fashion of their day. And they came here for the fair weather only, arriving in June with the first run of salmon up the Beauly River, staying on through the blooming heather for the grouse shooting in August, and into autumn colours for the stag stalking. When the first snow flurries capped Beinn a' Bha'ach Ard to the west, and frost crisped the fallen leaves drifting round the house at night, they scuttled back to their fine Anniesland town house in Glasgow. Estate workers who lived in the village here at Aigas cleaned up behind them and shut down the big house until their return, seven months later, with the swallows and the warm flush of spring.

The Oswalds did not want to live in a tacksman's house. They were Lowlanders who mistrusted everything to do with Gaelic Highlanders. Anyway, they were too rich and too grand to be seen to be summering in a cramped and scruffy eighteenth-century house. They were also too mean to knock it down. Instead they commissioned a well-known firm of architects, Mathews & Lawrie, to design a Balmoral-lookalike castle of their own. It was to be appended, stuck on, as it were, to the façade of the tacksman's house; entirely swamping it round with carved sandstone finery and battlements so that the uninitiated would never know the old house existed. Their date is carved into the gables of the high frontage: AD 1877, almost as if they thought future generations might be uncertain in which epoch it was erected.

Nearly one hundred years after that carving, I had followed a car's tyre tracks up the frosty drive more out of idle curiosity than with much hope of finding a new approach with which to pierce the armour-plated indifference of the council officials who had refused even to discuss selling the property. I walked past the parked car and in through the wide-open front door. The plaster realisation of Africa and the snow had gone and the broken skylights had been temporarily shrouded in polythene sheets. Somebody had cared, at least that much. It was well below freezing and ice-crystals shone around the still-gaping hole out of which Africa had fallen. 'Hullo-oo!' I called. 'Anyone there?' My voice rang round the chill emptiness of the great hall. No answer.

I wandered up the sweeping, imperial stairway and round the gallery above. I called again. Still no answer. The evidence of a failed institution was everywhere. Brown and cream paint peeled like sunburn; cracking green linoleum smothered every floor; and a lingering, omnipresent stench – an acrid cocktail of stale urine, disinfectant and floor polish – caught at the back of my throat. Another open door led me to a second, smaller stairway. On the next floor I called again. Nothing. Wartime iron hospital bedsteads were heaped untidily on a landing. Seeing a third open door, now leading into a tight spiral staircase, I began to ascend a dank, cobwebby tower. At the top, now seventy feet above the rhododendron jungle, an open roof door led me blinking out into low, momentarily blinding sunlight and sabre-edged air. A man stood with his back to me on the mansard roof of the great hall some twenty feet away. I opened my mouth to speak but my words were swept away by the surreal stage set of the ice-gripped forests and the shimmering glen. Below me the river burned like a golden slug trail straggling through pale fields as my eyes followed it out of sight and lifted, squinting, to the silent, crystalline peaks in the west. I don't know how long I stood there before the razor air slicing into my cheeks and lips brought me back to earth.

The river and its ice-forest had peeled me back like the strains of a distant piper, flighting across mountains, vaulting cloudbanks, across rolling oceans of time and events now washed aside, as insignificant as moulted feathers shed in mid-flight. I was back on the scummy marshes at Margam, back in Cornwall, picking along the glutinous tide-line, turning the death litter with my boot. Bob was there on the tower beside me: 'Don't ask bloody stupid questions, lad. Look for yourself and you'll see soon enough.' I shivered.

The timing was portentous. Had I known before I scaled the tower; had I met the man downstairs in the hall, or beside the rhododendron tangle ten minutes before, I might well have walked away from Aigas. Away from the wild possibilities now spinning in my head, away from the spiralling sense of time and place now burnishing my vision.

'Who are *you*?' challenged the burly man in a raincoat who had turned and seen me for the first time.

'Er, I'm a prospective buyer.' My words tumbled out, scarcely knowing what I was saying. 'Do you mind if I look round?'

'Please yourself,' he said, scribbling on his clipboard. 'Take a last look while you can 'cause it'll no be here next month.' He didn't bother to look up from his writing.

'What do you mean? What won't be here?'

'I'm just here to assess the scrap value,' he continued dismissively. 'They're going to demolish the whole place.'

Troubled, I drove up the glen with ice crunching beneath my wheels like broken glass. I didn't like the house. It was spiky, jarring, coldly hollow, like its castellated pretence. It was pompous and unfriendly, its echo mocking. Yet the place beneath was hallowed. Much later I was to discover that the Aigas site has been continuously occupied for four thousand years. Four thousand years of people like me had lived and loved and worked their life-chances into the soils of Aigas. Four hundred centuries of birth, death and decay in this place beside the ash tree I had not yet even noticed. I felt as though I had been chosen, like Daniel in the burning fiery furnace.

Bronze and Iron Age relics surround us here. Aigas is a place, not a house, the notched waterfall, from the old Druim Falls that used to crash through the gorge a quarter of a mile downstream before the dams were erected. It is favoured by its geology and its southerly aspect and bounded by the river. It is a place where a hundred and sixty generations of men, women and children have danced the eternal dance and sung the eternal song. Beneath the northern sun this place delivered up to them its nutrients, its shelter and its soft, bubbling water. Here they shuffled and reassembled their genes, broke rock and trod the paths of fate. Some left their marks for us to read, others, like the leaves of the ash, in innocence returned their nutrients to the earth that had spawned them.

God knows how many buildings have existed here across the millennia: groups of huts and bothies, enclosures, encampments, houses, cottages, hovels, barns and byres. Only God knows what else happened here over that enormous span of occupation. It was a place of sanctuary, with constant fresh water from the loch and the spring that feeds it, cold and clear as an April morning. Within the natural shelter of the glacial valley wall there was pine and birch forest for fuel and fertility in the friable soil terracing down to the lush meadows on the flood plain below. Hallowed. Little wonder it has a long history.

It was the place that gripped me, not the edifice; it was that momentarily dazzling, petrifying view. For a few minutes on the tower that day the clouds had stopped, the river slid to a shimmering halt. I had snatched at the fly and now I was being led away, nose up, robbed of instinct and equilibrium. The sun and the sharp air were sealing me in ice, blast-freezing me for a different purpose later, like a beetle locked in amber. But, I pondered, the Victorian house was not quite a hundred years old. There was good life in it yet. I thought of the bearded masons with their clay pipes skilfully assembling their finely carved blocks. I imagined the teams of joiners, two of whom I later came to know by name, who had laughed and joked as they created from raw imported planks the panelling and the shutters and the elaborate architraves around the doors. I thought of all the care and skill lavished upon this building – for little enough reward.

The decision to demolish it, to wipe it out as if it never existed, could only be political. The new council was embarrassed at the advanced state of neglect: too expensive to repair and convert to another use and too risky for the employees of a new authority, fresh into new jobs, to sell on the open market. It had been neglected badly. Someone might ask awkward questions.

SIX

Swifts in My Tower

Whilst this planet has gone cycling on according to the fixed law of gravity, from so simple a beginning endless forms most beautiful and most wonderful have been, and are being, evolved . . . there is grandeur in this view of life.

CHARLES DARWIN, 1809–82

I had some awkward questions of my own to resolve. Past the frozen glen and the bright mountains beyond there were some harsh realities to face. Looking back now, after all these years, I wonder that we ever made it. Flicking through my old notebooks, I find myself daunted now in a way that I simply don't recall back then. If it was youth, then thank God I was young and fit. If it was folly, thanks for the smiling oblivion. If it was destiny – and I wonder how destiny pays the bills – then I don't know whom to thank. At least I was not alone. The constant enthusiasm of my first wife, Sorrel Bentinck, in those early days, with three tiny children at her feet, was a factor I could not have managed without. And at least my notes were honest. I didn't like the house then and I don't love it now, although we have grown comfortable together as it has surrendered up its blessings to us all.

How does an impecunious amateur naturalist convert a crumbling mansion into a field studies centre and make it work without any experience or much idea about what he is doing? A good start was to gather around me a team of young, strong, enthusiastic and like-minded people who were prepared to work for virtually nothing and who shared common ideals and values. And then you just hope that 'way will show', as pioneering Quakers used to say.

How, twenty-five years later, do you sit down to write a book about a house you don't much like? Fortunately it isn't the house that has kept us here, nor is it the house that has shaped my view of the Aigas place and the Highlands around us. The house serves only as a focus: a pinpoint on a map of much wider, deeper consequence. The house just *is*, in its inimitable nothing-else-quite-like-it-round-here way; and we have mostly the Lowlander Victorians to thank for that. If it is imposing, it was they who made it so. The real Highlanders who have occupied and worked this gentle, tired land for centuries may have had many faults, but bombast was not among them.

Thank God, too, for my notes. (It is a writer's chore and a naturalist's discipline to keep notes – there is a typed log for every day we have existed in this place.) And it is thanks to my own crude jottings and our journals that I can relive those first heady days when the news came through that we had successfully purchased Aigas House. Twenty-five years later they are very revealing and more than a little sobering.

House is gaunt, unfriendly, v. cold. Huge rooms, v. high ceilings – daft. Impossible to heat. Plumbing rusty and crude. Lead pipes everywhere. Wiring cloth and rubber covered – lethal. All main rooms converted for dormitories – hand-basins, bedside lights. Lino floors stink of urine. Plaster on ceilings and walls badly cracked – unsafe – needs renewing. Skylights over hall collapsed – replace urgently. In old house woodworm rife – can push my finger into floorboards. Ceilings look dodgy. Sash windows nailed up. Copper pipe and tanks have been ripped out. Roof leaks badly in at least nine places. Lead on roof perished or missing altogether. Slates need replacing. Can't find a single room I want to live in.

Another page deals with the exterior:

Trees growing out of gutters. Frost split most cast-iron rones and downpipes. Harling [stucco] falling off everywhere. Paint non-existent. Eleven broken windows, some huge. Conservatory collapsed, only foundations left. Rear entrance a mess – corrugated iron and rotten timbers. Greenhouses totally derelict.

And then, far from acknowledging this catalogue of despair, the mood brightens; it begins to turn interesting. There is a page headed 'Reasons For Buying' – then a list:

1. Swifts in the tower. 2. Bats in the roof. 3. House martin nests on the façade. 4. Roe deer in the rhododendrons. 5. Rabbits everywhere – and buzzards. 6. Red deer droppings all over the lawns. 7. Hares in the bamboo and red squirrels in the conifers. 8. Wonderful tree collection – needs work. 9. Big Victorian rooms v. good for lecture room, library, dining, etc. 10. Good office space. 11. Kitchens huge and larders with brilliant slate shelves. 12. There are 13 lavatories, 9 baths, 27 hand-basins, 4 slop sinks.

Underneath as a footnote I have scrawled 'bloody cold'. That arctic day must have slowed the blood through my skull so that only its positive impressions downloaded and lodged there for good. It was January 1977. Two days later I came again, but with Andrew Matheson in tow. He was (and remains) an old friend who was also a land agent and chartered surveyor cutting his first professional teeth in Inverness. Together we crawled through roofs and lofts, peered into dank cellars, probed joists and rafters with our penknives and beamed our torches under floorboards. I remember his parting observation very well: 'If you are daft enough to buy a house of this ridiculous size and shape, you are unlikely to find one as well built or so badly maintained.' His chartered professionalism cost me a bottle of whisky.

I laugh now at how one little thing, a detail, can vault one over huge hurdles. I didn't know how badly I wanted swifts in my tower until they presented themselves to me. I can't explain such an impulse – I had never previously lived in a house with swifts in it. But I had read David Lack's ornithological classic *Swifts in a Tower* (required reading for all serious naturalists of my generation), the seminal study of the birds breeding in the tower of the University Museum at Oxford. In 1948 Dr Lack installed nest boxes in the roof of the tower. They are there to this day and constitute the most studied and filmed colony of swifts in the world. Like all great milestone works it had set standards, cut deep. Ever since then something inside me wanted swifts in a tower of my own, ideally with house martins cementing their muddy pellets under the eaves and swallows skimming in and out of the barn. At Aigas only the swallows were missing and it was to take no more than a year or two to put that right.

The European swift, *Apus apus*, is not a *Hirundine* – not of the swallow and martin family. Swifts don't even sit in the same taxonomic order as the swallows. They belong to a separate group with nightjars, the *Apodiformes* – the legless ones. But their scimitar wings and common insectivorous hawking behaviour seem irresistibly to group them in the mind. When Andrew and I climbed into the huge Victorian lofts at the front of the house, even though it was midwinter and the nearest swift was arcing across African skies several thousand miles away, I was enthralled and speechless. The swifts' nests beneath the louvred roof vents where these virtually legless birds darted in and out all summer long were three feet high. They were history heaped in dung and grass. They were tousled haystacks of grass, feathers, winged seeds and the decomposed faeces of decades of fledglings piled one on another for a hundred years. A century of swifts returning year on year to add a few items of flight-snatched debris to the growing pile. Absent birds were pulling me on board.

I counted the days until the swifts arrived. The house martins came first, and the swallows skimming low over the fields and the sand martins down on the banks of the river, and then, one bright May morning, they were here. They arrived on the 18th that year; they have done so more or less every year since. Sometimes it is a little earlier and sometimes a day or two later, but the 18th is indelibly inscribed in my mind as the date for the swifts.

It is many years now since I last spent time at the swifts' nests – although I did take Hermione, now ten, up there recently to see for herself where these screaming aerial acrobats went to lay their eggs and raise their young. This June I returned there on my own for two hours to rekindle the buzz, spark up my memory banks. But back in those early days it was an opportunity to indulge some serious natural history, to re-enter Aladdin's cave and to glean gems of hard truth from direct observation. I wanted to be able to talk authoritatively to our visitors about these birds whose screaming presence was such an inescapable feature of the Aigas summer.

In Roland Ascroft, who joined us as an early ranger in the field centre team, I quickly found a co-conspirator. Roland was a zoologist by training. He was keen to do some recording of the swifts and to hone his zoological skills. He and I hauled a folding armchair up into the loft and with beams and timbers nailed it into a reclining position in front of the most prominent nest. We rigged up a crude spot-lamp so that we could pry into the private lives of these mysterious birds of such extremes – the brilliant eye-squinting skies of summer and the arid, dusty darkness. We took it in turns to shut ourselves in the hot and airless roof for hours at a time to watch and discover.

The fact that the first seven reasons for buying the place paid scant attention to the page-and-a-half-long catalogue of real and potential disasters reveals my vaulting optimism – or vaulting something. But before the armchair had made its way to the loft, before I could become acquainted with the nesting swifts, first of all I had to become a builder.

Our urgent priority was to make the place wind- and water-tight. In their rush for grandeur and martial effect the Victorians had overlooked one fundamental rule of architecture – the roof

failed to cover the outside walls. In order to achieve battlements it had been necessary to run the slated mansard roof into lead valleys concealed behind the crenellated parapets and corner turrets. Water collecting in these valleys was supposed to escape through the outside walls in cast-iron downpipes and lead spouts tucked into the corners beside the turrets – all very fine until gripping frost closed them off, sealing them solid with ice. Then trapped snow and rain built up on the roofs for the ensuing days or weeks until a full, releasing thaw. If, meanwhile, we lit the fires and ran the creaking and throbbing central heating in a vain attempt to keep ourselves warm, then the heat escaping through the uninsulated roofs transformed the snow into a trapped lake with nowhere to go but down through the house. To add to this oversight, careless and unthinking council employees in hob-nailed boots had tramped about in the lead valleys, penetrating them in a thousand invisible punctures. That first interminable winter we lived with water cascading down the interior walls virtually every time it rained. We danced around buckets in passages and tripped over them in the night. We sat huddled around the fire in anoraks praying that the meagre warmth we generated wouldn't reach the snowdrifts poised high above us. My daughter Amelia, who was a toddler at the time, now tells me that her earliest memory is of her parents constantly emptying buckets of water.

We migrated from room to room as we ripped up floorboards and brought insecure plaster crashing down around us in clouds of choking dust. Gradually we dragged out and replaced leagues of ancient wiring and scores of obsolete electrical fittings. We tore out the ubiquitous hand-basins and slop sinks and enough copper and iron piping to fit out an ocean liner. We heaped acres of green lino and dozens of sordid mattresses – the unwelcome legacy of the old folks' home abandoned in upstairs rooms – into huge funeral pyres on the lawn. As the sparks flared into grey winter skies we watched the years of their terminal isolation brighten and burn away. It felt as though we were liberating souls.

One day we had to dismantle some Victorian panelling in the great hall. We were installing new cables and needed to drill a hole through the broad sandstone wall behind. We eased the fine woodwork from the place where it had stood unmoved and untouched for a century. As my willing helpers lifted it gingerly away from the wall a cry of delight broke from my lips. There, in bold carpenter's pencil script, was a message thoughtfully and purposefully inscribed for us on a rough board nailed to the back of the panelling. This incongruous old house was speaking to us at last. It stopped our work dead in its tracks and we spent the rest of the day celebrating the find.

1879 is an awful year in the country. There is no less than 2 banks [closed] down and about 18 masters [tradesmen] in Inverness alone. Whoever will be taking this down may be thinking on the men written on this board – where they are laid low – never to lift jackie [jack plane] more – him who had this job failed [went bust] when it was near finished. Such a joller lot of men never worked. Alex. Munro and Rodk Johnston was the two men who made this. [Signed] R. Johnston.

Now, quite suddenly, out of nowhere and with the arresting aura of a ghost, a highly personal past was beginning to emerge. At that stage, apart from the names of John William Gordon-Oswald and the tacksman Robert Fraser on the deeds to the property, I had no knowledge of any personal history here. For me Highland history was as yet concealed beneath its glossy romantic wrapping of the Bonnie Prince and the Celtic fringe. Aigas was a rapidly deteriorating shell of a mansion house with some sections clearly older than others, tucked away behind its snow-frayed conifers and tangled rhododendrons in a Highland glen. It didn't relate to real people, nor real events. Now, entirely unexpectedly, a semi-literate joiner called Roderick Johnston had stepped out from behind the panelling, telling us the name of his mate and giving us poignant insight into the economic conditions of the Victorian Highlands.

1879 *was* an 'awful year', both for Glasgow and for Inverness. For a few months that year the economy of Scotland was rocked by scandal. The City of Glasgow Bank, with an important regional office in Inverness, collapsed. What was to emerge in the ensuing months was that the directors of the bank who, to the uncontainable delight of the religious establishment in Scotland, were revealed to be prominent members of the Free Church (the Wee Frees – the nonconformist Presbyterian breakaway group that left the Scottish Established Church in the Disruption of 1843) had recklessly over-invested their customers' funds in highly speculative land deals in the United States and the rapidly expanding Empire. They had bought heavily into the Mississippi Railroad Company (later to become the Western Union) and also into the New Zealand and Australian Land Company, both of which proved to be disastrous and fraught with fraudulent intrigue. The collapse of the City of Glasgow Bank brought down the Caledonian Bank, the headquarters of which was in Inverness, causing it to close its doors entirely from August until December that year. The two closures were responsible for the bankruptcy of the eighteen master tradesmen (among many others). So severe were the economic shock waves from this collapse that the Free Church directors were fully investigated, found to be fraudulently negligent and imprisoned for their greed. It remains the only British case of a bank's directors ever being jailed for misapplication of corporate funds.

How much of this scandal our two Victorian joiners understood we shall never know. But there can be no doubt that it was the hot gossip of the moment and those working men must have gone to their beds each night deeply afraid that its impact would rebound directly upon them. It may well have inspired them to write their message on the board. Fortunately for them, the Gordon-Oswalds, although a Glasgow merchant family and almost certainly affected by the crisis in some way, were also very wealthy and in a hurry. They were determined to finish the Aigas job regardless of the economic constraints of the moment. This was their cabin in the hills, their summer retreat for genteel sport and recreation in high fashion. In its battlements and its glossy panelling they had invested their hopes for social acceptability in the years ahead. Some things just have to go on.

I have often pondered the serendipity of that discovery. I have never found anything of such historical consequence in the house since. There are broad screens of panelling, shutters and ornamental woodwork throughout the Victorian rooms on two floors. Not only could he have pinned his message to any of it, in any position, anywhere in the house, but we could have chosen any of a hundred other places to drill our hole. It seemed then, and still does, quite remarkable that we should have happened across it so immediately and at a moment when we badly needed something to spur us into uncovering the real story of the place. My debt to the two jolly joiners, Roderick Johnston and Alex Munro, is huge. Despite exhaustive researches in local registers, graveyards and archives I have never found where they are laid low, nor anything else about them. I don't know whether they were local men or migrant tradesman brought in for the Aigas job – Johnston and Munro are common names throughout Scotland. Wherever it is they are laid, all I can say to them is that we have 'thought on' them now for twenty-five years – probably far more than they ever imagined their tiny act of history might inspire. Their little board with its rusty cut-nails is a mounted exhibit in the common room, eyed, fingered and pondered by tens of thousands of visitors over the decades. More significantly than that, their actions proved to be the first piece in the jigsaw of Victorian Aigas. The actions of the Wee Frees and the turmoil within religious society not just in Scotland but throughout the world were to provide us with more direct links to the Oxford University Museum than just Dr Lack's study on swifts. At the very moment in 1879 that Roderick Johnston and Alex Munro were hammering nails into this huge roof, their world, and especially that of their sponsors, the Gordon-Oswalds, was about to be turned upside down.

When the foundation stones of the grandly Victorian Gothic building that was to be the Oxford University Museum of Science were laid in 1855, the Church and the world of science co-existed in relative harmony. Funds for this exciting, extravagant building came largely from the sale of Bibles – a highly profitable trade in England since William Caxton had set the world a-reading at the end of the fifteenth century. But therein lay a dramatic irony that was to rumble on for another hundred years. As the building progressed over the next few years, unknown to the lofty rectors of academia, Charles Robert Darwin (not long back from the Galapagos as naturalist on board HMS *Beagle*), and Alfred Russel Wallace (researching the Malay Archipelago) were absorbed in a world-changing correspondence of deep heresy. The younger Wallace had sketched out his thoughts on the theory of evolutionary mechanism, which chimed with Darwin's own fresh observations in the Galapagos. Together they agreed a plan to publish the faith-shattering theory of evolution by natural selection. It finally emerged at a meeting of the Linnean Society in London on 1 July 1858. It was to be the most revolutionary work of modern scientific imagination.

The belief that God had independently created every form of life was long established and fervently held, not just by the Church but by the whole fabric of Western society. In 1650 the Irish archbishop James Ussher had miraculously established a date for the creation of the world as we know it in his *Annales Veteris et Novi Testamenti* (*Annals of the Old and New Testaments*). Doubtless with divine inspiration he had plumped for 4004 BC. Who could possibly counter such definitive authority? This (now) bizarre and unlikely diktat was to run unchallenged for a hundred and fifty years. At the turn of the nineteenth century creationists like the Reverend William Paley still ruled supreme. It was he who in *Natural Theology*, published in 1802, expanded his argument that only God could have dreamed up such amazing design as, for instance, the human eye, or the feathers of a peacock's tail. With the glowing confidence of real dogma, he zealously pursued the watchmaker analogy – to have a watch there *has* to be a watchmaker.

In 1820, at Cromarty, only twenty-five miles away from Aigas, a remarkable young stonemason named Hugh Miller, whose strict Presbyterian upbringing had been steeped in Paley's creation-ism, was busy shaping his soft red sandstone; but increasingly he did so with a troubled look furrowing his brow. 'It was the neces-sity which made me a quarrier that taught me to be a geologist,' he was to write later in his autobiographical account of *The Old Red Sandstone*. On the foreshore near his home he had discov-ered the 'marvellous library of the Scotch lias'. Close examination of this rock revealed to him 'a sort of boarded book'. This shale-like sedimentary rock, in places as soft as dried mud, contained page after page of fossils thinly laid down one upon another, just like a book:

I found the pictorial records of a former creation in every page: scallops, and gryphites, and ammonites . . . at least eight or ten varieties of belemnite; twigs of wood, leaves of plants, cones of an extinct species of pine, bits of charcoal, and the scales of fishes.

His skills as a stonemason enabled him to 'open' these rock libraries with ease.

The inescapable evidence of evolution, particularly from fos-sils, evidence that was causing scientists to mutter darkly in private, had been conveniently explained by Jean-Baptiste de

Monet de Lamarck in his *Philosophie Zoologique*, published in 1809. It was the not-too-contentious theory of the inheritance of characteristics acquired by environmental conditioning: that by stretching their necks ever longer in the perpetual competition for food, the successful giraffes would reach more feed, grow stronger and be able to pass their longer necks on to their off-spring. Here was an evolutionary theory which did not directly challenge the original creation by God, but just nudged things along in a logical progression. Lamarck had seen the wood, but missed the trees.

In 1829 Hugh Miller came to Aigas. The fault line here, which separates the conglomerate 'pudding-stone' from the hard meta-morphic mica schist (and affords us the peculiar scooped-out hollow in which we sit), attracted his interest. In 1830 he made a discovery of fish fossils that were to bring him fame and scientific recognition as one of the founding fathers of geology. When he tapped open a sandstone boulder near Cromarty he found 'spines and small ichthyic bones . . . glittering rhomboidal scales, with a few cerebral plates, and a jaw bristling with teeth'. As Miller matured as a geologist so he came to realise that the earth could not possibly have been created in the six days described in the Book of Genesis. The creation was coming under general attack from the early theorists of evolution and Miller found himself trapped between the evidence of his own discoveries and his reli-gion, 'the central passion' of his life. He was to make it his personal 'sacred charge' to attempt to reconcile these two diver-gent and divisive beliefs. So he postulated his own theory of successive creation – the idea that the Bible's six days corre-sponded to a succession of great ages. He was to produce a great outpouring of persuasive insights in *Footprints of the Creator*, *The Headship of Christ* and *The Testimony of the Rocks*. It is thought that this intellectual exertion overtaxed his failing health. The years of inhaling stone dust had given him silicosis of the lungs, chronic and incurable.

In his last years Hugh Miller was increasingly troubled. It now seems inevitable that the momentum towards evolution – a notion he hotly disputed until his death – would sooner or later have rendered his theory of successive creation redundant. It would also have kicked from under him the central platform of his beliefs. In 1856, just three years before the publication of Darwin's great work, tormented to distraction by what is now thought to have been a brain tumour, Hugh Miller shot himself with a single bullet to the chest, and so died the Highlands' most famous geologist. He was only fifty-four. Later, his protégé, the celebrated grandee of geology Sir Archibald Geikie, was to write: 'I do not think that the debt which geology owes to him for deepening the popular estimation of the science has ever been sufficiently acknowledged.'

When *The Origin of Species by Means of Natural Selection or the Preservation of Favoured Races in the Struggle for Life* was published, it drove an irreversible and devastating wedge between the worlds of science and the Church. Although the book carefully sidesteps the issue of whether nature and man were created by God, the issue was not long in surfacing. It was there by implication – Darwin's central contention was that *all* life is subject to natural selection. A year later it came to a head in the famous debate, hosted by the now completed University Museum, between Samuel Wilberforce, Bishop of Oxford, and Darwin's fiery colleague and disciple Thomas Henry Huxley. The debate was turned to Huxley's favour and became instantly famous for his mocking insistence that he 'would rather be descended from an ape than a divine who used authority to stifle the truth'. It was to be another ten years before Darwin was to come clean himself. In 1871 he finally published *The Descent of Man*, postulating a direct evolutionary link through the anthropoid apes.

What remains so remarkable about Darwin and Wallace's work is that, quite beside the pressing and constraining beliefs of religion, they had no idea of the mechanism for the transference of variation from one generation to another. They knew nothing of genes, the building blocks of inheritance, or of the science of genetics, which was so powerfully to underpin their theory. Only a few years later (1865) the Austrian Augustinian abbot Gregor Mendel had been tinkering with garden peas. His research into plant breeding had led him to conclude that there were distinct laws at work governing the nature of inheritance. He did have the advantage of Darwin's theory; a copy of *Origin* annotated in his own hand still exists. Mendel's notes, entitled *Experiments with Plant Hybrids*, were published in 1866 in a little-known journal. It was not until long after his death that his meticulous observations achieved recognition.

Mendel's work lies at the heart of everything we have subsequently come to understand about heredity and natural selection. He cracked Darwin's puzzle. What Darwin and Wallace had figured out was that in natural populations many more individuals are born than can or do grow to maturity. Every one is an individual, slightly different from its siblings and its parents. In the 'struggle for existence' – the endless competition for food and to breed – those with differences, however tiny, which better equip the individual for survival are selected by nature to live and pass on that advantage. Darwin never worked out how this happened. It was the great omission from his work, and he knew it. He could never have dreamed of the extent of the random combinations of opportunity for change an individual inherits from its parents. It is this random selection of genes on the chromosomes of every individual of each species that gives natural selection its unlimited opportunities for change – that enables a swift to become a swift.

High above the theology versus science debate in Oxford, breeding swifts were screaming their frantic circles around the central tower. Even as they spoke genes were combining in the sky. While the interior of the museum was to be filled with dead specimens, natural selection for this most highly adapted bird species was acting out its seasonal drama. Dr Lack was to install forty double and sixty-seven single nest boxes so that there was space for one hundred and forty-seven pairs of nesting birds. This was no mean study.

Although Roderick Johnston had given us the date of 1879 on his interior work, the sandstone gables bear the mason's engraved date of 1877. It seems likely that, with landscaping, the Victorian house may have taken fully four years to complete before the Gordon-Oswalds moved in. It was precisely then, during the years 1876–80, that the Darwinian debate raged at its fiercest. We were later to discover that the Gordon-Oswalds had been apocalyptic Adventists – Plymouth Brethren – who would have had no truck with the profane articulations of science. They were stuck in 4004 BC. They adhered rigidly to the belief that not only was man created in the image of God but also that He was coming back any day to put everything right. Here at Aigas Darwin's name would have been spoken only in scorn.

At that time in Britain natural history was still a respectable and genteel enquiry into the wondrous world of God's creativity. The Gordon-Oswalds would have had no quarrel with our predilections for nature, but my need to search for deeper explanations of the natural world around me – my insight conundrum – they would have held to be a weakness of the mind, as drink and sex were weaknesses of the flesh. The age-old philosophical questions – 'Where do we come from and where do we go when we die? How should we conduct ourselves in between and who is to be our guide?' – would have presented few problems for John William and Eugenie Diane, his wife. Had they known that there were swifts nesting in their roofs, and had they believed the medieval legend that they were agents of Satan, perhaps these fascinating birds would have been evicted long ago and mesh nailed over the roof vents.

The folding armchair and the lamp are still here. I ease myself into the dusty seat. I am four feet from a swift on her nest. Gently

I focus the beam on to her sooty, curving form. She does not move. The feathers of her head and nape are layered like the slates above me on the roof, each one wearing a paler curve at its rim, like ocean waves on a choppy day. Her throat is pale. Her tiny black bill mirrors the curve of her aerodynamic head and her colourless sunken eyes, Oriental and inscrutable, stare at me in an unblinking, unrevealing gaze. No wonder this is called the Devil bird, or the Develing, the Skir devil or the Devil's screech. People have always been wary of things they can't explain. For centuries we knew neither where they came from nor where they went when they so suddenly vanished. Their common screaming presence around church towers and their darting disappearance into dark crannies seemed to suggest they were agents of the Devil sent to mock and to haunt the houses of God. Some, like the sixteenth-century Swede Olaus Magnus, Bishop of Uppsala, seeing them dip to the surface of water to drink, believed that they rocketed themselves into the mud at the bottom of ponds and lakes, where they survived the long winter. Even the great eighteenth-century English naturalist Gilbert White instructed men to dig in the ground in his search for hibernating swifts.

This is a mystery in dark curves. It is a bird unlike any other. It is enclosed by wing, trapped within its own parentheses. The rigid blades of its curved primaries extend far beyond its tail. Its genes must be curved. Its legs, such as they are, are invisible. It shuffles rudely on its belly. Its scrape of a nest, loosely gummed with saliva, is hard against the gable only a few inches below the louvres where it makes its rocketing, roof-piercing entry. I wince as her mate arrives. A black projectile hurls itself at the tiny day-lit aperture, a feathered dart stabbing home, right on target every time. The accuracy and speed are astonishing. This bird can fly at one hundred and five miles an hour.

Outside, the others – the gang of perhaps non-breeding juveniles honing technique for when their turn comes – are circling in wide, screeching arcs of catch-me-if-you-can. The air ripples with their frantic passing. Their wake casts dust into the thin sunbeams that slice across the roof floor. For a moment I am a lighted mote dancing in the beam. I become a blur, dazzled by this extraordinary bird.

Take one bird. Take an ordinary perching bird, a passerine such as makes up more than half of all known living birds. It has a beak and two eyes, two legs and four toes, a tail and two wings and a set of major and minor pectoral muscles bound to its breastbone to make the wings work. It has to have at least one mate. It has to copulate to fertilise its eggs and it has to find a place in which to lay them. It must find a reliable food supply sufficient to feed itself and raise its young. The world is full of food and there are thousands of niches it could fill. Throw in a good seasoning of competition and you end up where you started, with a passerine just like half the known birds living today. You have a thrush or a robin, a redstart, a blue tit or a wren. Some have special colours; others have special beaks, like Darwin's epiphanic finches in that remarkable evolutionary laboratory, the Galapagos. Some, like the peacock, have found a mating advantage in a special feature such as a tail and have gone for it. Peacocks have hauled themselves off on their own little whirlwind of adaptation, investing all their effort into a sublime outpouring of stupendously absurd tail. Nothing so whimsical for the swift.

Something different happened to the swift a long time ago – a very long time ago. No one knows exactly when, but it was probably in the Eocene, some forty million years ago. Swifts split off; they chose not to stay perching. Something or somebody back then took to one side the perching progenitor of the seventy known species of swift in the world today and whispered in its feathered ear. 'Ignore what everybody else is doing,' it said. 'You are going to have to distort a fair suite of your genes. Forget the land and the multitudinous food supplies down there. Give up perching and abandon your legs, swivel your toes around so that you can only land on vertical surfaces. To heck with trees and worm-cast lawns – make do with a crack in a cliff (of which there are very few). Grow a pair of wings so long that they'll prevent you from ever doing anything but flying in circles and, while you're at it, never roost again. Sink your eyes into the side of your head so that you can fly at a hundred and five miles an hour without making them water. Then go and live on gnats and moths. And, oh, when you've perfected all that, never sing again, but scream like a dervish!'

The hen fidgets on her three pure white eggs. She is living two lives: one out there in the gilding sunlight and the other in the hot darkness of her future. She is made for the light and forced to creep into the dark to perpetuate her kind. These are the only times she will land in her possible eighteen years of life. This incredible bird sleeps, eats, drinks, mates and even dies on the wing, drawing huge looping circles around its own existence like a child's first scribblings on a blank sheet. Only its eggs and fledglings need to share their gravity with the earth.

At night our swifts ride high. As darkness falls they spiral higher and higher, surfing the invisible currents of the wind until they disappear from human view. There they sleep on rigid, involuntarily flickering scimitars, endlessly inscribing their rapid circles in the night. To feed, they graze the wind. On a fine day a pair feeding young may snatch twenty thousand flying insects and thread-trailing spiders from the air. Dr Lack identified over one hundred different species in the food brought in to the young. From the tiniest gnats and the ditheriest moths to wasps, bees, hoverflies and lumbering beetles; nothing airborne in chitin is safe from these ravening, hawking, untaloned scourges of the insect world.

This bird is tied to the ebb and flow of its food supply. In bad weather when insects don't fly it will weaken and starve but, incredibly, the young are adapted to survive in the nest for up to three weeks without food. When the season draws in and the insect harvest recedes with the chill nights, the swift must follow the autumn south to a more insect-laden climate. It skims the enriching air far above the weather all the way to southern Africa. No one knows what draws it back again. In a lifetime a swift may fly well over four million miles. One famous bird – adult D3082 – was ringed in the Oxford Tower in June 1948. Obligingly it chose to die there sixteen years later in June 1964.

Sitting here, I am taken back to those early years. Watching swifts on the nest is not the most adrenalising experience. There are long periods of stifling emptiness when the bird sits tight and I nod off to sleep in the heat or muse over the tireless riddle of animal behaviour. I probe my torch beam around the roof. The long-eared bats are still there in furry, twitching bundles jammed into the tight apex of the ridge. As my light stirs them their ridiculous ribbed ears extend and rotate like the radar scanners they are. Their tiny black eyes sparkle like sequins in velvet. Roland and I sat up here for scores of hours. I remember staring at the rafters and the joists and imagining Roderick Johnston and Alex Munro and their pals laughing and joking through ribald days, hearing the ring of their hammers and the rhythmic song of their handsaws. I recall calculating the weight of the thousands of Ballachulish slates resting obliquely above my head. I remember hoping the nails were strong.

Rather than disturb her by climbing from this smelly old chair I wait for my bird to decide she needs to feed. She shuffles to the vent only slightly less awkwardly than I shall to the hatch. She launches. A flash of silver sunlight catches her flicking wings. If only I could pitch myself into the fine air. The roof ladder seems a crude descent after two hours of sharing the private life of a swift. The eggs seem to glow in the dark. I struggle out feeling empty. Part of me has gone with her, is at this moment skimming the tower honouring the day with a long-drawn scream.

SEVEN

Wasps and Winds

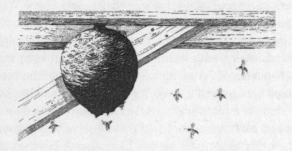

Ever since the dawn of creation people have craved an understanding of the underlying order in the world. Today we still yearn to know why we are here and where we came from. Our goal is nothing less than a complete description of the universe we live in.

STEPHEN HAWKING, 1942–

I stand underneath the ash tree thinking about the history it has seen. The three hundred years of people who have shared their lives with it and the soil I stand upon. Leaning against the rough bark I can scarcely bear the images of the Culloden aftermath, then the people drifting away and the nineteenth-century reinvention of the place Aigas as a grand sporting estate. After the Gordon-Oswalds die out comes the sorry era of the old folk's home. History is restless and exhausting.

As I turn away to return to the house a little wind skitters in, as is the way of these glens. The U-shaped glacial troughs, this one running twenty-two miles to the south-west, attract winds and breezes in every season. The Highlands don't have a sirocco, a mistral or a chinook; nothing so awesome as the Italian north wind, the tramontanta, which withers grapes on the vine, or the Greek euroclydon, which shipwrecked Paul of Tarsus while crossing the Mediterranean from Sidon to Italy – although I think we deserve one: perhaps Boreas caledonensis, an earthward fling of the aurora borealis, felt but not seen, or maybe a visitation of long airs, in the Gaelic *an ar-a-mach neo-shaicssinneach*, an invisible uprising.

Instead, we live with winds like breath, damp and warm, like harring on a mirror, or sudden angry blasts, as from pursed lips you would blow to evict a fly from your page. Sometimes these are so sudden and blade-like that well-grown Sitka spruces are snapped off halfway up, cutting a narrow swath through a planta-tion thirty feet from the ground. In autumn and winter wide gusting surges come swirling in from far out in the Atlantic and are flung upwards when they collide with the Highlands' moun-tain spine on the west coast. They rattle through the peaks and high passes and are sucked down again into the whirling void that straddles the glens, a vast upland wilderness of moors and snow-fields for which this land is so renowned. At such times the woods become a tumultuous sea for days on end.

People don't live up there, and never have, apart from long ago in a handful of summer shielings. They were little stone and turf shelters, anonymous now as a few boulders in the heather. Highlanders camped there while tending their livestock during the long-daylight days of high grazing. No, all the permanent houses, cottages, homesteads, farms and crofts are sensibly tucked into hollows, like Aigas, down on the edge of the flood plain or up on the rim of the valleys, or in between, if the geology of the valley wall allows.

These great glacial valleys, often a thousand feet deep, are known all over the world as glens. It is a word evocatively locked into the nostalgic psyche of all Highland Scots. Their hearts and minds have been so completely contained within these thin ribbons of intimate human settlement, sometimes twenty miles long, that even after several lifetimes away, and for all the magic and romance of the high hills, it is of the glens that they still longingly speak.

Blasts of ocean pick out the gaps in the hills. They are drawn down into the glens and scour through in a torrent, hurling everything before them. It is not unusual to see waterfalls spilling over the edge of the glacial rim – normally a vertical cascade of white water, rudely snatched at the rock lip and spun upwards again, thrown back to the sky by an invisible wind-surge roaring the rough utterances of the mountains. In summer much kinder drapes of moist air slide off the heights as a nylon sheet slithers off a table, soft and fluid. They pour into the glens like warm milk, channelled by their own sighing momentum.

The ash tree stands back from the edge of the valley, slightly tucked in, which may be why in its long life it has not blown over. But the uppermost branches bearing its outer skim of sentient green scales, translucent with sky, hang into the airflow so that they are almost never silent. Even on sultry days when I long for a breeze to freshen through the house and gardens, the ash seems to ignore us, enjoying its own private conversation up there, cryptic and aloof. It humbles me with its great presence, like a cathedral.

I'm heading out. Today is warm. It is a day apparently without air through which I am forced to swim. I need to escape and to pull in some wider sky for myself. There's too much going on down here. Leaving the house, I slide through the tall, arched plate-glass doors that partition the great hall from the entrance. I pass the common room, once the Gordon-Oswalds' dining room, now a sitting-cum-lecture-room given over to the field centre for the general day-to-day use of our guests and students. The door is about an inch ajar. A thin strip of the action inside tempts me closer. I can hear Duncan Macdonald explaining about insects to a class of fidgety eight- and nine-year-olds from Teanassie Primary School, three miles down the glen.

'Who do you think has made this?' His soft Borders voice wraps them in friendly enthusiasm. I can't see what he's holding up. I think it's a nest, or a cocoon, perhaps?

Duncan is our environmental education officer and has been with us for nine years; a teacher of the truths, stark and glowing, mankind often chooses to ignore. Thousands of children have fidgeted their way into nature here.

'Bees!' they yell, excitedly.

'No, not bees. Close, though. Try again.'

Silence. A few giggles. I can see a boy wide-eyed, galvanised with curiosity. Now I know what it is. I fight back an urge to prompt the little boy from behind the door.

Earlier this summer a badger dug out some wasps from under a larch root in the woods behind the house. That morning Duncan found the crater of dry forest soil and wafers of comb spread around, scattered like a dog in a dustbin. The nest was picked clean, the whole angry swarm and all their eggs and grubs, all licked up; so much lunch. The common-room shelves have been cluttered with huddles of papery cells ever since – that's what it is.

Years ago I took a wasps' nest out of the Aigas roof. It hung from a rafter like a huge paper lantern, bomb-like, resonant with threat. I made up a crude stethoscope from a coffee tin and a length of plastic tube and pressed the tin to the nest, the tube to my ear. It was like pressing my ear to the dome of some great Roman basilica wherein a constant droning litany rose and fell; murmured responses echoed, rippling through, unintelligible but strangely personal, as if they were praying about me. But it was in a bad place for wasps to be. They were terrorising the bedrooms of girls who worked in the household. They got lost in the roof and wall cavities, emerging crossly from beneath skirting boards in the night. They droned their menace around these rooms until

I gave in to the complaints and reluctantly silenced the nest with a vile powder puffed in to the entrance, a crack in the slates above, where the workers processed in and out carrying food and wood pulp for the expanding swarm.

The nest was so lovely, so finely crafted. It was an intricate mesh of shell-like scales mouthed together in a papier-mâché weld. I couldn't bear to destroy it. I cut it down intact and mounted it in an open display box so that visiting children and adults could share it. For ten days it was a source of great interest until one morning our duty ranger came to me in alarm saying that the common room was full of wasps. At first I thought that this was some sort of divine retribution; that the dead had arisen and swarmed back in anger to claim their own. The room was full of wasps and they were mightily cross, not to say outraged. They were everywhere, crawling all over the carpet and chairs, buzzing frantically on the windows and angrily dive-bombing anything that moved; several of us were stung almost immediately. Slowly I realised that it was my fault. I had killed all the living workers, wiped out a whole generation, stilling the buzz so that it appeared dead. Far from it: deep inside hundreds of grubs were quietly developing and hatching, untouched by the deadly powder, festering anger and revenge. The buzz had returned to the nest unnoticed until, perhaps in collusion, perhaps at random, that morning they came rampaging out to face their aggressors. It took us days to overcome them. The nest had to be removed to a tree and left there to exhaust itself of eggs and larvae until it buzzed no more.

In the field centre library I found an old book on coping with house pests. It said: 'if the nest can be doused in paraffin and set alight it is most effective'. I bet it is. Perhaps the Duke of Cumberland wrote it in his spare time.

The day-to-day business of a field studies centre is often unexceptional. Like every job it has its routines and its rules, its tedium and its moments of drama, but to most of the world it is an unknown. 'What do you do there?' I get asked by blank faces who perfectly obviously have not the first notion of what field studies might be or even what one could possibly find to study in a field.

'People come to us to learn about nature . . . and the wildlife and the history and archaeology of the Highlands.'

Aigas is a place where people can come and learn with the help of local knowledge. There are no set agendas. Our task is to provide the means for learning about the Highland environment – its geology, climate, archaeology, flora and fauna, its social history and the history of the land, its people. We take all-comers: schools, universities, clubs and societies, corporate groups, the general public – anyone who is interested in taking a closer look, peeling back the past, discovering what really shapes the land and people's lives.

We deal in texture.

I'm off up to the loch. This is partly escape – I've had enough of writing for today – and partly because in a while Duncan and the other rangers will be taking his class of fidgets up there to meet some insects for themselves. They have a pinewood and a marsh, a pond and a boggy heath and lots of wet willow woodland where they can explore. It is a summer activity all children love. Discovery is the essence of learning about nature. It quickens the pulse, keens the senses and colours the imagination. The woods and the marshes, the loch and the murmuring burn are waiting like hay: life's particular secrets, there to be found.

Like Thoreau, we have a cabin. Ours is called the Illicit Still. And like his, it's built of second-hand timbers, right on the edge of the loch, its portals decked out over the water. Here I can sit and spy on the rites of environmental education going on all round. I can sit quietly and work, binoculars at my side, so that when I hear a distant shriek I glance up and pull focus across the water on the bossy girl who has been pushed over in the marsh. Or I can see which boy has ventured into the bit of bog he was told not to, and now has lost his boot. Sometimes the rangers link all the children together with a ball of string, each child representing a different life form. It is an eco-game illustrating the web of life, the absolute interdependence of all living things. I spy on them floundering about in the heather, getting into tangles and perversely tugging on the string when they're not supposed to, or refusing to feel the tug which signals that they have been caught and eaten by a predator in the food chain. Sometimes I want to go and join in. It is a delight Thoreau never knew at Walden Pond. He was too busy moralising. I love to watch it happening from a distance, letting the pleasure of our work flow over me like the Highland breeze, nameless and invisible, which wafts their happy cries across to me. I chuckle. 'What is it, exactly, you do here?'

Today is now hot, but it's much fresher up here. The timber deck seems to absorb heat. I place my chair so that I can, too. I pick up my book. The cabin's rough pine cladding creaks and cracks as the boards twist and split. This makes its walls and its eaves a haven for wildlife. They're all welcome. It surprised me how quickly they moved in.

The Illicit Still is a small fishing hut, a place of refuge for our few friends who whisk their wet and dry flies, elegantly looping out across the loch like ringmasters' whips, for its wild brownies and a few rainbow trout popped in for good measure. We built it ourselves, family and field centre staff laughing together with our joiner, Billy Horne, who has driven joy as well as nails into every roof and door-post, every joist and every rafter of this place for the past twenty years. It is hard to imagine doing a building job without him; I have come to rely upon his agile eye, his ready wit and the ringing laugh of a man who loves his work. He has the hands of a master craftsman, deft and sure. Touch and feel are as much a part of his thinking as the intuition that guides them.

We were using up old materials, anything left over from previous jobs, and cutting fresh timber poles straight from the spruce plantation beside the loch. Our own pine boards, an inch thick, we had milled at the local sawmill. There was much need for imagination and extemporisation.

'This beam won't fit.'

'Why not?'

'Because it's too short.'

'Well, shorten the building then!'

And much cause for mirth among the gang of rangers and friends who helped out.

Every day someone had to stand up to his or her chest in the loch to hold the vertical deck poles upright as they were pinned into position. We took it in turns. Others just fell in anyway, or dropped their hammers and had to dive to recover them, or, accidentally stepping on unfixed boards, toppled in with a yell and a splash like pirates walking the plank.

It is said that words written in tears and in laughter are read in tears and in laughter. It is a maxim that taunts me daily. Aigas has taught me to believe it is also true of buildings. The Still has come to be a place of perpetual, rotating delight. Unlike Thoreau, we encourage friends and family to use it. Often their faces seem to reflect the burlesque of its fabrication. More laughter and simple ribald fun rippled out across the loch and was hammered into that shell of timbers than into any other I have known. Over and over again it delivers up its broad smiles, its infectious joy.

Most of the timbers were untreated. In a wet climate this is unwise: the forces of decay never refuse an invitation. Rot never sleeps. So we anointed them with a coating of preservative, sticky and cedar brown, which would keep the fungus and some of the bugs at bay, at least for a while. Not so the pipistrelle bats. The uneven edges of the pine boards, clinkered one over the next, inevitably left small gaps: thin slits, where if you tried hard you could see up into a small, dark cavity. As the boards dried, so some of these gaps widened, watched, it is clear, not by nocturnal eyes – bats are not known for their eyesight – but by probing night-radar far keener than Billy Horne's eyes or mine.

Now that I know what to look for I have sat and watched the prospecting process right through. ('Stop asking bloody daft questions, boy. Sit still and watch and you'll find out soon enough.') Like swallows checking out nest sites each spring, the pipistrelles, the commonest of British bats – pips we call them – fly in low and swoop up, bombarding the boards from underneath with very high-pitched sonar bleeps, inaudible to us, hovering momentarily, before flickering away again and out over the loch. From time to time the field centre borrows a sneaky gadget called a bat detector that allows you to eavesdrop electronically on any bat's ultrasonic soliloquy. (I was amused to see that it was made in Russia.) Once tuned in to the right frequency it crackles like a grasshopper, statically charged. Those ultrasonic bleeps must tell them whether the cavity beyond the crack is to their liking: deep enough, broad enough, penetrating far enough in to be worth exploring further, occupied or vacant. Back he comes, skimming in over the water, straight through the criss-cross log railings, sweeping low over the deck and, with a barely audible rustle of membranous wings, alights vertically on the rough boards, clinging on with toe and thumb claws, while the active little head inspects the entrance. They often hold this position for several seconds, during which other bats flit by, chittering and squeaking loudly as if encouraging, or perhaps rudely barracking the explorer. If it is to his liking – and it only has to be a tiny crack – the pip creeps in. What happens then is pure comedy. He pops his head out of the entrance and yells his triumph to all-comers. It is a game, visibly enjoyed by several players, something akin to 'I'm the king of the castle', or perhaps just shouting, 'Look what I've found!' and 'I got here first!' Far from the ultrasonic emissions they use for locating prey, these are highly energised chitterings that can be heard by the human ear very easily from many yards away. I have no idea what they really say, but the response is electric. Every other pipistrelle in the district arrives to have a look and approve or disapprove the new location, bickering in a continuous fly-past of squeaky comment. I have watched a dozen bats drawn in by this performance, all flitting past at high speed, swooping low and checking it out, all accompanied by exultant squeaky crescendos from the new lodger. Bat-chat.

Pips live in colonies. The Still is now an established colony producing young every year. As the boards have continued to warp, more cavities have opened up and made it easy for them to penetrate the roof and the walls: a bat village. I no longer know how many there are. On fine summer evenings I watch them emerge; excited chittering inside the walls and then tipping out, in ones and twos, still bickering like children coming out of school. But they're well-nigh impossible to count because they are emerging from cracks all over the cabin, on all four sides at every level. I charge no rent. If each one is gobbling midges and mosquitoes all night long, they are welcome indeed.

I have my feet up on the deck rail and I'm reading Gary Snyder's *Axe Handles*, smiling compliance with a fellow spirit: 'What I came to say was teach the children about the cycles. The life cycles. All the other cycles. That's what it's all about, and it's all forgot.' My spirit eases back, shedding static after history, wasps and bats. Something clatters across the corner of my vision. I look up. Rattling wings say dragonfly. But it wasn't quite right for a golden-ringed *Cordulegaster boltoni*, the biggest and the rattliest of the eight species of dragonflies and damselflies we boast on Loch Cuil na Caillich, although it makes a goodly racket with its four stiffly oscillating wings. Whatever it was has gone. I read on. Then I hear it again, harder, more clackety, and it comes in short, unfamiliar bursts without enough hover. Now I know what it is, and it interests me. I want to see it. For the moment even *Axe Handles* can wait.

This afternoon another prospective tenant is exploring the fence of spruce poles that surround the cabin. I stand up. This time I see it. It rises from the horizontal top rail and ratchets forward in a short, purposeful flight of only three feet or so. It lands closer to me and I can see it well. It is a wasp, but no ordinary wasp. This is *Uroceros* (literally, tail-horn, *u-ros-eros*, like rhinoceros, the nose-horn), the greater horntail or wood wasp. I see them in the pinewoods every year, but only since the cabin rails have been erected have I really come to know them well. By chance we have done what nature does in a wild wood. We have laid down the spruce poles like fallen trees, leaving the bark on, horizontal and waiting. Dead wood is a benediction to a wood wasp. Even the coating of preservative doesn't seem to bother *Uroceros*. It's convinced it has found the very thing God has told it to go and look for on a bright July afternoon: fallen trees nicely drying in the sun, expanding their fibres. To this complicated insect my rails are an irresistible match with its genetic printed circuit. She's hard-wired; on course for ever, like the sun.

It is clearly a wasp, a huge wasp, just like a hornet but bigger and more alarming. It's not social but solitary – downright anti-social, to put it charitably. It's all spikes and spurs, like a dragoon. It measures some three inches long from the gyrating, probing points of its long, segmented, bright yellow antennae to the red and black spike of its shining lance that protrudes, as fierce as a scorpion's sting, from beneath its tail. It has spent millions of years perfecting its menace, its threatening heraldry and its astonishing array of patently lethal ordnance. From its glossy black thorax spring six bright yellow legs, the rear pair of which, like a grasshopper's, seem to have been made unnecessarily large, as if for some devilish trick as yet unclear. It's actually harmless. It should be renamed the greater spoof-tail. What looks utterly convincing as a huge double sting, quivering from the tip of its long, yellow-and-chocolate-striped abdomen, is in fact nothing of the kind. One is a hoax – a sting that isn't a sting – a pretence, as useless as a stage-prop, a complete non-event. The other is a highly functional ovipositor closely resembling a full-scale drilling rig. It is the emergence of this rig that I now witness at close quarters, and it is one of the most remarkable feats of insect engineering I have ever seen. It is, frankly, inconceivable. It is also the stuff of nightmares.

The female *Uroceros* is bigger and more frightening than the male. She inspects her fallen log for just the right quality, the right feel. This she seems to perform with her long antennae. They tap and feel the wasp forward, slowly and diligently, one tiny step at a time, minutely inspecting the surface of the log as a blind man progresses down a cracked pavement. If it's wrong she abandons that spot and clacks off to try another place, maybe

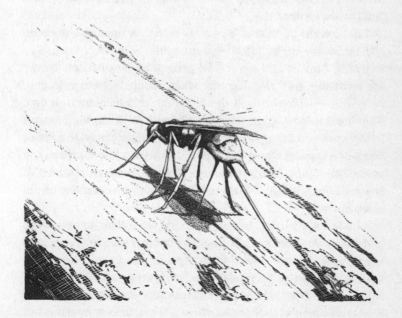

only a few feet away. But if it's right she settles, moves forward until the selected spot is immediately beneath her. She beds in, beginning her beguiling, mesmerising dance. Slowly at first, forward a bit, back a bit, turn to the left, turn to the right, repeat: a solemn barn-dance, like in a silent dream, mute and sinister. She is rising up from the log on ever longer legs; steps and manoeuvres getting smaller until she is jigging, vibrating on the spot, on tiptoe, antennae poised and trembling with trance-like expectation. Then – O wondrous illusion of the woods! – that red and black lance that appeared to be so evil miraculously unhinges from a concealed articulation beneath her belly, like a cavalier suddenly producing a hidden rapier from beneath his cloak. She tips it downwards until it snags on the roughness of the bark. She presses lightly to embed it and then, with the hooks and barbs on the feet of those powerful rear legs firmly anchored and her body arched high, she reverses over it, forcing it down and into the woody tissue.

I am caught up in this. I came here for an hour's voluptuous idle under the milky afternoon sun with the perfect excuse of watching Duncan and his playful gang at a safe distance. Now I am levitating, hovering like the wasp, alongside and engaged, locked in, unable to resist the climax of this elemental drama. The world is new again. Here is wildness at work. It's nature's most extravagant fling, like a cheetah scorching across the Masai Mara or a hummingbird flashing iridescence while it probes the private parts of a flaming hibiscus. I am flushed, exhilarated. If anyone comes along I shall talk gibberish only Aladdin would comprehend.

The lance is vertical beneath her. She has fallen on her sword and she sways mechanically, seeming to force it home. I expect to see it burst through her thorax, impaling her from below like a specimen about to be pinned upside down in a collecting box. The dance is rhythmic, regular, sensuous – Ravel's *Boléro* or the wild, throbbing insistence of *River Dance*. She is nursing her lance, not upwards through her, but down, down, deep into the tough lignin of the log, coarse and fibrous. The ovipositor has a serrated tip. It saws and drills simultaneously. Her wings flicker in sharp bursts, vibrating the lance. The strong rear legs are arched, sprung like a trap. She hums electrically. She is a power-tool in chitin, braced and defiant, conquering wood. She is straining like every schoolboy who has tried to force his compass points into the desktop. She can't sweat, her cheeks can't glow, her gasps are secret, undisclosed. But I can see how hard she is working. I am sweating for her. Something in the labour of her sway tells me she is breaking rock. Little wonder she has to look menacing. All this ritual is taking minutes – time lost me long ago – maybe a quarter of an hour, twenty minutes, and still she shows no sign of letting up. Many insects use camouflage to protect themselves while static, like the peppered moth – 'else some bloody bird'll come by and pick it off'. But this female contraption goes for the 'get me if you dare' approach. Everything about her says, 'Keep off! Beware! Danger! Call my bluff at your peril.' Aposematic. Nature's warning system. Bright stripes and threatening shapes – in this instance directly mimicking the hornet – to ensure that no opportunist predator will come by and snatch an easy meal. Who would want to? I think she's safe.

Finally, at exhausting last, she's done. The lance has penetrated half an inch of grainy fibre. That's one-sixth of her body length powered into timber. It is the equivalent of me forcing a gimlet and my arm twelve and a half inches into a log – a feat of unthinkable endurance, mechanical and terrific. There, in what she deems to be the veriest spot, with a palpable heave of spasm, she has placed a jelly-bubble of soft white eggs; only five or six (she will rattle off to do this all over again somewhere else – nature does not place all its eggs in one log), which will continue this feast of invention in perpetuity. Once hatched the grubs will bore deeper, thoughtfully filling the tunnel behind them with digested wood.

Slowly and delicately, never hurrying (why would she?), she undrills her nether organ. She rises up again, on to the fullest notch of her unwinding. The lance flicks out and a step forward permits it to angle back and fold upwards, like an old-fashioned boxwood rule, closing back under her tail. Did I hear it click into place? Her antennae flicker, testing the wind. She wears an aura of smugness, a job well done. For a moment she basks, wings flashing sunlight, then she lifts off, clattering loudly. How she must love the rush of light airs. Perhaps she has a name for the Highland breeze?

I stand up and stretch, catching my breath. My knees are sore. I look round. I am alone. Duncan and the class of children have gone from the marsh. The woods are silent, sun now beginning its long glissade, round towards the mountains in the west. A breeze flutters across the glinting water. There should be a name for this wind.

EIGHT

The Night

I am he that walks with the tender and growing night.

WALT WHITMAN, 1819–92

Nights come in glory and in fury, in sorrow and in peace, just like days. Tonight it is the stars. I am drawn here, to this private place of moon-filled emptiness where I can bare my thoughts, waft them off like ether. By day this place is nothing special, just a slight hollow in the high moor, a pockmark among many such on the complexion of the hill, but at night, this kind of late September night, it is a collecting disc for the vibrations of the stars.

It isn't a lonely headland where the smouldering sun crawls crab-like into a fiery ocean, nor is it a sacred mountaintop such as drew others, like Moses, to salute their God, although it does lead on up to our little mountain of the red kite, Bad a' Chlamhain. No, it's just the high ground that overlooks us and to which we turn first when we need whatever it is in high places that makes us seek them out. So it is neither poetic nor holy ('They shall not hurt nor destroy in all my holy mountain'), nor even particularly awesome. It is just a place I discovered by accident one day, coming down the hill late into the summer twilight, a convenient resting-place that bore me up and gave me back my wind.

In the middle is a boulder. It sits here, like an altar stone, as though someone thoughtfully placed it. I am absolutely certain no one did. It's far too big and, anyway, why would they? A rock the size of a small car stuck out in a hollow on the moor? No, I am quite sure it belongs here, freed from the icy grip of the glacier, just dumped and settled in its own place, like us all.

On that first occasion I stayed an hour to watch the night stalk the glen, a pale summer moon trailing its coat up the gleaming river. I watched the purple heather at my feet close up shop, and shadows merge to the blackness of thunder before the moonlight crept into them, pale-edged and chill. The night was drawing me in, marshalling my attention, as though something important were about to happen. The high moors echoed with the hollow fluting of curlews. Rowdy oystercatchers alarmed the wet meadows far below. A coven of hooded crows rowed furtively past, about some fell business I wasn't meant to witness, evil and apocalyptic, better under cover of darkness. And then, as the cloud thinned to nothing, white stars began to emerge in blocks, like someone turning on streetlights on a vast, galactic grid. That first night I had difficulty in leaving and kept looking back over my shoulder. I thought then that I should return here, and I often have.

Tonight this stone at my back is dry and cool to my fingers, the night anticyclonic but not cold: weather and stone in unison. Only rarely does September produce a frost. There is no chance of that tonight, but I brought a down vest and have my hands thrust deep in pockets. I have been waiting for this particular night. When we have a spell with clear skies it is almost always on an easterly air stream, just in from Russia, sere and desiccating, transparent as white wine. A high-pressure cell has dropped in and evicted the humid westerlies with their bullying clouds and petulant winds, slamming the door at the mountains' rim, shutting them out into the Atlantic whence they came and where I often wish they would stay. I know it will bring clear nights and one of them will be like this, calm and magnetic. For three nights I have gone to bed willing the restless breeze to pass. Tonight I don't want to hear trees and heather, bracken and the soft boxing of my own ears. I want the stillness that lifts me up, splits me open, lays me bare. I want whatever gave Whitman his wild, ranting song: 'Still nodding night – mad naked summer night.'

It is not dark. It never is unless there is total cloud cover, deep and woollen, and although tonight there is only a lemon segment of moon, there is plenty of light for walking carefully through the heather. I settle against the stone. I have not the faintest notion why I come here, except, of course, that I want to. But I cannot explain why. I don't dig for explanations any more. Some things just are. I hope nobody bursts the bubble. I do not want to be told that my haemoglobin grips tighter to oxygen in starlight, nor do I want to discover that, like cannabis, lunar magnetism frees up a few jolly endorphins. Science may be all very calming if you have a headache, but it does nothing for wonder, or for awe, or for magic, or for chilling out, as Hermione would say. I am here because tonight I just need to be here.

As these random thoughts shimmer through I catch the first distant strains of wild geese from somewhere high above. They are due. In the last few days I have heard from friends to the east that the first pink-footed geese have arrived on the mudflats of the Beauly Firth and are feeding in the stubble fields of the Black Isle. It is their time. The Arctic, where they have nested and reared their fluffy young through the long daylight months, is battening down. Life there is growing new fur, going underground or just plain leaving. Photosynthesis is chilling out up there in Greenland, Iceland, Lapland and Spitzbergen. Summer grasses and herbs – goose fodder – have long since stopped renewing. Chloroplasts are sinking back to earth. The valley flats and wetland meadows are grazed bare and the nitrogenous evidence of gathering goose numbers litters the ground with fat, white-tipped caterpillars of green excrement. The Pole Star is signalling.

They stand about in cliques and haggle noisily. They're jumpy. They take off and inscribe apparently pointless honking circles, only to land and haggle some more. *Zugunruhe*, the Germans call it. And then, one bright star-cluttered night, something in their streaming blood, something irresistibly genetic, snaps into a surge of irreversible motivation. One bird, perhaps old and experienced, which has tingled with *Zugunruhe* many times before, runs and rises, crying out. The haunting, hysterical cry of wild geese seeds the wind. The rest follow – at first in packs of a dozen or twenty, quickly followed by more as they circle out to sea and back again, gaining height. In a few minutes they are high and straggling across the night sky in huge skeins, hundreds of crying geese scrawling through the stars. Those who are left behind will not stay long.

From now on our nights and days will be full of their heady music. Many tens of thousands of greylag and pink-footed geese pass over us either to winter here on the tidal lochs and firths or to press on further south. These above me are invisible. They are too high, well above the mountains, some three or four thousand feet up. I scour the dome in vain. Stars flicker deceptively, playing a game. Is that geese crossing? I can't tell. Unless they happen to straggle across the moon I can only tingle with them, sing to their wild song: 'Press close bare-bosom'd night.'

The late Dr Ernest Neal published his monograph *The Badger* in 1948. By the time I read it in 1960 it was a natural history classic, establishing a method and a style often to be emulated. I had been given an orphaned badger cub to raise, so my schoolboy enthusiasm for these gentle, stripy-faced weasel-bears knew no bounds.

Yet Dr Neal's book stirred new awakenings. Here was another unexplored chamber in Aladdin's cave. It seemed as though there was a world going on out there that I wasn't supposed to know about; a world belonging to owls and foxes, bats and badgers, not to us, and which was treated purely objectively by the adult human world, and with unarticulated disdain – a sort of aloof disapproval, present but unspoken. It was as though animals of the night were up to no good, like burglars. Even science seemed wary of them. One read about them, noted their physiological adaptations for the night, collected their skins and skulls, made casts of their spoor and that was that: nocturnal, almost as if that were the end of the matter, nothing more to be said. No one had yet suggested to me that it might be possible to get to know more of these creatures and their crepuscular undertakings, to step inside their world on their terms, not ours – to dare to chart the ethereal gift of darkness.

The book opens with a descriptive chapter in which Dr Neal takes the reader through the experience of badger watching on a June night. He builds excitement as they sit in the dusk waiting for the badgers to emerge from underground. I found it galvanising. At the end, one sentence lodged in my mind: 'As we tramp home by torchlight we wonder what the badger family is doing; are they looking for beetles under the dung in the meadow, or digging for bulbs in the wood, or is the mother teaching her cubs how to find nests of young rabbits?' I wanted to discover the night.

A few weeks later I copied, word for word, large chunks of Dr Neal's book into an essay on badgers and submitted it for a school biology competition. Such was my fourteen-year-old naivety that it never occurred to me that anyone else might have read this classic almost as old as me. It seemed that no one had. I won first prize. Then one day, just before the prize-giving ceremony, I was summoned to the director of biology's room. Tommy Wallace, as I was later to know him, drew on his pipe and eyed me piercingly but warmly over the top of his horn-rimmed glasses. My entry lay open on the desk. 'I'm so glad you won the prize,' he began. I squirmed silently. 'I am sure you did a great deal of research but, you know, in science it is usual to acknowledge one's sources, otherwise someone might think it was all your own work.' I was impaled on those eyes. His words spun like bathwater inside my emptying brain. 'I think it would be a good idea if you gave me a list of the books you have read for this work and I shall add a bibliography to your excellent essay, don't you?' he asked gently. Yellow fragrance curled from his pipe. Forty years later I could describe to you stitch by stitch the tweed jacket he was wearing, tell you the number of gold emblems visible on his navy-blue tie tucked beneath his camel pullover, and I could draw the pattern of the crimson carpet. Wherever my eyes fell images like hot shards branded my clouding retinas. I can still smell the sweet authority of tobacco. 'Yessir,' I muttered. I wanted the earth to rupture between my feet, for a thunderbolt to strike the bell tower and to bring it crashing down about our ears. I prayed for God to roar in from the Chapel Quad and snatch me up in one of His mysterious ways I was always hearing about. No one in the world did I wish less to think ill of me than this gentle, kind, wise, inspirational master who alone among nearly four hundred other males in that place understood my passion for nature.

'Are they looking for beetles under the dung in the meadow? Digging for bulbs in the wood?' There was only one way to find out. For a few years I was to become nocturnal. It is a habit I have never quite managed to throw off. At school I was to find my own badger colony, creeping out of the dormitory after lights-out to spend hundreds of hours in their company until they became familiar with my presence, their cubs running to my feet to find the peanuts I dropped to entice them. Just then, through a natural history friend, I had met up with a remarkable and extraordinary middle-aged spinster named Eileen Soper, who lived with her sister Eva in deep Hertfordshire countryside. They were both talented artists. Eileen also wrote, publishing several books on wildlife, all exquisitely illustrated by her delicate drawings and watercolours. Fittingly, their house was called 'Wildings'. In my school holidays I travelled to Welwyn so that I could spend time with this most accomplished naturalist. She was to teach me field-craft techniques I have revisited a thousand times. She even sent me packages of peanuts at school so that I could entice my badgers to the same level of intimacy she had achieved with hers and later we corresponded for many years. It is partly to Eileen that I owe my love of the night. In her book *When Badgers Wake*, published in 1955, she observes: 'It may be that badger-watchers, in company with bird-watchers, are not entirely human.'

After her death in 1990 Duff Hart-Davis was to publish *Wildings – The Secret Garden of Eileen Soper*, the story of those two ladies' bizarre existence with wildlife invading their home at every level: dormice in the sofa, squirrels in the roof, muntjac deer in the porch, blue tits weaving their mossy nest behind the curtains; and, of course, the badgers.

Daylight and colour are the succour of human toil. They conspire to bring joy to the meanest task, wash our waking hours with ever-delighting art and form. The human eye is arranged to make the most of them both, but at a general level. We should never overlook that there are arcane elements of detail and the spectrum we cannot begin to see (gamma, infrared, X and radio waves). The adder and nocturnal owls, for instance, use infrared vision to home in on their warm-blooded prey. Our vision is limited to that slice of the spectrum in the range from red to purple, and our light receptors can only determine large life forms. A sample of pond water looks clear until we examine it under the microscope and discover the teeming organisms it holds. It is only in very modern times that we have even suspected their existence. We have little idea what it must be like to live with the vision of the golden eagles that float across our Aigas sky, six thousand feet up. We have to rush for our binoculars even to identify them. With binoculars built in, they are eyeing our every move.

The light-receptive cells in our retinas that interpret colour – the cones – are positioned in the centre, where directly viewed images fall. To either side the cones give way to rod-shaped cells that deal mostly in monochrome. Army training teaches soldiers to look slightly to one side of an object at night so that the image falls on rods, not cones. It works, although it takes a while to become accustomed to navigating by tangential vision. It's a skill to be acquired, like roller-skating. You have to trip over a few logs and blunder into a tree or two before mastering the art. When you have, when the little tricks of technique clot to form a mesh of unconscious reaction, when you no longer flinch at unseen foliage touching your face, or start at sudden night sounds like the shriek of an owl or the snapping of a nearby twig, another world begins to emerge.

This is the night world that holds no fear for my dogs, the Jack Russell terriers, Ruff and Tumble, who sift the wind for hard information about the sex, age and species of other animals, as well as being able to read how long ago they were there. The same goes for Barney, my horse, grazing in the field with the cows lying, breath-steaming and cud-rumbling, beneath a crescent moon. This is the world of roe deer tiptoeing out of the birchwood and of badgers snuffling and grunting in the dew and, it so happens, of most other common mammals around us. We can have little concept of their rarefied world of scent and hearing acuity. Some male moths can detect a single molecule of pheromone shedding from a female abdomen more than a mile away. The night is loud with bat shrieks far above our crimped deafness. In the deep oceans of the world whale song is pitched so low that it will carry for thousands of miles. We need heavy technology to hear it.

Colour vision is the exception in mammals. Most see only in an extended range of black and white. Animals with colour built in, those which mobilise colour for their own singular purposes, can, of course, see colour – tropical fish, insects like the small tortoiseshell and *Uroceros*, and most birds, for instance. But mammals like those around me at Aigas every day, deer, sheep, cattle, squirrels, pipistrelles, dogs, foxes, pine martens, shrews, live their lives in an unchromatic world of black-and-white film, especially those which prefer to move about at night. Yet for all the apparent joylessness of monochrome, they all share a life-enhancing compensation that most of us humans live our entire lives without suspecting, far less sampling. It is as though we are blinded by colour – swamped, so that we sideline the other senses we possess. We have lost the use of the tuning knob. We can no longer bring all our senses into balance, as they can. Without the distraction of colour, for them dependence upon sight is diminished and toned down in order to let the other senses in and take over – other senses which, in the unending odyssey of evolution, are often finer-honed for the task of survival than sight alone. I am humbled by the knowledge that the other animals around me here at Aigas are living on the land, their home and mine, in a broader, grander, sharper, more focused reality than I am.

In many animals scent and hearing predominate as darkness falls. Sight isn't abandoned, it is still there, on duty, but its importance is reduced. It is demoted so that the others can pull focus. Sight is relegated to the margins of sentience, a ring around the twitching core. It becomes a facility for detecting movement, rather than for shaping images, for confirmation rather than for naming the moment of truth. Many times I have stood as still as a graveyard angel and been scrutinised by wildlife: deer and badgers, antelope, elephant, moose and beavers, rabbits, hares and squirrels, hedgehogs and even sharp-eyed predators like foxes and wildcats. They have examined me from head to toe, eyed me up and down, drawn my image into pools of deep suspicion. They have floated me across visual sensors, checked me out against aeons of pictorial memory-bank and then discarded me as dross, as so much texture on the tapestry of the night. But if for a sliver of a spilt second the visual image can be combined with the finest thread of wafting scent, or so much as the sound of a swallow or a thumping heart, identification is instantaneous and electric, like snapping on a light and seeing the whole horrifying picture in stark relief.

Nocturnality is a relative concept. It is a convenient term with which we like to disguise our own inadequacy. Very few nocturnal animals either know it or obey it. Most are catholic, choosing the time of day to feed or move or attend to their private affairs that best suits them – always that which best meets their needs for survival. Here, north of the 57th Parallel, nocturnality is also seasonal. From early May until August any animal choosing to move only in darkness goes hungry. By the summer solstice the night recedes to only ninety minutes in twenty-four hours. With clear skies there is no significant darkness for several weeks. Hunters must hunt in the light or starve. It also provides the 'not entirely human' observer with a God-sent opportunity. Here, our latitude permits the June sun just to dip below the north-western horizon. It skims along out of sight for a stretched moment of twilight and surfaces again in the north-east at an angle so obtuse that darkness becomes a gesture, a mere flicker of monochrome like a signal aberration on a TV screen. Just as the Inuit have highly specialised words for snow, so Highlanders have their own word for the elastic evening interval of sunlessness and twilight: the *gloaming*. In Shetland it's the *simmer dim*, in Norway the *skumering*. The Swiss have an *alpenglow* that highlights the mountain peaks long after the valley villages are closed in darkness.

From early May until August the gloaming is a delight, our mountains jewelled in sunlight, and at the head of the glen the high peaks are cushioned in the ermine of lingering snow. By September, nights and shadows are stretching their limbs, reaching out. The sun bends to the mountains as if it has to hurry off, somewhere else to go about its business. The light falls with it, draining away so that you think quickly: What must I get done before dark?

So here I am settled against my stone, long after what we call nightfall but which is really night-rise. The air hums, raising its cool, familiar murmur. The geese have gone now, passed on, trailing their wildness across throbbing stars. The hill around me is opening up, not closing down. It is breathing freely again after the rush of the day, opening its shirt to let the sweat out, throwing unused solar radiation back to the sky. For an hour I am doing just that. The day's junk needs to be let out like dishwater. I am alone in a great auditorium, settling for a grand performance, expectation rising, head cleared, players up there all poised, hanging like ripe fruit, charged with promise. I close my eyes.

When I opened them a few minutes ago the night had changed. In that short time I seem to have readjusted the inner workings of my medulla oblongata to a new setting. Like stopping down the camera lens and resetting the DIN, I am no longer programmed for day, or even for the gloaming. I am tuned for night: fully awake, seeing, hearing and absorbing. This is my 'still nodding night, mad, naked, bare-bosom'd and tender'. This is the point. This is *why* I have come. For years I have striven to know this place well. In order to talk about it and to help others discover its truths, I have sought to explore its every mood. I have to have a firm notion of what is going on out here. I need to know it by day and night, in summer and winter, in all its finery and on those *dreich* (a good auld Scots word meaning 'hard to bear') days of rain and wind when we creep indoors and choose to forget that life *is* going on out there. If I don't strive for the whole picture the jigsaw puzzle won't be completed.

Often there are lichens I don't know, or mosses whose names I can't remember – but I'm no longer bothered by that. I can always go and look them up or ask Jessica, our botanist, or one of our enthusiastic rangers, to help me out. Identification has long since ceased to be pivotal to understanding, or even very significant to me. What matters now is living the whole show, somehow becoming a part of it all. Sometimes it seems to me that just about all the science of natural history has been captured, measured, radio-tagged, monitored and data-banked, but thankfully not the religion of it. I have to explore the three physical dimensions in which our little Aigas world is built, and use the fourth one, time, to figure out its meaning. This place is a great symphony that I love, the score of which I have been learning by heart for years. I don't need to know the names of the second and third violinists or even how many there are. I just want to see with the composer's eye and hear with his ears. The night is just one more movement.

The sky dome is no longer charcoal; it is the soft purply-green of a port bottle held to a bright light. The stars are palpitant, drilling presence earthward. They crowd in, pressing. Now I see more behind; the most infinitesimal and countless specks of distance are thronging in from far beyond. There are four hundred billion stars in the Milky Way alone, of which the sun – our life source – is just one. Awe settles around me in drifts, pure and chill.

I lift my binoculars to Pegasus and trace the long legs, the arching neck. Times ten they are as brilliant as a diamond chandelier. I can sense Galileo's excitement when in 1609 he stepped up the magnification of his newest invention to thirty and saw for the first time ever, among many other things new to science, the four new planets revolving around Jupiter. Six months later he was to discover Saturn's rings. I don't need a telescope tonight. It isn't detail I seek. I just want to see what the migrating geese see, to sense the *Zugunruhe*, to feel the pull and understand a little of the godless cyclical magnificence of which we all are but an immeasurably insignificant jot.

They are all there – the ones I know and the unfathomable innumerabilia I don't: the Bear, the Plough, Andromeda, Orion's Belt . . . Venus is close, burning low and warm, Mars is flushed and rowdy, Saturn is coy. The Milky Way is like a wild slash with a shining sword. And there is the Pole Star, fat, low and calling, guiding me as it has a million generations of birds exploring latitude for their own special purposes. It is our treat. The Southern Hemisphere has no Pole Star. Consequently most great bird migrations like those of these geese are found in the Northern Hemisphere. The Pole Star is closest to the celestial North Pole (about one degree off) and is bright and prominent above the horizon. Handy for a goose.

Early last century somebody observant noticed that migratory songbirds kept in cages displayed nocturnal restlessness during their normal migration period. German ornithologists named this *Zugunruhe*, but only when Gustav Kramer published the findings of his experiments in 1949 did the world of science begin to take *Zugunruhe* seriously. He worked with the red-backed shrike, the whitethroat and the blackcap, three European species known to be night migrants. He kept them in circular cages where they could see the sky without the distraction of any city lights. As night fell in each autumn of the experimental period, his birds faced south and fidgeted: *Zugunruhe*. In spring they danced to the north. But it was not until 1955 that Franz Sauer and his wife Eleanore demonstrated conclusively that stellar navigation was a reality. They conducted many experiments similar to those of Kramer, also using blackcaps, whitethroats and other European warblers of the genus *Sylvia*. The significant difference they recorded was that directional orientation ceased when the sky was overcast.

Now convinced that stars were important, the Sauers moved their cages to the Olbers Planetarium in Bremen. The results were electrifying. First they placed the birds under a dome of diffused light. For many consecutive nights their captives' movements were entirely random. No pattern emerged. Then they projected an artificial spring night sky on to the planetarium dome. The birds immediately oriented to the north-east, the direction of their normal spring migration. When exposed to skies not characteristic of the migratory season the birds became completely disorientated. *Zugunruhe* was celestial and real.

The moon has slid to the south-west. I suppose it is past midnight, although I can't read my watch. The hour is irrelevant; it is time passing that matters. The silence is a continuous cosmic roar as when a hi-fi system is switched on but playing nothing; down my spinal column life hums deeply like surf thundering in distant breakers. Ptolemy's stellar music is cerebral, not celestial. Like Gustav Holst I compose my own. There is a rare interruption: a tractor throbs and a dog barks somewhere far over the other side of the valley. Deep in the heather somewhere behind me a shrew is yelling abuse, probably at another shrew. They are feisty little predators, always bickering. Both impinge momentarily, like a pinch, reminding me in whose gravity I am pulsating. Otherwise just weighty, loaded stillness. I sit in a drum of silence. Just me and the stars and their music still singing in my head. I can feel my spirit begin to spiral upward. I have to hang on to the rock.

At one time I thought that if I dipped into particle physics a new meaning to life would open up to me. And it did until it lost me. I might as well have tried to dip into a black hole. I came away baffled and wrestling even more profoundly with my insight conundrum. It seemed to deny me the raw throb of my own exis-tence. Einstein embarrasses me. There's something glib about celebrating his undoubted genius without being able to compre-hend a jot. $E=MC^2$ is as much a mystery to me as God. I have failed utterly to convince myself that a gramophone record play-ing continuously for a thousand years ends up with its outside edge older than its centre. I cannot imagine what the world would look like if I rode on a beam of light. I have enough trouble imag-ining the number of stars I can see above me.

It is all very well for brilliant cosmologists like Stephen Hawking to claim to have come close to revealing the thinking of God by the cryptic contortions of mathematics. For lesser mortals a black hole remains an unthinkable figment of unlikelihood; far less can I countenance being sucked into its singularity or ultimately emerging from it as human beings. It would be interesting to know how far beyond the Introduction the twenty-five million people who bought *A Brief History of Time* managed to get. For most of us there is a compelling argument for striving to understand our immediate environment rather than rendering it meaningless at an astrophysical level.

On my way down I happen across a narrow path that leads me into the pinewood. The night of the forest is another world again, a black hole of its own. The stars are lost now, only sporadically signalling to me through black tree-fingers clutching upwards. I have to slow right down. The path is barely discernible, a black thread winding across a darkling forest quilt. The moonlight that was enough for the moor is inadequate now. I move carefully and stealthily from trunk to trunk, eyeing their solid blackness at the edge of my vision and moving in until my hands reassuringly caress bark, crinkly and safe. I wait and listen. In here I am not alone, not for a moment. Nor shall I remain undetected for long. I can creep and tiptoe as much as I like but I am a total amateur in this night world. All I can do is settle down with my back to a tree, as Eileen Soper taught me to, and wait, wallowing in unfiltered experience. I watch the moonlight seep through the branch tangle above me like mercurial rain.

The ground falls away from me down towards the loch. I can just see the water gleaming through the black pine-columns pillaring the bank. Mallard are flighting in and bickering. Others rise, quacking harshly. They wing invisibly away over the canopy above me. A sharp cry breaks through the trees. The heron only has a curse. Night or day it's the same rough-edged, bucolic expletive, monosyllabic and damning. I can't see him but I can picture him gliding in on hollow wings, resting his heavy bill on his breastbone, long legs dropping to the shallows where he will stalk frogs and trout fry in the silvered marsh.

Long ago there were brown bears here, and wild boar and wolves, and beavers dammed the pools in the burn. But they are all gone. Man was too numerous and too active. The forests were too small, too accessible. Crops grew too slowly and livestock was too precious. Competition was stamped out. The last wolf in the Highlands was killed in the eighteenth century, apparently in about six places at once, so there is a 'last' for Lochaber, a 'last' for Sutherland, a 'last' for Moray, and so on. The last of this glen was killed in the remote and lonely forests of Guisachan twenty miles from here a few years before the 1745 Jacobite Rising. A few years before that, another well-recorded incident very close by reveals as much of the Highlanders of the day as of the few remaining wolves.

In their *Lays of a Deer Forest*, written half a mile to the east of us at Eilean Aigas in 1845, John Sobieski Stolberg Stuart and Charles Edward Stuart tell of a place called Creleven, near Struy, the village only three miles over the hill from where I sit. They were the colourful but questionable 'Pretenders' to the Scottish throne who claimed they were the grandsons of Bonnie Prince Charlie and his brief marriage to Princess Louisa of Stolberg-Gedern, and that their father had to be raised in secrecy for fear of retribution by the Hanoverian Crown. This notion appealed to the Lord Lovat of the day and he permitted them to build the fine Eilean Aigas mansion on the twenty-five-acre island in the River Beauly. There, swathed in tartan, they set up a court and attracted a retinue of romantic followers.

Their story goes that as Yuletide approached, not having an iron girdle (a heavy iron baking plate with a hooped handle for hanging over a fire) large enough to bake her New Year's bannocks, a Highland woman walked out east from Creleven to Struy to borrow one from a neighbour. As she was returning she met, as the Pretenders put it, 'with one of her gossips, as wives may do'. They stopped at a cairn formed by large rocks that had fallen from the valley wall and were overgrown with heather and whortleberries. Unknown to them the rocks concealed the den of a large and hungry wolf. At this point it is important to note that in European folklore the wolf regularly kills and eats humans – Little Red Riding Hood *et al*. The reality is that there is no hard evidence of wolves attacking and consuming people anywhere in the world, unless cornered or defending themselves from human attack. However, the tale insists that the starving wolf couldn't resist the smell of the two women gossiping at his door, so he begins to emerge. But the entrance to the den is tight between boulders and lies immediately below the two women so that they suddenly see his head appear at their feet. 'Had they been women of the present day,' the Pretenders observe in 1845, 'they would have shrieked and fled, like some of their sex from a mouse, and others from a cock-chaffer; but the wife of Creleven knew with what she had to deal.' With commendable presence of mind, she ups the heavy girdle and fetches the poor wolf a blow, 'with such good aim and vigour that it brained him on the stone which served as the block for his emerging head' – an ignominious end for so legendary a forest beast.

So nowadays the Highlands is left with four species of deer: roe and red, some fallow introduced to England by the Romans, and feral Japanese sika, mostly escaped from parks, no effective means to control their numbers, and a handful of small mammals. Our big game, such as it ever was after the last Ice Age, and the grand ecosystems that fixed them all in their special niches, is now only a healthy twinkle in the eyes of restoration ecologists. It pleases me to know that the same genes that hold these old pines erect also heard the timber wolf howl.

As the minutes pass I am aware of constant movement. Wood mice skitter about over the needle litter. A tawny owl is hooting off to my left, and another, probably this year's youngster, is answering it with a regular un-owl-like 'sker-reek' away on the other side of the loch. A clumsy beetle of some kind is clambering across the scaly bark of my tree trunk. I can hear its hooked feet clacking and scraping close to my ear. I am thinking about moving lower down. I will enjoy being closer to the mallard on the loch, even if all I can see is the moon-stream from their wakes as they ski in. But just as I press my knuckles into the soft forest litter and flex my shoulders, I become aware of a low snuffling coming up at me from somewhere below, away down the slope. I freeze.

Silence.

It's gone. All I can hear is that damned beetle in my right ear, creaking like a gate. Perhaps I imagined it? No, there it is again, clearer now. I hold my breath to listen intently – something no deer has to do. Nor can I rotate my ears, so I get an incomplete picture, floating fragments, clusters of image with their own black holes. I have to guess. I think it must be a hedgehog. They are regular in this wood. I find the shiny twist of their black droppings along the forest paths and see the little snout probes in the needle mulch where a beetle has been caught napping. I hope he will come and gobble mine. But something is wrong with this hedge-hog. Its snuffling is *profundo*, a little too gruff, too intermittent and somehow too strong. The snort is powerful, authoritative, a little tetchy, not to be fooled with.

The hairs on my neck begin to rise. A tingle of recognition sparks at my brain's core. I know this sound. I know the author of this elemental grubbing, grunting, snuffling wheeze. This is no hedgehog. In fact, any hedgehog in the vicinity would do well to tiptoe smartly away. I know exactly who this is. 'Oh! It's my delight on a shining night in the season of the year,' goes the old poacher's song. This is the friendly daemon of my boyhood woods. He is coming to gild my starry mission, bringing the wild wood to me in all its dark, secretive, fungally and needly truth. In its mouldy fecundity this is real forest. It is nature's climax. It's a perpetual, undulating arpeggio of turning, churning nutrients, all down the long, iceless millennia. Its inexorable travail ensures that there is always a beetle to crunch, ever a nest of wood mice to rootle out, always a tuber and a rhizome to gnaw and a patch of bluebell bulbs to grub up. 'Are they looking for beetles under the dung in the meadow? Digging for bulbs in the wood?' Yes they are, O my soul! That is just what he is doing, and no doubt his friends and family, too, scattered about this hillside outside the range of my singing, soaring senses. It is Brock, the badger. If the last wolf itself had popped out from behind a pine with a scar on its head, I could not be more thrilled, no more uplifted. This mammal above all others taught me natural history, led me by the hand to discover his stoical, benevolent ways. He is endearing, reliable, consistent, benign. He is tough, brave, self-possessed and irascible. And he is immortal, locked into the legends of so many places: Brockenhurst, Brockbridge, Brockford, Brockhampton, Brockley, Brockhall, Brockwood, Brockworth and Brockton. Not four miles from here is a place and a pub called Brockie's Lodge.

The word badger, Dr Ernest Neal assures us, comes appropriately from the French, *bêcher*, to dig. But the name evocatively built into the fabric of British and Scottish folklore is much older. *Brok* is the Danish for badger, also in Irish and Welsh; in Highland Gaelic it is *brochlach*; *brockit* in Old Scots means having a white stripe (a brockit cow has an unusual white-striped face); all assimilated from the same Norse word.

In his all-absorbing classic *The Goshawk*, T.H. White witnesses the death of a sow badger ('I held up her muzzle and looked into her small opaque ursine eyes') and celebrates those badgers that live beside him in his Buckinghamshire woods:

> Brock: the last of the English bears: I had been proud that her race lived in the same wood with me. She had done nobody any harm. Her home was tidy, her habits industrious by night, her claws and forearms agriculturally strong. Hob would be a good name for a badger.

The nineteenth-century German naturalist Carl Christoph Vogt writes: 'In fable the badger plays the role of a peace-loving, gentle and cautious Philistine who loves beyond everything his comfort, his family and his home, but who may become furious if alarmed or disturbed in his habits.'

He comes on. There is no wind and scent is his principal ally – not that he has much to fear in these woods. Badgers have few natural enemies except man, and hereabouts they go unmolested. They live down in the Tomich of Aigas woods, less than a mile from here. There are seven active sets and half a dozen others currently not in use. They are deep burrows tunnelled far into the sandy bank so that huge spoil heaps form great mounds outside each entrance. I regularly see their signs in the woods and we know that they pass through the gardens from time to time; their rootling in the dewy grass for earthworms leaves its own special signature. I am also proud that badgers live in my woods. Every once in a while we find the skin of a hedgehog turned inside out. The badger is one of the few predators that have learned to cope with their matted spines. He comes on.

Now he is only ten yards away. Slowly I realise that the dim path I followed down off the moor was, of course, his. Badgers are obsessively habitual, persistently using the same paths that radiate out from their sets in all directions. I am sitting not three feet from this one. I can scarcely believe my luck. This fellow is grubbing his way home from a feeding foray. I can see his stripy face. I wrest my eyes a foot to his right. The friendly moon-striped face is clearer now, and he's digging again. *Phorrt!* He snorts the peaty soil from his black nostrils. I can hear his powerful jaws chomping. Whatever he's eating must be vegetable for the molars to have to work hard. He is a true omnivore. I can see the monograph's dentition chart: 3:1:3:1 on the top and 3:1:4:2 on the bottom including the vestigial premolar, so minute that 'in preparing a skull for a museum it could easily be overlooked ... The molars are considerably flattened to facilitate the grinding-up of vegetable food.' Whatever is now being ground to mush is also being worked by a soft, wet palate. No one taught this Philistine to eat with his mouth shut. There is nothing genteel about a badger, nothing so contrived. He is at it again, ripping at the fibrous roots of something with his long front claws, 'agriculturally strong', to reach a hidden succulence. A tree root is in the way and he grips it in his teeth and rips upward. It snaps sharply and he tugs again, breaking it off and discarding it with a shake of the head. Now he stops and listens. His head is up and turned to one side. His snout quivers and twitches, flicking upwards in little jerks as if he is tasting different levels of the night. I wonder if he has caught my scent on an eddy of breeze. I know he won't see me, badger eyesight is poor, but his sense of smell is formidable.

He comes on again. Pad, pad, pad, pad . . . I can hear his claws rattle on the stony path. I hold my breath. He is only six feet away. He stops and shuffles to one side, a foot or two off the path where he seems to be plucking at something with more jerks of the head. Eyes to the side again. The vegetation is low and dense in a little clearing. Of course, I mouth to myself, wanting to shout. It is bilberry, *Vaccinium myrtilis*, the Highland blaeberry, the whortle-berries of the luckless wolf den. And it is September; they are plump, round and full. His dessert is forest bilberries, fresh-plucked under a tilting, smiling, crescent moon – his delight on a shiny night. I am very proud that he lives in my woods.

Twice he turns to look at me. The glistening nose at the end of the pied face is inscribing Ws in the air as he floats molecules of essence across his palate like a wine taster. Something is not right. Something not of the pinewood is infiltrating his gentle, 'inter-parietally ridged skull with permanently articulated lower jaw'. O, my friendly Philistine! You have nothing to fear from me, however raw I smell to your wise old nose as fine-tuned as a baro-graph. He is back on the path – three feet, two feet, one . . . I could touch him now. He stops and sniffs my protuberant boot, steps back, skirts it warily, almost crossly, and stops again. There is a frozen moment of uncertainty. I hear his gut rumble and his short breaths. He is so close that I can smell him now, a dark, wild, organic musk like a tramp's. He swallows, an audible spasm of muscular intimacy at the very warp of his being. I am breathing his hot breath. 'Not entirely human' seems to be his verdict – insufficient to merit undignified flight. Purposeful and unhurried, he turns away and trundles up the path – his path – whence I came. I turn to see him go. His shaggy, bear-like silhouette brands my brain. He is an indelible effigy of the night.

NINE

Continental Drift

The art and science of wildlife conservation is that which
brings stability or regular rhythm into disturbed habitat,
beauty and balance into the wilderness itself, and renders it
productive of materials and spiritual values.

SIR FRANK FRASER DARLING, 1903–79

It's Sunday and I've been given a class. We have a group from
California, just in. They look a little fazed, although it never ceases
to amaze me how well our guests throw off the effects of long-haul
travel. Seven thousand miles in under twenty-four hours, one fitful
night in a strange bed, half a pint of decaffeinated coffee, a bowl of
porridge and here they are, their American-ness rippling like a
flag, keen as cologne and with expectations soaring like eagles.

I'm torn between wanting to meet them, find out who they are
and why they came, and needing to get on with today. They're here

to learn about the landscape of Scotland, particularly about the Highlands. This group is composed of students of land use. They are college alumni expanding their environmental and historical horizons, with a few gratuitous Scotophiles sprinkled in. I have a skim of a notion of what they expect of me; they must know that I have met many like them. And we both have some hard data to go on. They will have checked us out, read the text we mailed and scrolled through the website where we expose ourselves to the world, all smiles and promises. I have a name list, and I know about their institution. I know some of them are academics; others are wives and husbands, associates with a common interest in land.

It's a good start, but it's never enough. Groups come for a week, ten days, two weeks and still it's not enough. It takes days for preconceived perceptions (not to say prejudices) to slough off as the adder sheds its scaly coat, revealing the bright reptile beneath. I come with Lucy whose consummate people skills far exceed mine – she just loves people. She is already in there, softening, smiling, issuing grace. Joyce Grenfell used to say to complete strangers at cocktail parties: 'Do you like string?' I can't see it working here. I need time and space and a chance to share images, shafts of light, clouds. Sometimes I wish I could walk in with something quintessentially Highland that *wasn't* tartan or the pipes, something that would get them all spurred up for this four-dimensional allegory that is the Aigas place, our home. But I stick with the handshake and the smile, however inadequate they may be.

I must accept that this is the nature of our work. These are our students drawn in to discover and learn. Some folk come shining in, beaming presence like a gift; others come and go like clouds, drifting through. We can never hope to reach them all at the level we should like to, although we try hard enough. Time and again I just discover that, after all, I share a real bond with a particular individual and – *damn!* – it's time for them to leave. 'If only I had known earlier,' I hear myself saying over and over again.

So I shall spend today mining, breaking through. I want to be the rough stone against which they can begin to rub and split their travel-worn skins. Right here, right now. We are here to deal in real feelings, real muddles, real joys; the Aigas world being lived and shared by each of us in our own pernickety way, bright and clean. It's about seeing and understanding; those two. That's what we do.

I scan the list. There is a Macdonald, a Gunn, two Macleans, two Campbells, a McKey and a Frazer. Eight out of twenty-five have Highland names, probably many more have links. There is something psychogenetic at work here. You can't shake off Highland roots; they keep coming back at you like kippers. Many of these folk will be the descendants of eighteenth- and nineteenth-century Highland émigrés to the New World, of whom some were searching for a better life, while many were cleared – shunted into emigration because they had no other option. The McKey and the Frazer were likely to have been Mackay (or Mackie) and almost certainly Fraser. Spelling varies greatly and anyway either the émigrés themselves or the registry clerks listing arrivals in the USA a hundred and fifty-odd years ago were probably at best indifferent to spelling, at worst illiterate.

Some will know their Highland descent, arriving primed with hot connection; some won't. Some will enthusiastically agree that it hasn't just tugged them back here, but that it's a *raison d'être* which colours their very being. Others will look mildly ruffled by the notion, a little uncertain. They may feel envious of the ring of authority surnames award to our scattered tribes. If you're not ready for the power evinced by the Highland clan mystique, it's like being told you're not entirely in charge. Folk can feel horribly left out. Care needed. I go for the greeting. Hands shaken, smiles closing gaps, soft words shedding edges. Mercifully for me Lucy is an expert at this. Her love of people shows. She is beside me purring gentle waves of welcome.

Today my problem is time. Not just the time I have to explore our subject – this morning, starting right now, under the mackerel sky of a failing summer – but the last two hundred years of continental drift. The Scotland of Robbie Burns and the Bonnie Prince, of Brigadoon and Scott's Waverley novels is mostly myth. If it isn't two hundred and fifty years out of date, it's either been adapted for mass consumption or it never existed in the first place. In the case of Sir Walter Scott, the leading protagonist of the Scottish Romantic Movement, it was then (Waverley novels, 1814–28) and still is a tangle of swashbuckling legends accidentally exported all round the world by the hundreds of thousands of expat Scots and their descendants. Not surprisingly they chose to perpetuate those emotion-tingling bits that best spurred their self-indulgent nostalgia. It runs deep; it comes with the Scottish surname. After a while myth becomes indistinguishable from fact, especially from afar. Even if the truth of a situation is revealed it's immediately coloured by long-ingrained perception, believed only reluctantly, or perhaps not at all. The obvious analogy in reverse is cowboys and Indians. The reality had to be a million times more drab than the epic fiction we have chosen to nurture. I don't want to learn the real history of Wyatt Earp or Jesse James, sordid and dull.

A walk in the hills would seem simple enough, but even to address the landscape factually I have to pierce the armour of historical distortion. Sometimes it's hard going. Folk like their myths endorsed not shattered. Today, I somehow have to tell them that the blooming heather moors of August, 'ye bonnie banks and braes', are largely man-made, a result of centuries of deforestation, the product of habitual burning and overgrazing – degradation is the word ecologists use. Somehow the soul of the heather has entered the blood of people like these. They pick a sprig in a hushed, wondering way. I must be careful not to degrade my class. When he was very old I once asked the celebrated Highland war hero, diplomat and historian Sir Fitzroy

Maclean whether after such a long and eventful life he could sum up Scotland. 'Yes,' he said with alacrity, 'things are never what they seem!'

We're headed up the hill. I lead; the group straggles out. A ranger gently herds, sheepdog-like, from behind. We stop and talk plants and trees, building familiarity, allowing folk to catch up. Sometimes I think we should study human group dynamics, not natural history. We do more of it.

Continental separation took the Americas away, but their wildlife, their flora and fauna, are often remarkably similar to ours despite the thousands of miles that separate them from us. We explore some easy examples to shore up the familiarisation process for our student guests. Take, for instance, the red deer (*Cervus elaphus*) and the North American elk (*Cervus canadensis*). They are not-so-different cousins stemming from the original elaphine *Cervus* that browsed the ancient Asian continent (probably the source of all deer) in the Pleistocene era up to a million years ago. Their common ancestors trotted off to the west to colonise Europe, and east into the New World. They still produce approximately the same antler conformation, their bodies and colour remain pretty similar, and their diet is more or less identical. They occupy approximately the same ecological niche in marginal forest. The big difference is size. The American elk is huge; a big bull can achieve a thousand pounds in late summer. A big red deer stag in Scotland is a third of that live weight. Environmental factors in North America favoured big, strong individuals. That is what polymorphism does in nature. That one is called an elk and the other a deer is an aberration perpetuated by the first European settlers in the Americas. They weren't great naturalists. The first bird they saw with a red breast they named a robin. It's actually a thrush. The first carrion eater was called a buzzard: properly a New World vulture. The largest deer they confused with the broad-antlered Scandinavian elk, *Alces*, which is an entirely separate genus of deer better known in English as a moose. While these misnomers may have been comforting to homesick settlers, their legacy is widespread confusion. 'You call that a *robin*?' transatlantic visitors exclaim when they first see our pert little redbreast at the bird table.

Even more remarkable are the many more organisms that can't run or fly into remote places to start off new populations. In plants there are hundreds of very similar varieties that have dispersed themselves around the globe. They extend their range inch by creeping inch, or by seeds projected a few feet at a time, by floating on the winds of chance, hooking into fur or feather, hitching an uncharted ride in a rumbling gut, washing down rippling streams or swirling across great oceans, lakes and seas. Wherever they pitch they have to adapt from their common lineage to suit this or that new habitat, soil or climate. It is a powerful illumination of genetic resilience that over such distances and down so many millennia they can face so many different environmental factors and still remain virtually unchanged.

We spot the delicate yellow flowers of silverweed, a *Potentilla* they know well, and beside the track we admire the orange-tipped, golden pea-blooms of bird's-foot trefoil, *Lotus corniculatus*, which made its way to America in the turn-ups of emigrants' trousers. We laugh and joke. I can almost make these migrants feel at home.

A thought passes through. If geographical separation is responsible for speciation – the creation of new species – perhaps these Americans are on their way to creating their own. Normally when an animal population is separated off by a mountain range or an ocean, by a drifting continental plate or even just a river, it quickly adopts its own local characteristics, folding them in, undiluted by what it left behind. They've certainly done that. It develops its own ways, sounds and social groupings – done that, too. Biologists call that a *race*. Tricky word. The migration of Celtic peoples round the world over the past three thousand years has resulted in many different biological races: the Welsh, the

Bretons, the Belgians, the Galatians – the 'false bretheren' to whom St Paul loosed off his ferocious epistle – the Galicians in north-west Spain, the tribes of Ireland, the Highlanders. They all proudly tote their differences and their local adaptations. None, to my knowledge, has made it yet to subspecific status, but that is where the logical conclusion is heading. And what about Nova Scotia? Cape Breton Island? Some say they are now more Scottish than the Scots; wear more tartan, hurl more hammers, toss more cabers, reel more reels, hold their rituals more dear, ever more zealous the ancestral dream. Has Scotland, like the elk, become bigger and glossier over there? Grown bulkier antlers? Some days it seems like it. My retro-migrant Celts are here to check out their origins. I must tread warily.

We trail up the moor like a multicoloured worm slowly extending and contracting itself along a ribbon of path. Sections of the tail curl and clot around an object of interest then wind off again, hurrying to reconnect with its body. I talk about blanket bog, something most of them have never heard of. It's a black quilt of peat wrapped over the subsoil. It rounds the contours and fills in the hollows. I force my crummack three feet down into a soft spot and fail to find the bottom. Astonishment spreads like fog. Then come the questions, they look, question and look again. Most had never given a thought about what might lie beneath the heather.

'This is a peat bank, last used between the wars . . .' We stop at a symmetrical declivity in the moor, squared off by a neat-minded crofter. I jump three feet down into the soggy hollow. This is a frontier of understanding: a way in. Gently it lays a shadow over the ethereal idyll of Highland life. It tamps down the hype. It's something new, a phenomenon non-existent in the New World. We're juggling with new words, new concepts, new knowledge. I flick from face to face, watching thought processes congeal like cold porridge. 'Folk came up here to cut their fuel from the ground. They dried it and carried it down to their cottages in creels on their backs. If they were lucky they had a pony with panniers. Most didn't.' I stoop and tug away thick sponges of sphagnum moss with my fingers, history filling itself in. Underneath the exposed peat bank glowers darkly. I pull out a knife. The dark, fibrous stodge cuts like Mississippi mud pudding. I hand a slice up to the nearest onlooker. They are surprised by how heavy and wet it is, even in summer. 'This will *burn*?' asks a lady in shades and a sun hat.

We talk about the formation of the peat, the long dark winters, the acid rocks and the unforgiving cold that stops all microbial and fungal plant decay dead in its dank, non-humic tracks. Carefully we revisit Dr Isabel F. Grant's grim testimony: 'a half-naked hungry people living in mud-floored hovels, peat smoke blackening their faces, before it drifted out through a hole in the dripping roof, the sole room shared all winter through with starving cattle'. I have to keep reminding myself these are their ancestors I'm talking about.

A man mutters to his wife, 'Small wonder they left.'

'It accumulates at about a foot of peat for every thousand years.' I climb out of the pit. They look around. I reveal other, older peat banks to them, grown in like old wounds, barely discernible scars on the face of the hill. You have to know what you're looking for, but once shown, they're everywhere. Silence. They gaze round, spotting a new one here and another over there. Disbelief thickens the air for a few moments before the scale of the human toil and the pathos that accompanies it begin to sink in. Midges graze on our ears and necks.

One day I shall pluck up courage and stage a full re-enactment. I'd like to start at first light on a good summer's day – that'd be five o'clock – walk them up here and say to this couple: 'Right! Here is your peat knife. [A long, two-angled blade on a spade handle.] Off you go, that's your bank over there.' And to another pair: 'You take that one.' And to dot the whole group around the moor in pairs like nesting gulls. Then I would say to them: 'You have sixteen hours of daylight ahead of you. This is perfect peat-cutting weather. You aren't going to get many days like this and if you don't cut it now, stack it properly to dry with gaps so that the wind can blow right through it, you won't have the fuel you need for the winter. One cuts and hands up, the other stacks. Off you go!'

I would tell them that they need at least thirty-five tons per cottage to get through the winter. They can probably only spare two weeks a year in which to cut it because they have so much other work to do on the croft, so they have to be sure to cut and stack at least two and a half tons today – starting now.

Then I would sit back and watch. 'And oh! By the way,' I would remind them, 'you have no other source of heat at all in your croft cottage, except a few sticks of firewood gathered from here and there and your tallow candles. No electricity, coal, gas – nothing. It has to cook your food, boil your water, dry your clothes in the long, wet winters, and heat your space. This is it!'

Where is Brigadoon now? How does *Braveheart* fit into all this? If life was so tough, from what gleam of gilded inspiration did they fashion the *pibroch*, the exquisitely poignant classical music of the pipes?

A few years after I came to live in this glen, back in the early seventies, I was driving home from Glen Cannich one night when a deer leapt across the road in front of me. I swerved and hit the roadside fence. I extricated the car from the tangled wire and drove on home. The following morning I threw a few fence posts, a coil of wire, a hammer and some staples in the back of the car and set off back up the glen to mend the fence. As I hammered away, a crofter emerged from his tiny corrugated-iron-roofed cottage thirty yards away. He thanked me warmly for repairing the damage and invited me in for a dram. On the way in I passed his peat stack: many tons of immaculately cut rectangular turfs stacked like black ingots, order and neatness reflecting their value, a patchwork of thoughtful symmetry buttressing the leeward gable.

Roddy Murchison was seventy-four, his wife perhaps a year or two younger. They had been there all their lives. They lived in a cottage so small that it was little more than a name beneath a tin roof. Such cottages are referred to as a 'but-and-ben' in Highland parlance. It was a native building wrought from the ground and the sweat of native hands. It looked as though it had grown out of the soil, rather than being built upon it. They told me proudly that the 'electric' had just arrived, a few weeks before. Wires had been crudely installed over the ancient herbaceous wallpaper to a bare bulb that hung, shadeless, like a solitary pear from the centre of the ceiling. The walls were yellowed with age, nicotine and peat smoke. Dark smudges ringed the ceiling above the glass chimneys of two fluted brass oil lamps, elderly and picturesque as if out of a nineteenth-century photograph. A black kettle whined on a stained cream range. A decrepit old collie, as blind as a potato, lay rumbling suspiciously against the warmth. A box of peats rested beside the hearth. They had no television; their radio was a battery transistor on the table. Roddy told me that the main use they had for the 'electric' was to see to light the oil lamps. Then he turned it off again. 'And it is very handy if we've to get up in the night.' They neither trusted it nor wanted to incur its cost, which, they had been warned, could be high.

His wife, Morag, suffered chronic rheumatoid arthritis. She was sorely crippled and sat in an old armchair utterly dependent upon Roddy for everything. Her diseased old bones were packed and cushioned round with foam rubber crudely cut with a kitchen knife. A few months later I heard that they had given up the croft and gone to live in council accommodation in Inverness so that Morag could be near the hospital.

We find a high, dry bluff for lunch. We are flecks of colour in a rolling ocean of purple, as one sometimes sees a cluster of marigolds and poppies defiant in a field of yellow corn. Up here the breeze disperses the midges. It's warm. The sunlight is thick and vague, too idle to bother with shadows. The distance is absent, lost in a haze of deceit, and the mountains doze behind a veil of innocence. Today is episcopal, all purple. I try to guess what's going on behind the shades and the film of Jungle Juice. What did I think when I first saw an arid goat-created desert? How did I react when I first saw shoulder-high chaparral chamise in Californian sheep and cattle country, rolling out as far as the eye could see, the soil raw and bleeding away beneath it? Both are the man-imposed degraded landscapes of grazing and burning. Both caused by man doing what he has always done. 'Be fruitful and multiply and replenish the earth, and subdue it.'

It's Aldo Leopold's 'life of wounds' all over again. If man hadn't interfered so devastatingly, so every-damned-last-inchedly, perhaps nature could have repaired the damage, kept on painting in the gaps with diversity instead of letting a few dominant hard-nosed survivors run riot. Heather and sphagnum moss. I look round. Blade-edged sedges (*Carex*) and swipes of pale wavy hair grass (*Deschampsia*) illuminate the wet flushes. Deer grass (*Trichophorum*) bristles like hedgehog spines on the exposed peat ridges. Crimson and lime-green sphagnum cushions bulge exquisitely in the hollows. Yellow spikes of bog asphodel nestle among rough rugs of purple moor grass (*Molinia*) and mat grass (*Nardus*), as dense as its name. The moor is beautiful, unquestionably so, in its wide, mournful emptiness, but there is no tree to be seen. Native forest has been expunged from this place, cleared like the Highlanders: banished. And it has been kept out by the millennial perpetuation of the same grim tactics thought to be the only answer to human survival.

Fraser Darling branded this landscape a 'wet desert' in his cogent and unsettling report on 'the Highland problem', *West Highland Survey*, published in 1955. The book was condemned by the Church and by government officials of the day who were embarrassed that they had commissioned it in the first place. They managed to delay its publication for seven years. Politicians regularly dislike the truth. The *actualité* can be awkward.

The moor is beautiful but largely unproductive either for itself
or for anyone else. It's good at growing peat and the red deer have
adapted to it, becoming small and wiry compared with those
living in forests throughout Europe. It's home to the meadow
pipit and the darting falcon, the merlin, the size of a thrush. Red
grouse like it and have spawned an industry with myths and legends all of its own. Hill sheep and hardy cattle do well enough in
the short summer, but they hardly thrive on it. In winter it fills
with shimmering frozen snowfields across which the starving
deer pick their searching way, devouring every last sprout of
greenery that sticks up through the crust.

No hope for a struggling tree.

So it stands as a remarkable testament of man's ability to
reduce his habitat, to fail to understand and to discard the bless-
ing of nature's munificence. Take too much today and you wreck
your tomorrow.

Even a haphazardly managed renewable resource – in this
case native pine and birch forest with its patchy meadows and
swamps, its proud pine stands and soft birch glades – is an infinitely preferable habitat for man and his livestock. It delivers
shelter, fuel, construction timber, fruits and game, and it renews
soil, all free. But just as the tribal Arab Bedu couldn't resist
increasing his wealth in goats on the savannahs of the Nile Basin
and the Sahara, so the tribes of the Highland hills wanted ever
more cattle, more sheep, more deer – whatever grazing mouth
was in fashion. The forest just kept on giving way, falling back
with the grim dignity of a respected enemy, retreating to the high
windswept gullies and lurking furtively in burn-cut gorges like the
Jacobites themselves. Suddenly it was gone. Heather, sphagnum
and the rough grasses and sedges moved in, building peat and
smothering the minerals and nutrients needed for other seed germination. The vital spark was doused, the healing cycle cut off
before it even got going. An accidental monoculture of wet heath
spread like plague. Aided and abetted by a declining climate, it

infiltrated at will, quilting every damp hollow, systematically asphyxiating every dry knoll and every broad upland slope. Its low, cloying photosynthesis welcomed only its own. It caused the inexorable eradication of species after species of life-enhancing, soil-creating organisms that needed the intricate mystery of forest cover to survive. It was, to borrow a coldly charged phrase from Professor Chris Smout, 'a major modification of the natural world'. Not content with wholly altering the landscape it diffused itself into the folklore of the Highland people, celebrated in melancholy verse and song, echoing the mournful story of a broken people woefully departing their impoverished native land. Small wonder they left.

Sometimes I am gripped by the enormity of what man has done – is still doing despite the ubiquitous lessons of history – not just to our patch of Highland hill, but to the globe. I shut it out. It doesn't bear thinking about too much. It spoils lunch.

Things happen and we don't know why. I don't know what to make of destiny beyond it being the course of an individual's life, one's lot. The notion of predestination is alien to me – just plain unlikely. Yet, looking back, few events could have had more impact on the way I would spend my adult life than taking up pen and writing one day in 1972, out of the blue, to that one man whose books had opened my eyes to the reality of the Highland hills: Frank Fraser Darling. It seems to me now that had I not written that letter I might never have started a field centre for the Highlands – its first – nor would I have arrived in this place called Aigas and come to love it so well. If there was a germ of a vision in my head it had not presented itself openly to the light of possibility. I am not even sure now why I decided to write the letter. I was footloose and uncertain of any direction other than that I did not want to return to industry. I hoped that I could write for a living. One sentence was to change all that.

'Why don't you create a field studies centre based on your home?' came the reply from the most eminent ecologist in Britain, of whom I had asked whether there was a future for nature tourism in Scotland. 'I have long thought that the Highlands was the perfect place for such a thing and it has no such facility for learning home truths at all.' These words of encouragement from a man whose writing I had so admired, the author of ten books on Highland wildlife and wild places as well as his greater academic works. Why not indeed? It seemed such an eminently logical idea.

Much later, after we had met and spent some time together in the field, he expanded on his idea. 'The mistake,' he told me, 'of conventional field study centres is that they are too often cold and institutional. They preach from the lofty heights of science down to the poor demoralised layman. As such they are unfriendly and will not encourage people to them. If you are to pursue your idea of a centre for the Highlands, make it your home, too. Make them feel welcome.'

We try.

I cannot sit on this window ledge of Scotland and just watch the clouds go by. This moorland landscape, of all the diverse scenery that surrounds us, is the one that has become our daily bread. The very least I can do is try to help others to understand its past, share its predicament.

'This is degraded moorland,' I begin to explain as they munch their ham and salad rolls. 'It is neither good heather nor is it natural montane grassland.' There is a real story to tell here. Something they can get their academic teeth into after the rolls. The day awards itself a debate. We're happy to sit a while.

I tell them that it is struggling in a man-inflicted morass of chronic ecological impoverishment. The land is exhausted after centuries of unwitting abuse. The break-up of the climax forest was followed by the loss of its precious soils: the slowly accumulated natural wealth that underpins everything else was exposed to the wind and rain. It washed away. That happened a long, long time ago. So long ago that no one remembers trees here, not even the songs and legends. Perhaps they were felled for fuel, or set ablaze to drive out wolves, or perhaps it was just the creeping tide of agricultural clearance. Or maybe, later still, the last trees were sold for profit or converted into charcoal and carried away in the panniers of Highland ponies to be sold to iron bloomeries far away at a time when the Highlands had nothing else to give. Maybe it was an overlapping combination of them all. Only the ancient bleached roots protruding from the all-preserving peat tell us that it was once a broad forest of pine and birch. Too many sheep, too much burning; now too many sheep and too many deer still compounding the problem.

We begin to discuss deserts. Old deserts, new deserts, wet deserts and dry deserts, cold and hot. We trade parallels, teasing out their own experiences like picking winkles. They tell me about Amerindians burning vegetation to make hunting easier. We're breaking through. Up comes the logging out of the Pacific North-West and the spotted owl. I share the glow of comprehension. Continental separation is reversing itself right here, right now. Everyone joins in with an anecdote or an illustration. 'Soil,' declares the lone Frazer triumphantly, 'no matter where you are, it all comes down to the soil.' We all agree; it is a global problem, man's greed. We head off into tropical rain forest. This is good.

I think we knew a good bit about the land when we came here twenty-five years ago, but I don't believe we had any idea of the extent to which interest would accumulate around the seminal work of our mentor. The father of Highland ecology saw beneath the scruffy grasses and the stunted heather in a way no one had before. He unravelled the historical trail of impoverishment and related it to the unhappy story of the Highlanders themselves. A whole new window had opened on the Highlands. It was one that was to come to dominate our lives in the years ahead. We asked him to open our field centre in 1977.

I remember a car drawing up. A big man with a thicket of black hair eases himself unsteadily from the seat. With the help of a long stick with a carved ram's-horn handle he unfolds to his full six feet and more. He smiles broadly, leaning on his crummack. His right hand holds out an offering: a book. It is a treasured volume from his own library. It is a present wrapped in the spontaneity of real giving, William Mackay's *Urquhart and Glenmoriston – Olden Times in a Highland Parish*: the two glens immediately to the south of Strathglass, our glen. It is the 1914 second edition, long out of print and as rare as a midnight wedding.

Sir Frank Fraser Darling snipped our ribbon across the broad oak front doors of Aigas in 1977 in the company of our staff, a few friends and family and one or two Highland journalists. There could not have been a more appropriate person. He was then right at the end of a distinguished professional career dedicated substantially to the Highlands. He had cast his seeing eye across the world and returned to Morayshire to retire. He left us the legacy of true greatness. The depth of his work as an international ecologist is still improperly understood and his philosophies are not yet universally shared. He made a rough-edged comment in 1950, as he sat being interviewed on the fifty-fifth floor of the Rockefeller Center in Manhattan, that they knew more about his *West Highland Survey*, one of the world's first great works in human ecology, than did most people in Scotland. The special research fellowship he won from the Rockefeller Foundation was to enable him to mobilise his intellect and provide him with a world stage.

For all his lifelong association with the Highlands, Frank was only part Scot. He was a Yorkshireman with ancestral connections to the Border country, and it was there, to some high and bleak upland farm, that he was sent aged fifteen, he told me, 'to rid me of the farming bug'. It did no such thing. He learned to use a scythe, load a coup cart with hay, to milk, to spot a sheep struck with the fly, and (his lasting pride) to handle a wool dray with four horses in line. For a scientist who was later to maroon himself and his wife and child on such remote islands as Treshnish and North Rona for protracted periods of natural history study and wildlife observation, and who was to struggle single-handed with a Summer Isles croft and make it pay (just), it must have been a vital training.

'The intellectual life has never been enough,' he wrote of himself, 'and every now and then I have wished to withdraw and work with my hands.' He became a skilled drystane dyker, a most testing trade, and extended his interests far beyond the bounds of prescribed academic life. A passionate interest in the arts enabled him and his wife Christina to recreate an old dilapidated country house in Hertfordshire. Together they designed the interior, and decorated and furnished it with fine period furniture and art treasures collected from all over the globe. He collected and drank fine claret, completely flooring his wine-buff American hosts at a luncheon when they demanded his opinion of a particular vintage. He savoured the ruby liquid for a few moments and then pronounced: 'This wine should be drunk alone with a woman.'

This was a tousle-haired giant of a man whose huge hands had caressed the ancient stones of the hermit monk's cell he rebuilt on North Rona. His needle-sharp mind and no-nonsense opinions were eloquently expressed in the 1969 Reith Lecture, *Wilderness and Plenty*, and in his outstanding natural history of *The Highlands and Islands* with John Morton Boyd in 1964. His works were widely read both by a popular audience and by academics, and his reputation expanded across the three continents in which he had worked. 'There is no personal god for me,' he wrote in an autobiographical article, 'nor could I be such a fool to myself nor a knave before god to pray to him.'

I took to visiting him at the end of his life and sitting with him in his home at Lochyhill in Morayshire. He was a sick man but his brain burned as bright as a star. He took me to the window of his study, looking out over Scots pines and the forty-mile view beyond. 'There are the Soutars and Tarbert Ness, and on a clear day I can see the Duke of Sutherland on his monument on Ben

Bhraggie.' These were hills Fraser Darling had climbed and pondered and then exposed in his quiet, eloquent, literary way. I don't
know whether it was destiny that brought us together and
inspired our venture, but I do know that it was quite exceptional
good fortune.

'We are born with our complement of genes and grow with the
accidents of our environment,' he writes. 'There is not, nor can
there be, with all our political eagerness for doctrinaire notions,
any equality of opportunity. I accept this and hold that in humility
we should strive towards our potential. If we are favoured we can
practise the aristocratic ideal and show forbearance for those less
fortunate than ourselves.'

The day has been good. We have climbed a little higher, seen
a little farther and spun the globe a few extra rotations. Our group
has sorted itself into mini-groups so that we progress across the
moor like a troop of baboons, in families and little cliques, chattering. The Campbells and the Macleans have rediscovered their
Gaelic heritage and found a common link back home. Their forebears arrived in Hampton, Virginia, in the same year, 1838 –
perhaps even on the same boat. Things like that often happen
here.

We have teased out those two giants of global environmental
understanding: biodiversity and polymorphism. We have tackled
Darwin, and Lamarck in the nineteenth century, and debated the
Jesuit palaeontologist Father Teilhard de Chardin in the twentieth, whose attempts to bring science and God together caused
him to be gagged by Rome (yet again). We have rambled around
the contemporary work of Professor Edward O. Wilson, the orig-
inator of the term *biodiversity*. We have raked over the
impoverished Highlanders and their degraded landscape;
explored some of their lost options resulting from their lack of
biological diversity. We've toyed with fundamental ecology, with
and without human intervention. We have even drawn some conclusions: that cultural and biological diversity walk hand in hand.

Human survival for a hundred thousand years has depended upon our ability to adapt to widely differing environments from the Inuit on the Arctic ice to the Bushman in the arid desert. Our ability to do this, to make these changes for survival, is a result of polymorphism, the genetic capability concealed within most species to adapt to new conditions. 'Now that the Highlands are opening up,' poses the lone Frazer, 'with new blood rushing in, perhaps we can reverse some of the negative ecological trends which have threatened so much and driven so many away?'

We saw the scimitar-winged merlin in the distance, found *Lycopodium*, the stag's horn club moss, trailing its unlikely antlers across the bog. A pair of guilty-looking ravens corrupted the air with guttural croaks as they hurried away. They told us where a deer carcass lay. It had been picked clean by the ravens, buzzards and hooded crows and spread around the heather by squabbling foxes. Charlie Gunn finds the bleached skull with the stubby antlers of a late calf – probably a victim of the winter. We discuss the problems of survival in a harsh climate made harsher by man. We finger the skull and pore over the lack of minerals that the pathetic antler formation indicates. Charlie props it up on a boulder like an Apache totem. He backs off and bows to it, arms held high. Laughter and more discussion: some good old natural history thrown in to leaven the inescapable dough of genes, our continental drift.

They've opened up, sweated a little on the steep ground, found good heather for sitting in to get their breath back and – Oh my! – stumbled across a young rowan tree lurking in a rocky gully. No doubt a bird dropped the seed there. Bomb-like, wrapped in a faecal bubble, it was ready to burst where it lodged in the rock wall. It survived because no grazing animal could get to it, veering skywards like a bean sprout in a jam jar. It stands as a measure of the force of man's interference. One small tree alone in a day of walking a moor. We all agree. There's nothing wrong with nature, just with the way we treat it. 'Trouble is,' says a quiet man in steel-rimmed spectacles whom I have discovered comes from San Francisco and buys his khaki clothes from L.L. Bean, 'you don't give it a chance.'

'Who doesn't?' I ask.

'Well' – he smiles – 'I guess it's all of us.' He grins like a naughty schoolboy caught eating sweets in class.

I think of their lifestyle. I think of the Californian homes I have stayed in. The profligate use of energy, the cars, the aeroplane journeys, the lights of San Francisco at night shimmering across the Bay. I think of my own extravagances, those of my family. And then I think of Roddy Murchison lugging his peats from the hill and his crippled wife sitting alone at home.

It is twenty-five years since I saw their little house. Twenty-five years of progress. Twenty-five years of more consumption and dependence on electricity, technology, entertainment, all the junk we take for granted every day. Twenty-five years of distance from the simpler, cleaner world that Roddy Murchison knew. No wonder our guests have trouble relating to life here in the eighteenth century. In just twenty-odd years Roddy is history and we're spinning away from him, out of control.

We turn for home. Tomorrow I shall bring them face to face with what happens if you give nature a chance. We have been running our own moorland and woodland restoration project for twenty-five years: a few dozen acres of hope. Wet desert to sun-filled birchwood ringing with birdsong and a future. But first we shall attend to their bodily well-being. A hot bath and a dram, the chink of glass and the clatter of silverware at dinner and a chance to discuss the day beside a crackling pine-log fire.

TEN

Bella Macrae

Nor knowest thou what argument
Thy life to thy neighbour's creed has lent.

RALPH WALDO EMERSON, 1803–82

Very early on in my years at Aigas, on an April day of high anvil-headed cumulus clouds against a blue so radiant that I could scarcely force my eyes to take it in, I climbed the heather mile to the Iron Age fort. I was musing on the presence of man in this beautiful but paradoxical landscape, still struggling to come to terms with my own life being one more to stipple the millennia of uncounted beings this land has owned. I stood among the straggling whins eyeing the great trough of the glen a thousand feet below, watching cloud shadows tease across meander-waisted river fields.

To the west of my view a movement drew my eye to the Craigdhu croft. A scatter of cattle and sheep spotted the rushy parks like rust on a rose leaf. I raised my binoculars. A lone figure stood among the alders at the riverside, slightly hunched, with a long crummack in hand. Beside the figure a sheepdog lay obediently at rest. At first I couldn't determine who it was. It was too far away and although I knew of the existence of Bella Macrae, I had yet to meet her. That distinctive image I was to come to know so well – the old tammy hat and the muted tweed coat with a haversack slung across it, her crummack always in her right hand and black gumboots almost meeting the hem of her coat – was yet to be imprinted on my mind. As I steadied my gaze, resting my elbows on the heaped stone ruins, I knew that it must be her.

From my eyrie I spied on Bella for half an hour. Every now and then the sun flashed from her hand, drawing me back to look again. She was almost unmoving, just raising and lowering her own binoculars and occasionally taking a few steps to aid her vision as she watched her lambing ewes spread around the tiny fields. The day was bright with ambition. I was exploring my new home, testing its moods. I wanted to meet her.

It took me most of an hour to cover the three-quarters of a mile between us. I had to scramble down the steep valley wall and stoop my way through a jungle of broom and gorse, following sheep and deer trails and tunnels often precarious and savage. They tore at my clothes and often led me to the unseen edges of vertical drops so that time and again I had to retrace my steps uphill and find another route. I emerged at the Craigdhu roadside scratched and bleeding, plucking gorse spines from my arms and legs. Now it was I who was being scrutinised through binoculars. I dusted myself down as best I could. Bella had not moved more than a few yards and I still had to cross the two small fields to where she stood.

I have often wondered what this ageing crofter must have thought of the lanky, untidy youth striding towards her. I knew she would have heard of me, of course. News of incomers in Highland glens travels like birch seed on the wind, and besides, I had known Dunc MacRae from Oldtown of Aigas, our nearest neighbour and hers, for several months. (The two local Macrae/MacRae families are most particular about their different spellings. You might have thought, mightn't you, that after the first half-dozen generations of intermarriage, these two factions of Clan Macrae could have agreed a common spelling? Not a bit of it! Highlanders are tribal and unity is not a Celtic virtue.) It is also inevitably the case that when the big house changes hands, even though it had briefly been an old people's home since Mrs Gordon-Oswald died, more than usual interest immediately surrounds the new owner.

I was unready for the laughing blue eyes and the tranquillity in her weathered face. I introduced myself, apologising for my appearance. 'Aye, aye, I know who y' are, right enough,' she replied, looking me up and down. 'I thought it was elephants coming down the hill. Do you not use the roads?'

Bella wore her years robustly. She was sixty-six when I first met her that day and it would be wrong to say that she did not look it. For all its many compensations, a crofter's life is rigorous, especially so for a single woman. Her face had resolved itself into the lean lines of the fine skull and the strong jaw beneath, gaining much in power and character and passion. The eyes, slightly sunken, were framed in tangled crow's feet suggesting a smile of mischief and fun and a heart quite unexpecting. Her hands were the texture of old leather gloves, scarred and worn, the white skin folded and pliant, fingernails split and stained with outdoor work. Her cheeks were as smooth as patches of still water on a summer lochan. Silver-grey curls like apple-peelings emerged from beneath her bonnet and sprung in the breeze. Her tweed coat was a small hound's-tooth check, probably once of grey and purple. But years of the sun and the coursing rain had blended it to a soft uniformity like that of an old barn door, no longer possible to say for certain what colour it had originally been. The bonnet, which could have nodded respectfully to Sundays long ago, was now just an old hat. It was a thick knitted tam with a

graceless bobble on the top. Unlike the coat, it had clung tena-
ciously to fireclay orange, weakening only in paler patches where
something mildly caustic had splashed across it. The tops of her
black gumboots had been rudely cut down with scissors at the
front to stop them rubbing her shins; the fabric lining frayed
white and ragged. She wore thick brown stockings barely visible
in the gap between boot-tops and coat hem. The crummack she
loved so much was a hazel stick, long and slender, with a sheep's-
horn handle; it was uncarved and smooth with years of use,

curling elegantly back upon her hand. It became a permanent
extension of her arm and her eye. It was everything to her, as is
a bow to a violinist, and with it she played out the intricate har-
monies of her land. It was a prop and an extra limb; it was a probe
and a measure of the ground. It lent her authority over her beasts,

eased her over fences and ditches, and steadied her gaze. Its smooth comfort caressed the folds of her hand.

One day I called in to see her and found her *trauchled* – as they say in these glens – not so much angry as thoroughly displeased, but with a measure of hurt thrown in. She came straight out with it. 'D'ye see this?' she demanded crisply, fetching the stick from the corner at the kitchen door. 'See this, now!' she repeated, her anguish on full display as she thrust it at me. 'I've had this since I took over the croft from my father in 1951. I was at the ewes this morning and one tried to break back. I put it out and – snick! – it just gave way in my hand. Look at that now!' The horn handle had snapped off on the downward curve rendering the crummack useless. She passed me the broken piece and returned to her chair at the Rayburn stove, clicking and tutting and shaking her head as if war had been declared on the next glen.

The world of epoxy-resins had not included Bella, nor would it ever, so when I returned it to her two days later, apparently as good as new, she was amazed, fetching her glasses to inspect it minutely and not a little suspiciously. Months later she was still beaming her delight and waving it to me whenever I passed in the car.

In the following years Bella was to define crofting to me in a way no one else has. Crofters come in many forms. On the coast and in the islands, it often includes inshore fishing for crabs and lobsters, or spinning and knitting or weaving tweed, indeed any handcraft from carving sticks for tourists to making fiddles. It can involve boat-building and can combine itself inextricably with community life – the post, nursing, road maintenance, regular trades, forestry and many other activities; but almost inevitably it returns to the land. Agriculture, or at least basic farming, is at the very heart of its origins – a native people living off their land. Bella was never happier than when she was at work on her croft. There was about her an emanation, a landward resonance that pealed like bells, and of which I was deeply envious. The gleam in her eye, the ready smile and the calluses of her old fingers reflected the land as it, in its own way, bowed graciously to the labours of her hands.

Often I would just go to find her because I enjoyed her resonance so much. Her gentle philosophy drew me in. I wanted to learn from her – to watch her thinking with her hands. She epitomised that unhurried, thoughtful resourcefulness that is so often a hallmark of the Highland Gael. Over the years I have come to respect it and to enjoy working with it, albeit in a world where others would seek to homogenise and bureaucratise it out of existence. When the elements ganged up against Bella, scouring rain drenching her cattle for days on end, mud up to their knees, or when the snow piled into her little fields at lambing time, sufficient to drive most people to drink and despair, she would beam a gleaming row of National Health teeth and shake her head, saying: 'That's the way of it. What can y' do, eh?'

From the roadside I could look down to the river or up to the cottage. It would only take me a minute to find her. The entire compass of her world lay open like a book. One spring day I found her far down on the river fields clearing dried flood debris from the fences. If you don't clear off the branches and the rushes, the dead bracken and all the other flotsam that comes down and strings itself along the wire fences like Monday washing, when next the flood comes it strips the whole fence away with it. We worked together all morning, heaping the brittle vegetation into mounds and setting fire to it so that aromatic wood smoke stung our eyes and the bittersweet of campfires was on our lips. It was good work. At lunchtime we broke from our labours. 'You'll take a cup o' tea,' Bella announced.

I went to untie the wire holding the field gate shut. 'What're you fussing wi' that for?' she asked, mischief dancing in her wide, sky-reflecting eyes.

'I'm letting you through the gate,' I replied ingenuously.

She pouted her cheeks in high indignation. 'Pssht! Do you not think I can manage the fence?' Before I could answer she had gripped the hinge post and swung her leg over the wires, skirts to the wind.

When the bad September flood of 1965 hit Strathglass, Bella had just completed her harvest. The oats' sheaves stood three to a stook, dotted across the field in an ancient symmetry as elegant as fleurs de lys on a golden counterpane. The hot weather cracked like a plate. Cloudbanks of charcoal brimmed over the moors and thunder echoed from high in the Affric Hills. The flood came down like the Assyrian upon the fold, casting all before it. The new concrete and steel bridge in Glen Affric was swept away and for a few days the valley disappeared beneath an angry brown broth.

Reading the clouds and the muggy air, Bella had hurriedly mustered her cattle and sheep and brought them up the croft to the park beside the cottage, well above the flood line. But she had no time to move her harvest. Every last one of her golden sheaves was swept east to the march fence with Oldtown. There they were dumped against the fence in a long sodden line; rushes and uprooted broom tangled among them, with the ragged corpses of hill sheep from way upstream sprinkled in like suet dumplings in a vegetable stew.

As soon as the flood subsided Bella was out at dawn working the fence. She disentangled the sheaves, shook them out and retied them with twine. She bundled them together and slung them on to her back. On her bowed back she carried her entire harvest home that year, toiling the long half-mile back to the barn over and over again until she had recovered every one.

A croft has attracted many definitions: a smallholding, a subsistence farm not quite big enough to live on, a small farm entirely enclosed by regulations, and so on. In reality it is many of those things and much more. Emerging from ancient systems of dividing arable land among a tribal people and precipitated by the disaster (for Gaeldom) of the Battle of Culloden, crofts became any piece of low-value land to which the (troublesome) native population could be pushed to keep them alive. At the same time it tied them as a workforce to larger properties: the network of large farms and estates that were proliferating across the Highlands and would shape their future.

Crofting is alive and well, although absurdly uneconomic, in the twenty-first century. In his intuitive way, Frank Fraser Darling, who was strongly drawn to the crofting life and tested it in his own socio-scientific way by moving his entire family to the Summer Isles in 1939, defends it in *Island Farm* as a way of life rather than a viable occupation. He describes his time on the island of Tanera Mor as 'a shriving experience starting from scratch and reaching a peasant level of comfort in three and a half years'. Twenty years after Fraser Darling's death, although there is some recruitment into crofting from throughout the UK – often of folk disenchanted with mainstream life in a post-industrial society – most crofters today remain the remnant population of Highlanders left working the land after the nineteenth-century Clearances and the mass emigrations to southern cities and the New World.

As I have known it in my time, crofting possesses more than a little of the *primitif*. For many observers the day-to-day physical struggle with poor soils, long winters of brutal rainfall and almost non-existent returns would seem to be too much: the index of a man's value measured in endurance, unacceptable drudgery and a standard of living sometimes closer to that found in a third-world country than in urban Britain. But I believe this is to misinterpret the apparent paradox in which many crofting communities survived the proliferating materialism of the twentieth century. In Bella and her family I found no martyred doggedness or dumb heroism. Instead I discovered an enviable art of real accommodation, a self-reliance and an ability to make do and be happy with it. Crofters like Bella are their own capital, a concept barely recognised and certainly not valued by the growth-dependent economics of Hayek and Friedman.

History has awarded the crofter a set of instinctive and collective values that supplant the rational, more objective values of mainstream Western civilisation. Disposable income and leisure only become a *force majeure* when they are required to fill the vacuum left behind when a culture and a true sense of community cease to exist. Culture has no price. Even after long and successful careers away in the outside world, for their retirement, sons and daughters of crofts commonly seek to return to the community of their origins. For all the hardship of their history, and in common with American Indians, Australian Aborigines and many other relict populations whose traditions and values have been swamped by overweening Western ambition, crofters were then and still are a native people in occupation of their own land – albeit a tiny, impoverished, peripheral bit of it. Astonishingly, despite active suppression throughout the eighteenth and nineteenth centuries, the Gaelic language, Highland music and dance, their song, their poetry and their folklore have managed to cling on in the remote fastnesses of the glens and the islands. Bella had been brought up in a Gaelic-speaking household, but from the moment she went to school it had been discouraged as stringently as one might try to prevent a child from swearing. So she stored it away and kept it for just that. It appeared only on rare and worthy occasions – a tangle of venomous glottal aspirates and consonants hissed like a cornered wildcat, fervid and rank.

The native Highlanders' sense of belonging is not comprehended by the great generality of the English and the Lowland Scots, neither of whom possess it or, when they recognise it, consider it to be significant. It took me years to uncover its meaning and to understand its relevance to the land around me, something I could not glean from history books. It is to Bella that I owe that clipping of insight: what it really meant to belong – to *be-long* in a land. It was an imperceptible comprehension, as slow as a maturing wine, but one that for me, ultimately, would become seasoning: an enrichment of the place Aigas.

Bella was many things to which I was drawn, but above all she and her neighbours living on either side of her in those days, Colin and Dunc and their families and her cousins on the other side of the river, were all MacRaes – from the ancient Gaelic *Macrath* – Son of Grace; in later centuries to become Clan MacRae of ferocious fighting reputation. Their ancestral stronghold is one of the best-known landmarks in the Western Highlands, the reconstructed coastal fortress of Eilean Donan Castle only a few miles through the Affric Mountains to Kintail. Like Frasers and Chisholms, MacRaes are patrician, as noble as the landscape here, belonging in a way that one never thought to question, far less to emulate – in the richest context of that much abused term, *paysannerie* – a people of the land. They answer to this place as the Inuit answer to the booming pack ice, or the Sami to the dim forests of the north. Asking them where they come from is as fatuous as asking a Bedu if he belongs to the desert.

Such Highlanders possess a palpable sense of belonging – or rather a total absence of a sense of *not* belonging – which sets them apart. It simply never crosses their mind. Not surprisingly they have a word for it, and, equally unsurprisingly, it has no English equivalent: *dùthchas* (pronounced *dooch-hus*). But 'a sense of belonging' is hopelessly inadequate. Rather, as an expression *dùthchas* projects an indefinable oneness of spirit with the land and the centuries of cultural associations that attend it as clouds pursue the moors. It becomes a wholeness, chiming with the North American Indians in Chief Seattle's famous (and probably apocryphal) speech, 'We are of the land, the land is of my people. The earth does not belong to us, we belong to the earth.' A dictionary definition is more precise: 'of a native land, even a hereditary right to be there'. But it still misses the mark because it is the unconscious authority of *dùthchas* in the psyche of the

Highlander that affords them their eloquent reticence and the wry smile, the laissez-faire, the softly adjectival approach to life. Bella wore *dùthchas* as she wore her old coat.

It is hardly surprising that those Highlanders who scattered to the New World took their subconscious *dùthchas* with them, fostered it with the remnant trappings of a tribal society, recreating them as living icons of their past, almost inevitably overegging the pudding so that the St Andrews and Caledonian Societies, the Highland games and clan gatherings of the United States and Canada, of Australia and New Zealand, sport more and brighter tartan, more pipers and zanier traditions – and expectations – than anything back here. Nor is it surprising that three, four, five generations on it still tugs them back to whichever wee bit of moor and glen still fizzes from the depths of their long Celtic psyche.

When I came to know Bella much better I was surprised that she had never married. The faded black-and-white photographs she showed me of her youth pictured a fine young woman; there was no doubt that she had been healthy and strong. But fate had delivered the young Isabella into a world cut off from mainstream life in Scotland at a time when young men were leaving and never returning. She was born in 1910; just four years before the great conflagration of World War One in which Highland regiments were to suffer such grievous losses. It is the poignant legacy of ancient clan loyalty that every Highland village and township across the north and the west, and extending throughout the Hebrides, displays an elaborate stone memorial to the tens of thousands of young men, many only teenagers, who fell in that terrible conflict.

In the absence of young men, many women became crofters and adopted the family responsibilities for their land. Years after her death Pat MacRae told me that Bella had one day unearthed a box containing a fine string of cultured pearls. She opened it reverently and spoke wistfully, 'These were given to me years ago – but never mind all that.' Hurriedly she buried them again in a drawer. Pat never pursued the subject, but she told me that she thought that there had, once, been a suitor.

Bella took over from her father Duncan Macrae when he died. She adored him and lovingly tended him until his death. She was just forty-one. Until he became infirm she had 'jobbed about', as she put it, first working at Aigas House as a housemaid to the Gordon-Oswalds, living in a tiny servant's bedroom high among the turrets on the third floor. She told me that the house was rigidly formal in those days. The servants were not allowed to talk in the front of house and laughter and gaiety were frowned upon at any time. They were given a short cutting of candle to light their way to bed. When it ran out they were committed to darkness and their rooms until dawn. In later years she returned as a domestic helper in the kitchens at the very end of Mrs Gordon-Oswald's life. But she fell out with the bossy housekeeper who was a Lowlander from the Lothians. Bella was affronted that she wasn't allowed to wash up the fine china and glass in case she should break something. 'There was not a laugh in her,' she told me with a Highlander's historical disdain for their southern countrymen fully unfurled, 'about as much fun as a Wee Free on the Sabbath.'

That was certainly not true of Bella. She loved a ceilidh and a dance and turned out to such infrequent local events as often as she could. It was years before I could persuade her not to offer me a dram whenever I dropped in to see her. After several disastrous occasions when the whole day slid into a miasmal blur, at the risk of being thought rude, I learned to decline her hospitality firmly. But she never gave up. The very last time I saw her at home before she died, as I got up to go she tried one last time: 'Will you no tak' a wee dram afore you go?'

What Bella took over, aged forty-one, were twenty-five acres of rushy river flats euphemistically called arable land, all of which was prone to potentially catastrophic flooding twice a year. There was a pocket-handkerchief paddock beside the croft cottage, and a much older cottage now turned into a tractor shed and barn. This former Craigdhu from an unrecorded past was built upon a mound facing down the glen with its shoulder set to the prevailing wind. There was a stable for the croft horse where the mouldy harness still hangs on wooden racks along the wall; beside it a stone byre with stalls for four milking cows. Wooden-planked and corrugated-iron shanties and lean-tos had grown on to these ancient buildings, expanding them outwards like rings on a shell. This tiny empire contained the four cows in milk with calves at foot and a handful of *stirks* (good Highland word for bullock), and thirty-three blackface ewes – blackies. These animals were her joy.

As she aged, so inevitably she became less able to cope with the more physically taxing tasks of her croft. Her ingrained independence and reluctance to ask for anything meant that we had to check her out regularly, or rely upon Colin and Pat next door to tell us when she needed help. It took years for her to pick up the telephone and ask me to come. Even then she would hedge, hesitation hanging in her voice like mist over the river. 'Are you busy just now?'

'What is it, Bel? Do you need help?'

'Ooch well, I was just wondering if you'd be passing later on.'

Slowly I would extract from her that she had been down in the river fields for half the night watching a ewe in lambing difficulties. Her problem was that she could no longer catch the sheep in trouble. Even with the help of Nell the collie, the ewes were too quick for her. If she spied one lying down and pushing she would inspect it closely through her binoculars. After a while she would approach cautiously. Ewes with twins or breech presentations often need a helping hand. Sometimes they will accept help without a struggle, but others, despite the exertion of hours of contractions, will spring up and run off as nimble as a deer. So, year after year, the birth miracle became my most regular spring contact with Bella. It crystallised my chemical reaction to this ageless crofter and the land that owned her. Each April I longed for the phone to ring. It was also a climax in the Craigdhu calendar and she loved it. Her grin herded her cheeks up under her sparkling eyes where they shone like satin pincushions. She would scuttle down the cottage drive to the road and across into the fields before I could get out of the car. When I had caught the sheep she would settle down beside me, holding the ewe's head (she would say 'yow', like cow) by the horns and quizzing me as I worked away at the other end.

Between gripping contractions and with the help of a squirt of obstetric lubricant, a hand is gently eased through the cervix to locate the jammed lambs and sort them out. Often this means pushing a lamb's legs or head back so that it can be turned before pulling it forward again.

'Is it twins she has?' Bella would demand impatiently from the head.

'Yes, it is, but I think one may be dead,' I would reply. 'That could be the problem.'

'Ooch, I knew it!' she would announce. 'She had trouble with one last year. She's not up to twins, this one.' Or, tutting and shaking her silver curls, 'Ach, I'd rather have one good lamb any day. Twins is more trouble than the toothache.'

If the result was a total failure and limp corpses lay on the bloodstained grass, Bella would shrug her shoulders and say, 'Aye well, that's the pity of it.' But if we were successful and good lambs came wet and wobbling into her Craigdhu world her face would radiate pure joy. As I whisked the slippery little bodies round to the ewe's head to lick them dry, imprinting their smell and their taste – the essential mechanism for bonding mother and lamb – Bella would stand back and admire them critically, speaking as much to the ewe as to me. 'That's strong lambs, that is. Oh well, now! Very good! I'm pleased wi' her. That's a good morning's work.' Or then again, 'I don't think much o' that wee one. That's no much o' a lamb you've got there. Is that the best you can manage after all that work? It's got a lot o' catching up to do, that one has. You'd better be a good mother now!'

Sometimes she wouldn't be happy with a lamb I had presented to its mother. 'That's no right!' She would point with her crummack. 'It'll no suckle wi' all that muck in its mouth.' And I would have to prise open its tiny jaw with my fingers, like an orchid, lush and wet, and clear the sticky mucus from its nostrils. 'That's it now! That'll be it, right enough.' The smile would return, as wide and radiant as a sunset.

We would walk slowly back to the cottage, stopping every few yards to look back and see how they were getting on. 'You'll come in for a cup o' tea?' If I declined, saying that I must get back to my work, she would impale me on those blue eyes and add, 'I've pancakes just made.' She knew I couldn't resist for long.

As I came to know her well I sounded her out on the abundant wildlife on her croft. She missed little and on rare occasions she phoned me if something unexpected cropped up. She had no desire for specific knowledge and the concept of conservation was incomprehensible to her – she simply had no idea of the extent elsewhere of urbanisation, of industrial pollution or even of intensive agriculture; in her world there was little need of conservation; nature could look after itself as it always had. The Craigdhu wildlife belonged there as she did and she saw no cause either to give it a fancy name or to tinker with the order of creation. In environmental terms Bella's lifestyle was as sustainable as one could find anywhere in the developed world.

Breeding corncrakes disappeared from this glen in the 1960s and by the mid-seventies they were a rarity even on migration, passing through to their last stronghold in the north-west Highlands and the Hebrides. One day Bella phoned me to say that there was a strange bird calling in her hay field. I asked her to describe it. 'It's like a grating sound,' she said, 'calling over and over again.' And then she added, 'I've not heard it for years, but it was all about us when I was a girl.'

'So you know what it is?' I said.

'Aye, I think so,' she replied cautiously. 'I think it is a *corn-flake*.'

Wildlife that did her no harm she loved. She took me to the river bank and showed me the mudslide where she often saw the otters leave the water to hunt in the ditches and marshes for frogs and elvers. She spoke of them in hushed tones, saying there were still those in the glen who would come and trap her otters for making sporrans from their skins. She smiled at the primroses and the yellow banks of lesser celandine; with real glee she pointed to the pearl-bordered fritillaries tripping graceful minuets among her sheep. I told her their name repeatedly but she never bothered to heed it, referring to them only as 'that frilly butter-flies'. But foxes that came in the night and stole her weakling lambs, and hoodie crows that pecked out their newborn eyes, she scorned with a Gaelic curse and palpable anger in her puck-ered brow.

She shared her nocturnal pastures with the red deer from the hill in an agronomy ill-equipped to nourish more mouths than those of her own stock. Sometimes a dozen hinds would melt away into the river mist as she appeared on her lambing rounds at first light. 'Ach well,' she would sigh, 'it's their glen as much as mine.' And then she would glance at me with a little sideways look of mischief playing at the corners of her mouth. 'And it's good to know they're there if I go hungry.'

Bella was renowned the length of the glen for her sound hus-bandry and her eye for a good beast, especially cattle. She bred a fine crofting cow, Highland and Shorthorn being her chosen cross, and one or two old favourites she kept going long after one might normally expect a cow to survive, let alone continue to bear calves. One day she asked me to fetch a bull from a neigh-bour. As I was unloading it from the trailer into her field she was busy separating a very elderly cow called Morag from the others. Morag was twenty-three years old and her hips protruded like chimneystacks on a sunken roof. Her head hung low and as she walked her joints clicked and creaked like a wicker basket.

'She'll not take the weight of the bull now.' Bella shook her head as we eased the old cow through the gate into the next park.

'Surely she won't be bulling at her age, will she?' I asked.

'Ooh! Don't you believe it.' Bella laughed, blue eyes dancing. 'Morag'll not miss out if she has the chance.'

To carry her livestock through the long winter she made a barnful of hay rich in clover and kidney vetch, wild poppies, lady's bedstraw and cornflowers, as sweet-smelling as a vanilla pod. Most years she grew a football pitch of turnips for the sheep in winter, lifting them by hand in the autumn rain and sealing them into a clamp until needed. In the days before the ready availability of bagged feeds, she grew a six-acre field of wheat or oats. In the croft yard a scatter of brown hens scratched and pecked in the dirt, laying their sun-yolked eggs among the hay bales in the barn. At her door Nell lay patiently beside her water bowl waiting for her mistress to take her down to the river fields. 'I have everything here in these few acres that you could ask for, except money,' she said to me once, and then added wryly, 'and I've not much use for that.'

Cars and television have now fragmented and dissipated the communal spirit of many crofting townships, but in the prime of Bella's tenure she had her neighbours to call on for help with the really heavy work of harvest or hay-making, sheep-clipping or mustering her livestock for the mart in Inverness. Dunc at Oldtown and his son Finlay and his wife Pamela, Colin and his son Alastair and daughter Anne, and their near neighbours Henry Bain from Struy and Donnie Fraser, Culligran and the Frasers at the Knocknashalavaig croft, all came together to spread the burdens of glen life. No money changed hands during these exchanges of labour, but the host croft habitually provided an extravagant 'tea' of eggs and bacon or roast chicken and cold meats, followed by jam-laden scones and griddle pancakes dripping with home-churned butter, and homemade bread and heather honey from her own hives. Bella's baking skills are still spoken of today. Never would she have felt that she was on her own, nor that willing and experienced help was not close at hand.

These years of often back-breaking, happy and fulfilling toil among her family and friends had delivered up to Bella an independence of spirit that, when combined with the inherent self-sufficiency (*urralachd* – another Gaelic concept for which English has no single word) of the Highland Gael, made her impervious to the onset of modernity. She had never travelled. Every few years she went to Mallaig on the west coast two and a half hours away on the bus to visit relatives, and she once went to Perth, a hundred miles to the south. As a schoolchild she had boarded away at the Elgin convent, sixty miles to the east, as was common secondary schooling for the sons and daughters of Catholic families from the remoter glens, but that was the extent of her life's journeys. Offered the chance to go to France, on a pilgrimage to Lourdes with Colin's wife Pat, she declined, expressing suspicion of such foreign lands. My own view is that she had no need to travel. What she said of her home acres was what she really felt. Craigdhu and the little white church at Eskadale just across the river were her whole world, round and full. It was where she had lived and moved and had her being for more seasons than she could remember. It had fed her and clothed her and handed out joy and toil in equal measure. She went to her bed contented and rose happy to meet the challenges of each day anew. She had everything she could imagine wanting and she saw no need to ask for more.

Expeditions to Beauly for her 'messages' as a passenger in Pat's or Colin's car were regular weekly events, although she held motorised traffic in high contempt. Her shopping days were accompanied by the frequent screeching of brakes as she ignored pedestrian crossings and stepped out in front of cars without so much as a glance to either side. It was as though she

had consciously decided to reject modernity and tolerate it only
when forced to. In consequence she became evasive, not wanting
to give anything away. She seldom gave a straight answer to any
but her closest friends, almost as though she were afraid that
there was some new rule out there that would catch her out – not
so much paranoia as a canny wariness of any values other than
her own. When asked by the man from the Department of
Agriculture how many sheep she had she would don a worried
look, shake her head and say, 'Ooh, not as many as last year.'

Yet she read widely and listened to the radio, stubbornly refusing to call it anything but the wireless, and latterly she
occasionally watched a little television from a black-and-white set
with very poor reception. I don't believe she identified with what
she saw, choosing to remain distant from it, preferring to sit and
knit or embroider or go next door to enjoy the 'crack' with Colin
and Pat, rather than allow it to consume her evenings. I asked her
if she had a favourite programme. 'Not really,' came the reply
borne of centuries of suspicion and delivered with a funny little
twist of her head and a hovering grin. 'But it's quite good to know
what kind o' things foreign folks get up to.'

Among many other skills urgently needed when I first came to
live at Aigas were those of a plasterer. Ceilings had fallen on three
floors. When the weather gets into old buildings the plaster,
which is often over an inch thick, absorbs moisture and expands.
This fractures its grip on the timber lath that holds it in place; its
weight increases many times and, sooner or later, often when it
dries out again, it comes crashing down. The noise is alarming
enough if you are not in the room, but if you are it is potentially
very dangerous. Tons of plaster falling from six or eight feet
above your head can spoil your day.

In the great hall, where the curved ceiling is thirty feet high, so
much had either already fallen before we came here (Africa in the
snowdrift) or was ominously bulging that we decided to replaster

the entire area. It seemed to be testing our guests' enthusiasm a little too far to risk such weighty fall-out from immediately above the dining table. But where in this land of scattered settlements was I going to find a plasterer who could tackle a task of such ecclesiastical dimensions? Curiously, and in the portentous way that fate sometimes comes tripping along, the answer was almost next door.

Colin MacRae was supposed to be retired. He was in his late sixties and officially disabled. He had an artificial leg and his left arm was pinned permanently in a bent position. 'Officially' was as far as it went. I have never known anybody less retired than Colin. It just so happened that he was a master plasterer *and* my neighbour. He was Dunc's brother and lived beside Bella at Craigdhu, a mile up the glen.

Like many Highlanders in 1939, Colin signed up for his local regiment, the Lovat Scouts, to serve in World War Two. He was thirty-one and a qualified, time-served tradesman. He had worked a five-year apprenticeship for a master plasterer in Inverness and then branched out on his own. In time of war it was his natural authority and leadership that took him quickly through the ranks to full sergeant in the Pioneer Troop. He came through an active war unscathed until April 1945 – only a month from the end in Europe.

During the night of 11 April his squadron was ordered to advance to the top of the Gesso Ridge by way of a steep and rocky pass above Pradella in southern Italy. The leading platoon had experienced such difficulty reaching their objective that Sergeant MacRae was instructed to supervise the clearing of a better pass through easier ground known to be studded with enemy mines. He had served in a mine-disposal squad. At once, by himself and in the dark, he began to clear this new route, refusing to allow others in until he had made it safe. He located and lifted 'Schu' mines and 'S' mines and made it to the ridge, laying a tape as he went. Then he turned to go back over his work and lead his men through. He had missed a mine. It triggered, blowing off his left leg below the knee and shattering his left arm, as well as giving widespread shrapnel injuries to other parts of his body. Despite his grievous condition he never lost consciousness and shouted back to his men not to come in to help him. Lying in great pain, he continued to instruct his men in the work still needed to make it safe.

There were other incidents and more casualties that night, but Colin remained imperturbable and continued to advise and help as much as he could. Finally, still declining help for fear of maiming other men, he dragged himself out over a distance of fifty yards. His citation states that he saved the lives of many others and was cheerful and calm throughout.

In the surgical tent, thinking his patient unconscious, the field surgeon asked the medical orderly what was Colin's job. 'A master plasterer, sir,' came the assertive reply from the theatre table. Colin was not a man to have another answer for him. There then followed a discussion about how he would like his left arm pinned for holding the plasterer's hod. He was awarded the George Medal for military gallantry, a rare honour seldom more honourably earned. A few months later, wearing his new tin leg, he travelled to Buckingham Palace to receive it in person from the king.

Colin and his wife Pat became our good friends. He plastered ceilings and walls and patched cornices here for several years, teetering on trestles and ladders, doing the work of two men. He was a perfectionist, occasionally pulling down his own work because it wasn't good enough, cursing softly to himself as though some sloppy apprentice had done it. He wore an air of natural authority like a badge. From the start I saw that the other workmen obeyed him without quibble. One evening he and I were left working alone in the Aigas dining hall where he was replastering the ceiling thirty feet above our heads. His helper who mixed his plaster had gone home. I began to clear up. It had been a long, hard day and I was ready to pack it in. Colin had some plaster left over that he wanted to use up and began to climb the ladders up the high scaffold towards the ceiling. 'What are you doing?' I asked.

'I've a wee bitty left to do up here,' he said, still struggling upwards, his artificial leg clattering on the aluminium ladder.

'How are you going to get the plaster up?' I asked naively.

'You're going to bring it to me,' came the answer in no uncertain tone. 'The buckets are there and I'll have the first one just now, please. Don't hang about or it'll set.'

From time to time he called us out to help rescue Bella's sheep from precipitous rock ledges above the Aigas quarry where they had been tempted to graze without realising that they couldn't get back. Sheep are not well equipped with common sense. He would perch on the edge of the precipice, instructing those of us abseiling on ropes below him and directing us to the stranded sheep. Although living in the midst of his crofting family, Colin was not officially a crofter in the legal land-tenure sense. The twenty-five arable acres of Craigdhu land beside the river was crofted by Bella.

Colin died in 1985 at the age of seventy-seven after a long struggle against cancer. Pat told me that if he had a splinter in his thumb he would moan as if the whole world were against him, but in the long months of dying he made not a murmur. The whole glen mourned his passing. At his funeral old soldiers travelled from as far as the Faeroe Islands to honour their comrade. Cars stretched for two miles down the winding single-track road to the little white-harled Catholic church at Eskadale where he now lies with his first wife Margaret, Bella's sister.

I came here on a warm May afternoon to remind myself of this tranquil place and the two funerals where I had stood at the back of the crowd, apart, a bystander witnessing one of the last manifestations of ancient clan ritual. Here, with my back to the dry-stone wall, I watched the proud loyalties of the Lovat Scouts and a tight Highland community closing ranks to embrace its fallen soldier. I know of no more moving ceremonies than the shared carriage of the coffin from the church to the grave, that final reclaiming of the deceased by the whole community. Nowhere have I more deeply sensed the presence of *dùthchas* in all its tribal and primeval authority as I watched the honoured allocation of nine silk cords to male family members and closest friends. Then the moment of levitation as the coffin is borne up on their slender strings, that last web of mortality; and the solemn lowering, hand over hand, handing back to the land, to the brown clay that moulded and fed him and his predecessors, to rest.

Bella now lies here, too, in the same grave as her father, alongside Colin, among long-forgotten generations of the several branches of Aigas Macraes whose genes live on in the sombre faces that gathered that day. The ancient stones of pink Tarradale sandstone and rough-hewn granite stand in casual ranks in the gentle sunshine like soldiers waiting to be summoned to order for the last parade. Tall oaks and birches surround that little graveyard. The same pale green lichens, powdery and crisp, fleck both the tree trunks and the gravestones, somehow bringing them closer together, approving, embracing, belonging. The leaf is yet to burst. The white faces of wood anemones sprinkle the grass under the wall like a flurry of confetti. In another month shadow from the larger trees will quilt the mown grass and mingle with the deeper shade of the obligatory yew, holly and rowans, old and straggling, planted long ago at the gate and the perimeter wall to ward off evil spirits.

From where I stand at Bella's grave I can see across the river fields little more than a mile to Craigdhu and Oldtown and the spur of the Iron Age fort nudging the sky. Higher up the Aigas hill Bad à Chlamhain tops the burned-cork moorland in a blur of strident blue. The dry-stone wall embraces its graves with a soft, ageless caress, seeming to hold them apart from the tarmac road and the cars that sweep mindlessly by.

'Pray for the Soul of Colin J. MacRae of Craigdhu' instructs the stone's polished face in its particular Catholic diktat. Oh! I shall, I shall – and for Bella, and Duncan her father, and Angus her grandfather. I am happy to obey. I have no trouble with souls.

In the years before her last short illness Bella had worn her age just as she wore her old coat, with increasing affection the tattier it got and no longer able to imagine it new. She seemed to me to be the last of that dignity of crofters to whom age was its own embellishment. She was active and still busy crofting, but now with the constant help of Colin's son Alastair, who would succeed her at Craigdhu, until only two weeks before she died. When I saw her in hospital in Inverness a few days before the end she was a tiny, frail old woman awaiting her fate securely wrapped in the serenity of her faith. They had amputated her right leg because of a deep thrombosis in that foot. 'Now I can compete with Colin,' she said to me with a hint of the old gleam lightening her eye. She died suddenly a few days before she was due to be released from hospital. She was eighty-three. Although her family were ready to take her home to the croft, it would have been a cruel end for so independent a spirit, like chaining a dog that has always run free.

ELEVEN

Birds and Souls

And I have felt
A presence that disturbs me with the joy
Of elevated thoughts; a sense sublime
Of something far more deeply interfused,
Whose dwelling is the light of setting suns,
And the round ocean and the living air,
And the blue sky, and in the mind of man;
A motion and a spirit, that impel
All thinking things, all objects of all thought,
And scrolls through all things.

WILLIAM WORDSWORTH, 1770–1850

In the absence of the wolf, the lynx, the beaver and the bear, birds still ensnare our imagination, trill endorphins into our days, invade our affections, meddle in our politics, burnish our hopes, and nourish our dreams. Without them we should be as lost as Buddhists without Nirvana.

Aigas has awarded so much. In my mind the rim of its woods and the lambent shadows of its loch are a tabernacle of silences that grow and fatten like calves. The creation of this place is a concoction of subtle strokes; it's a hologram that toys with the viewer, twisting this way and that, teasing its inner self. The accumulation of years at its core delivers up to me not a single picture of dappling birchwoods or of amber water filled with bright clouds, nor yet that of moonlight on the loch, silvering its ruffling moods – one of my favourite images. None of these precious silences. Instead I find myself carrying around the jubilant gift of birdsong.

When I am travelling or working far away and I think of Aigas, perhaps because I have been particularly aware of birds all my adult life, it is birdsong that leafs me through my databanks of dormant nostalgia. If I hear a familiar ripple of song, a trilling wren or clamouring rooks, the liquid curlew or maybe just chaffinches claiming sovereignty over a spring morning, there and then I am transported. I am magic-carpeted off to a thicket deep in the garden, or among the twiggy avenues of limes and horse chestnuts, up to the high moors or into the birchwoods beside the loch.

Perhaps one of the reasons why Aigas has survived as a successful site of human habitation for four thousand years is that it seems to possess a soul. Souls are invested in the dark cranial recesses of those who find joy in special places. They are complex emotional responses happily beyond the reach of current science. Each generation discovers its own, pocketing them like bright stones. For me it is birdsong that most readily conjures up the soul of the place and has the ability to draw me back here, wherever I am.

On fine spring mornings I wake early, often with the birdsong brought to a crescendo by the sun impaling the day on slanting halberds of brilliance. It is three-thirty. That seems to be a witching hour that spins webs of introspection into my sleepless skull. I give in to it and slide out of bed, tiptoeing downstairs to make a mug of tea. Outside, I step into a swoop of fresh air and a musical surge of birds.

In June dawn comes ridiculously early in these northern lands. Visitors seldom believe us, exclaiming indignantly, 'I woke up to bright sunshine and looked at my watch. It was only two-thirty! I thought I was dreaming.' 'That wasn't a night,' someone once said to me, 'it was a passing thought!'

By the end of June my morning scherzo with a mug of tea is no longer dawn. It is day, full, rounded and hard at work. Photosynthesis is shaking out its skirts all round me. Chloroplasts are streaming like rush-hour traffic. Earthworms have trailed their dewy inches back underground, away from the blackbirds' tilted ears. Chaffinches and willow warblers are stammering out scales that never dull. Wrens trill feverishly. Swifts scream through in a rabble. Blackbirds and song thrushes, as rich as plum cake, compete from high places for virtuoso acclaim. Sawing great tits are felling whole forests. Robins scatter their tinkling octaves in air as fine as champagne. House sparrows are gossiping hysterically. A cuckoo, disyllabic and muted, dots the distance with semi-colons. The rooks are parading the sky, backwards and forwards like barrow boys in a busy street market, urgently pursuing their pressing affairs.

I stand in my dressing gown and slippers and sip my tea. This morning I can locate all ten thousand million neurones in my brain. Every last one. They're all on duty, all in unison, all humming electrically. The rook-throng scrawls its rough crotchets and minims across my empty staves, *larghetto, fortissimo, crescendo*. Imprinted. No wonder it follows me round the globe. Even now the insight conundrum won't go away. What is it for, this joyous eruption of wild nature? Do they, the birds, comprehend how exquisite their music is? Can it really be the result of chaos, a random exultation of single-minded purpose, arriving entirely by chance?

Every now and then I meet a jet-lagged guest who has also been drawn from his bed by the morning chorus and is wandering quietly through the gardens drinking in this symphonic introduction to a new country, a new place, a new experience. We greet each other with a nod and a smile. No explanation needed. We share a moment of silence together in the midst of tumult. One day a man in pyjamas and an anorak muttered to me, 'Damn me for a fool!'

'Why?' I asked.

''Cause I've lived sixty-two years and I never heard this before.'

Rooks belong to my English childhood, so to find them here in command at Aigas when I came was a buttress to my often-sagging conviction about our work. They are with us all the year round. A day never passes without a stream of them racketing like hooligans across my study window or clotting the red oak with loud, insistent silhouettes. They are persistent, rowdy, bossy, conniving, obsessively social and utterly peaceless. They are greedy and messy. Yet I would not be without them. Aigas would not be Aigas without them.

Every spring and summer the oaks and sycamores along the drive deliver a perpetual fall-out of twigs and watery emulsion to the road beneath. Returning from school, little Hermione skirts them wide with an anxious upward eye. It is as though a squad of industrial cleaners are at work up there, spring cleaning the tree-tops, flinging dustpans of winter into March air as rare as a fine wine. Eager decorators pursue them, swilling out paint pots of lumpy and chalky water, randomly tipping them from high windows so that they drip their whiteness through stippled branches to splatter the tarmac below.

Many years ago one warm spring day, my (then) six-year-old son, Warwick, went missing. Panic spread through the house and gardens like a fire in dry bracken. His mother yelled frantically for him and the field centre staff abandoned their work and joined the search, running and calling. People rushed to the ponds and up to the loch to eliminate that dark fear. We combed the woods and thickets in teams of two and three, calling and calling. How long had he been gone? No one was sure. An hour, two hours, possibly more. He was last seen happily playing on the lawn with his four-year-old twin sisters and Max, my Labrador. The old dog was still with the twins, who knew nothing more than that Warwick had wandered off into the garden wilds. A grim cocktail of adrenaline and dread clouded our words.

After an hour of searching, almost in desperation I climbed the spiral stairs of the tower to the parapet on the very top. Seventy feet above the lawns I scoured round the grounds with my binoculars. I noticed a throng of rooks circling vigorously over one of the big trees on the drive in a way that seemed to indicate that something had upset them. A thought flashed through: Warwick had quizzed us about the rooks' nests a few days before. I scrutinised the trees but could see nothing. I hurried down and out into the sunshine of late afternoon. Nearly three hours had passed since he was last seen.

I ran to the avenue with his mother at my heels. Feverishly we peered up into the huge trees. The limes were in flower, humming with the drone of bees, the great oaks were just bursting into leaf, horse chestnuts were spreading their lobed shade, punctuated by occasional specimen conifers, dense and lofty, planted by the Victorians a hundred years before. The rooks clogged the sky high above us as gulls throng to a plough. So loud and pressing was their clamour that we could barely hear ourselves speak. We peered into each tree in turn, scouring the twiggy maze for a bundle larger than the huge nests dotted through the tops. Foreboding tugged at our faces. When I came to a huge old Oriental spruce I had just about given up searching the trees. There lay his blue pullover abandoned among the wood anemones – a surge of hope at last. The rooks here were frantic, like us. The branches were thick and the dark foliage so tight that it was impossible to see into the core of the tree. I pressed against the scaly trunk and peered upwards through the branch tangle into the ominous cavern of its interior. At just that moment we heard from far above a sound that was unrook-like, a sound nearer a sob than a cry, a muffled, faintly hopeless call, choked and broken. It was Warwick.

I don't remember how long it took us to get him down. It required ropes and climbing harnesses. Rob Graham, one of our young rangers, as agile as a squirrel, reached him first and comforted him while I progressed up the trunk attaching karabiners and pulleys. The child was utterly exhausted. He had climbed ninety feet into the slender, swaying apex of that huge tree. 'I wanted to see what the rooks were doing, Daddy.' We lowered him gingerly to the ground.

Once he had scaled the heights and apparently satisfied his curiosity, he found that he could not get down. He shouted and yelled, screamed and cried, but as he did so the rooks alarmed around him in an ever greater and greater cacophony, drowning out his thin, tormented cries. He had been clinging on for three hours. In his pocket were the crushed remains of two addled rooks' eggs, five weeks old, putrescent and fetid, cold slime oozing out through the weave in his jeans. As the weeks passed and the tale was recounted at the family table, it became clear that by far his greatest regret was the loss of those two eggs.

All deep thought leads to the spirit. In my lifetime we seem to have been afraid to admit it and tackle it head on. It is as though science has done too good a job. It has tricked us into doubting anything it can't fathom with its artless disciplines. It has nothing to say on happiness or fortune, our culture or values, nor good and evil. It is contemptuous of anything it cannot analyse or measure, like art, and it casts shadows over the precious mysteries of intuition and instinct. Science has caused us to ditch some of the most vital gems of our past: the magic and the sacred, holiness and the spiritual direction that glued us together as human beings for so long.

I don't mean formal religion, although it's clearly in there, too, suffering the same fate, but I do include the deep sense of wonder that comes to me when I stand and touch the grainy column in a great Gothic cathedral. What I refer to are our inner emotional personae and the linking and the bonding that some ancient human societies still derive from their unashamed emotional interactions. Recently a visitor to Aigas remarked, 'TV makes a lousy god, it never gets as far as the soul.'

We still talk about souls, but only superficially now, even with mild embarrassment. Yet our emotions and sentiments are as alive and twitching as they ever were – some would say out of control: convulsing, casting about, circling like migrating birds blown off course, lost out at sea, desperate to find an island, a ship, an anything, upon which to land. Sometimes I feel that we need to pull our emotional responses back together, relocate them in a spiritual matrix we can all own and, in awe, sign up to, like Aborigines watching the sun dying behind Uluru. Perhaps we need to reinstate them at the very heart of our lives.

Is it so fanciful, this notion of a soul here at Aigas, this metaphysical ideal of inanimate life? Is the spirit so far-fetched? Most people would agree that they possess a nature other than the corporeal, that their creative and emotional personae deserve recognition and a name. Can we set aside our quasi-scientific embarrassment for a moment and rationalise it, bring it to heel sufficiently to understand ourselves a little better? Or am I to ignore the spirit, erect the palisade of Britishness, smile the inscrutable scientific smile and pretend that it doesn't exist? For years I was happy enough to do that, but it returned to me once too often, like a catchy song cropping up again and again. It forced me to turn and ask its name.

The soul notion has been with us for a long time. I am sure it was around long before Aristotle's carefully analytical mind articulated his thoughts in *On the Soul* some three hundred and thirty years before the birth of Christ. He can have had no idea of the resounding impact his thinking would have on the founders of Christianity and, consequently, our own view of the soul. Aristotle argued that things exist because they are made of material essence, *matter*, and that they possess a particular shape or function, *form*. A boulder and a house may both be made of stone matter, but the one is distinguishable from the other by its form. Form gives meaning and understanding to matter. All things have matter and form. It is *soul* that gives the meaning of *body* to an assembly of flesh and blood. In that sense it cannot be separated from living tissue. When we die this tissue perishes and the soul can no longer act on it. As a broken vase loses its form, so the body becomes a corpse. Aristotle's *mind* was that part of the soul that enables the body to think. If there was anything divine in Aristotle's conception of the human being it was the mind, and the mind was capable of providing experiences during a lifetime that were so exalted, as Stephen Hawking now claims, as 'to be close to the thinking of God'.

Through Aristotle's direct influence on St Thomas Aquinas and St Augustine, Christian culture was to mould the position that *mind* and the *soul* were to adopt in Western thought. As the centuries pass so science cuts deeper, and thinkers like the seventeenth-century Frenchman René Descartes, the founder of modern metaphysics, emerge to bridge the great intellectual disciplines of mathematics, physics and philosophy. Descartes, famous for his saying '*Cogito, ergo sum*' ('I think, therefore I am'), argues that some ideas are innate and God-given and that self-consciousness, or awareness, is the great achievement of the human species, elevating us above all other forms of life.

I am drawn to the somewhat clinical mind of the German professor Immanuel Kant (1724–1804), the founder of critical idealism. His most celebrated work, *Critique of Pure Reason*, is an enquiry into the limits of knowledge. He introduces the idea that certain knowledge resides within ourselves and is a property of our perceptual apparatus. He holds that our experiences are the texture and the form that lead us to comprehend the special and particular knowledge that lies within us. But Kant was no mystic.

He would not have believed that my insight conundrum would lead me to beauty and truth. Yet in Kant I was to find comfort for the idea that through the intimate experience of nature – through 'nature's rough congress', as Thoreau puts it – I might better discover myself.

At one level Albert Einstein dazzles me: 'The most beautiful and profound emotion we can experience is the sensation of the mystical.' Then again I am gratified to read, in *The Selfish Gene*, Richard Dawkins's able scientific intellect openly admitting that 'the evolution of subjective consciousness is the most profound mystery facing modern biology today'. Subjective consciousness and the mystical, those two. They are the fences of our Western culture that hedge most of us round, which ultimately frame the soul.

Others, such as the Inuit, the American Indian or the Bushman of the Kalahari, to mention three of literally hundreds of ancient, native and all too often dying cultures outside the swamp of material influence, have woven for themselves intricate webs of spiritual awareness within the natural world that transcend anything we in the West know or comprehend.

Many American Indian tribes correctly believe(d) the earth was their Mother Creator, that they and all of life were but dust. After death we all return to dust and it is this dust that recreates us. Here in the West ecology sees this as the recycling of nutrients and for some people this does translate into a wider respect for the whole environment. But for the Pueblo Indians, the Hopi or the Zuni, it is not simply nutrients that are recycled, but the spirit, too. All living things take their spirit from the dust of the Mother Earth, the Great Spirit. When death occurs the spirit returns to the earth as dust to be taken up again by some other life form. The notion of one's father coming back as a slime fungus or a wood wasp may not be very attractive to us, but to the Pueblo it was axiomatic: the very process by which they themselves came to be. Thus the respect that came from these beliefs

extended to all life and all nature. Stones, earth, the mountains –
even the rivers and the wind – all constituting a unified whole of
which they were an intrinsic and spiritual part. In this context a
hunt becomes an act of worship of the hunted by the hunter. The
deer consents to give himself up to the hunter so that his spirit
may be passed on to new life. The hunter carefully and respectfully lays out the entrails to feed the scavengers and the soil so
that the released spirit may extend as far and wide as possible.
They treated their own dead in the same way, so that their spirits
remained close by.

The bear, the salmon, the elk and other prey species vital to
their survival are honoured in carved fetishes in bone or jade, jewellery worn with reverence as we might wear a crucifix, but way
beyond pure symbolism, believed actually to contain the spirit of
the animal and to bring favour and protection to the wearer. It is
likely that their cave paintings and pictographs were also acts of
worship or magic: focuses of concentration upon the animal and
its spirit, which in turn guide the hunter's arrow.

Finding myself wholly in awe of ancient access to the spirit, I
turned for help to Dr Ieuan Evans, a young neuro-physiologist
bristling with state-of-the-art scientific confidence, who happened,
most conveniently, just at that moment to marry my daughter
Melanie. Together we explored the convoluted subtleties of the
human brain.

By a long stretch the human brain is the most complex association of living tissue known to biology. The cerebral cortex, I
discovered, consists of millions of densely packed nerve cells
interconnected in so bewilderingly complex a manner as to defy
description and to defeat the imagination. We know it is the
seat of intelligence and the higher activities of the brain.
Somewhere in there wafts the spirit and spins the soul. But just
where and how are still as much of a mystery as the soul itself.
It would seem that it has no seat of its own (are you surprised?)
but flits about within what are known as association areas that

link memories or emotions with experiences, like the pain and the memory associated with burning your hand: a million computerised telephone exchanges all buzzing with your own special, private messages, all in a space the size of an apple.

Inevitably it isn't that simple. The limbic association area, the important one for the burned hand, consists of the cingulate gyrus, the hippocampal formation, the parahyppocampal gyrus and the amygdala. It is probably the amygdala that spins you back to childhood at the whiff of a familiar smell, or by association with a particular sound – in my case screaming swifts, clamouring rooks and trilling wrens.

The amygdala is thought to link memories with emotions: to take you a stage beyond the childhood memory and to attach to it the pain, the joy, the laughter and the tears of its original association. Yet learning and memory are themselves spread around the neocortex in many different association areas. So it becomes apparent that Einstein's 'sensation of the mystical' – something very akin to the spirit – is itself only an electro-chemical frisson that sparks from ganglion to ganglion like a bumble-bee buzzing at random from exquisite bloom to exquisite bloom.

Whether that frisson can break free and sparkle alone through the dim labyrinths of extra-sensory activity as the Pueblo Indians would have it, whether it can survive as a spiritual afterlife, is a question better reserved for God and mystics, however appealing the notion – although I do find myself wondering whether on moonlit nights I shall flit through the pines at the loch, long after my nutrients have returned to the soil, dust to dust.

So what do I mean when I write of the soul of Aigas? Why after all these years of striving to know this place have I come to think about its soul? What truths has my self-indulgent love affair with nature delivered up to me? What I have discovered is this: that what I do and what I feel are both derived from my own private passion for nature. They are as much a part of me as my genes. They are my own strictly private frisson arcing within my own amygdala, not some inherently spontaneous faculty of the world of nature itself.

Joy and delight are nature's gift to those who seek it and strive to reveal its truths. Nature comes free and in full Technicolor. It is neither fussy nor personal. It recognises no cruelty, tolerates no flaws. It makes no promises and tells no lies. It is utterly original, constantly recreating itself anew, dazzling and inspirational. Its laws are absolute, without amendments. It just bowls along in its meticulous, random way, handing itself down from generation to generation, making the most of its rocks and its climate and its simmering broth of genes. For those who are fortunate enough to be able to know it well, it reveals the triumph of creation. In its birdsong and its trees, in the river and the mountains and the loch, in small tortoiseshell butterflies and its inscrutable trout, in its swifts and wrens and rooks, in its badgers and its pipistrelle bats, in the adder and *Uroceros*, in praise of all of these and more, the nature of Aigas has handed me my life.

At a weighty meeting of government officials some years ago I found myself sitting solemnly around a boardroom table arguing some complicated twist of environmental policy. I honestly imagined that I was applying due attention. I must have lapsed into silence. My old friend and colleague Dr Peter Tilbrook, who then directed the Nature Conservancy Council for the vast mountainous wilds of the north-west Highlands and Islands (and for its successor body, Scottish Natural Heritage), leaned across and whispered in my ear, 'Where are you?'

So often my minder in those hectic years of jargon-and-acronym-loaded papers and board meetings in far-off cities where we tussled with personalities more than with policies, every now and again, without a word, Peter would unobtrusively stretch over and turn my pages to the correct item. Trying to persuade uninterested politicians that they have a responsibility to look after the environment and its wildlife is stultifying and often deeply dispiriting. It cries out for distractions. I never had any trouble finding them. One day recently I had to hunt back through some old papers for a snippet of technical information. Scrawled in a margin in my own hand I found a vital annotation for Peter: 'Sparrowhawk – second window from left.'

Where was I? I don't remember. As often as not a scatter of jackdaws would tumble past the office windows and the mischievous and friendly 'Jack! Jack!' would harpoon my thoughts, towing them off to the roofs at Aigas where jackdaws habitually bicker and swoop while disagreeing which of the unused Victorian chimney pots was best to clog with their twiggy debris.

Then again I remember an energised discussion about whether a commercial salmon farm should be sited in a sea loch on the west coast. The afternoon was hot and airless. The meeting dragged on and on. I longed to go outside. My blurred eyes stumbled across the wearisome text. Then I read that the kelp beds were exceptionally fine in that loch. Something inside me began to awaken, to focus. I read that they had not been harvested for alginate for over a hundred years; that the loch was the last on that stretch of coastline to remain unexploited; that it was that great rarity in our manipulated landscape – pristine. It was too much. I was no longer trapped at the boardroom table. I was floating off. The cry of gulls was banishing my lethargy, a flurry of salt breeze scattering my papers. I could feel the crunch of fine shingle beneath my feet, taste the briny tang at the water's edge. I could hear the singing wingbeat of sea ducks bearing down on me, three in a line, silver-shouldered, white wing-bars flashing, irresistibly beckoning. There was nothing Peter could do to save me now. I was metamorphosing like Franz Kafka's awful cockroach, splitting the pupal case, involuntarily shedding my drab pin-stripes for the sharp, overlapping black and white and the soft dove-grey of plumage. I was out there now, riding the surface of the shinkly sea, as much a part of it as it was a part of me. I felt myself pushing off. Scarlet webs surged me smoothly forward. A bow wave flounced out from my downy breast. I was a merganser drake paddling across waving curtains of cinnamon and olive-green kelp, rocking with the swell. My probing, seeing head dipped beneath the surface as squadrons of little silver fish paraded in and out of the swaying forest of gold and green. I was flame-breasted and saw-billed in blood, bottle-green-crested and neck-ringed in snowy white. My ruby eye cast from side to side as the tide flooded me in and out of dark rocky chasms jungled with kelp. Bright beads of water rolled like pearls from my feather-scaled back.

For a few minutes I was all bird.

Mergini. Scoters, sawbills and sea-ducks, says the *Handbook.* *Mergus serrator*, the red-breasted merganser. Pisciverous, and serrated like a bow saw. Our commonest fish-eating sawbill is cousin to the goosander (much hated by salmon fishers) and the rare and delicate smew. The elegant drake merganser and his soberly conservative wife with a helmet of burnt sienna are found diving in every inlet and bay, skirting every estuary and probing far up every river. They are toothily snatching little fish from every sea loch and ice-ground fjord around our convoluted and wave-washed rim.

When you work closely with wildlife, as the years tick by, like learning a language or to play an instrument, one arrives at a moment when things unexpectedly and most agreeably click into place. They achieve a known status: complete, satisfying and fulfilling as a picture when you've finished painting it. They become data; logged in. You no longer have to think about them; they just come to mind, uninvited but always welcome. You don't have a choice. It's familiarity without the contempt. Intimacy by imposition and stealth; time served. A somewhat wayward analogy might be that of accidentally burning your hand on some hot item of everyday use. You didn't set out to learn it but you did, and once it's happened you can't unlearn it. The hand and the brain have come together and logged it for good – there even if you don't need to remember it.

Pain and joy are both waymarkers on the route to understanding. The joy nature is capable of awarding to the absorbent observer is just as lasting, just as vitally stored away. In response to the question 'How on earth did you know that was a merganser?' as a dim shape flashes past half a mile out to sea, enthusiastic birders say, 'Jiz' – a colloquial amalgamation of 'It just is.'

In World War Two our fighter pilots were trained to recognise aircraft to the finest degree of accuracy possible. The trainers made models of our own and German planes in matt black, as they might be seen in silhouette against a grey cloudbank or the sun. Pilots were presented with flashes of these models in every possible position and range and were required to make endlessly repeated snap identifications until they just knew them all. They were no longer thinking consciously, It's got kinked wings so it must be a Stuka. It was instantaneous – *Stuka!* – and straight on into the painfully learned evasive or aggressive action until it was reflex. It is claimed that many ghastly accidents were averted by this dogged technique; many British boys saved from the grievous blast of their own pilots' guns. It's what happens to a chaffinch when the dreaded sickle of a sparrowhawk looms. No time to check. Second looks are fatal. No good looking round to see who else is reacting. Just go.

Some birds and other animals do that to me in reverse. They seem to draw me in, sucking me down a tunnel of intimacy so that I end up imagining that I can see the world as they do. That bit of my brain, those few million neurones that have explored, eyed, pored over, pried into, Zeiss-scoured, garnered and secreted away so many thousands of mergansers over the years, has taken over. Sharp images have been flashed in, micron by micron, down the charged receivers of my bloodshot retinas, along hot corridors of optic electricity, to fix the merganser permanently in the mysterious synapses of my mind. That sleepy afternoon all those bright moments of flashing wings and scurrying wakes came together and claimed me for their own, towed me out to sea.

I have to write about the wren because it will out, like the truth. It is a fidget of buff-speckled busyness, a ferment of tiny insistence. It is a spasm of unfettered jubilation. Like rooks and mergansers, it's in too deep. It has fidgeted and spasmed itself into my own inner cave, my cerebral cortex, gone in like a bright stain and stuck. There for good.

Why the wren, you ask? Why this turbulent jot of restlessness? This oh so little bit? Why not the golden eagles that slide high over Aigas on fixed wings, or crossbills, or siskins, or the peregrine falcons whose frantic screamings echo from the walls of the Aigas Gorge? (You think the golden eagle and the peregrine *need* a better press?) The answer is relativity. Ounce for ounce,

trilling milligram for trilling milligram, the wren is more bird than the golden eagle, than the peregrine – than any of the above. From a wren you get more action, more pulse, more volume, more sheer bubbling joy, more cheek, more thrill and more downright damnable panache than you get from a dozen others put together. The wren nests in your broken drainpipe a yard from your door. It hurls chittering abuse at you from two feet away in a bush so thick it knows you can't see it. It darts into your wheelbarrow full of rose prunings and checks it out for aphids and scale bugs while you're having your tea. The wren sings like it's busting a gut. The wren has pizazz.

The wren lives in a cave – well, maybe not a cave exactly, but a crevice. But he is called *Troglodytes*, the cave-dweller. It's a good name. For a nest he builds a cave of his own. It has a domed roof, a tiny entrance hole and it's a tight little bundle the size of a cantaloupe melon wedged in deep tangle or jammed fast between the stones of a dry-stone wall. We leave piles of brashings from the woods dotted all round the place like beaver lodges to provide impenetrable jungles for the wrens to nest in. Every April I prise apart the spiny briars of a dense and ancient *Berberis* to peer in to where once I witnessed a stream of fledgling wrens emerge. I have never found a nest there again, but the memory brings me back year after year.

It is also called Jenny. As anthropomorphic nomenclature goes, I find that a poor choice. Jemima works famously for most farmyard ducks and Old Bill Brock admirably fits the badger. Shere Khan has a majestic ring for the *Jungle Book* tiger, and so has Tarka for an otter. But Jenny rankles. All the Jennys I have known have been gentle, feminine and kind. They've been soft without edges, warm and friendly. None of them could be less like a wren. The wren is feisty, rasping and bristling with edges. The wren is more like a Jack than a Jenny. It's all go, all hustle and to hell with the consequences. Jack the Lad.

I don't want to create the impression that I don't like wrens. I love them. I think they're astonishing little throbs of dynamism. They cause me to waste hours watching their antics. When they die I feel the burden of doom. They do a lot of dying round here. The Highlands is not kind to its second-commonest bird (the chaffinch gets top score). If you're that small, cold is a real problem. For all their pluck, winter carves them up. In a hard snap in the winter of 1986 the frost must have prised a nest box away from the tree it was nailed to. It was a closed box with a tiny hole I had hung beside the garages for blue tits. It fell to the ground. I went to pick it up and found a dead wren lying beside it. I cupped the tiny corpse in my hand and tried to breathe life back into its 8.2 millimetres of curved bill. It was no good. Its eyes were as firmly closed as a church on Monday. With a sigh I pocketed it to show it to the rangers and picked up the fallen box. It needed a new nail.

I was almost back at the house when I fancied I heard a sound. It was the faintest little scratching sound; so faint it almost wasn't a sound at all. It was more of a suspicion attached to a claw. I opened the lid of the box. To my utter disbelief it was crammed with wrens. Dead wrens. Wrens in a clotted jumble of huddled corpses. A mass grave of wrens. When I picked the first one out another came with it, the clenched claws clutching the feathers of the one beneath in a final, defiant clench. I was horrified. How was I going to live without wrens? Was this to be our own awful silent spring?

I ran into the kitchen and tipped the box out on to a tray. There were twenty-one tiny brown bodies on the tray. I had a whole tray full of silent springs. I stood in gutted disbelief, aghast. It was as if a bucket of gross injustice had been tipped out on to the kitchen table. And then ... and then, with hope rearing like a stallion inside my breast, one of them moved. A tiny leg extended a hooked claw and scratched hope into the afternoon. In a surge of optimism I gathered the whole lot up in my hands like scooping up a pile of walnuts and dumped them in a china bowl. I thrust the bowl into the bottom of the Aga warming oven.

For those who aren't familiar with the Aga, it is more of an institution than a kitchen range. There are British country houses that
revolve entirely around their Agas. As a means of cooking they are
archaic, expensive to buy, often unpredictable and by no means
economical to run, but they are indispensable. They are a fount of
cosiness in the nation's draughtiest houses. You boil and fry on
their sizzling plates and roast and bake in their capacious ovens.
Your dogs clutter the floor for their unending, life-enhancing
warmth. The length and breadth of the country teenage bottoms
in tight jeans are clogging Aga rails, caressing their mugs of
coffee, hogging the heat and denying kitchens to any other users.
Riding gloves clutter the warming plate and drying underclothes
are strewn above it like erogenous bunting. An Aga has four ovens:
one roasts, one bakes, one keeps supper hot while everyone fails
to come back from the pub, and the last one, the coolest bottom
oven, usually stuffed with drying shoes, resurrects wrens.

Which is exactly what it did. In under an hour I had twenty
wrens in a bowl, all fidgeting, all shuffling feathers, all treading on
each other, all ticking, all looking cross. Now I had the
Resurrection in a mixing bowl. From a fistful of feathered walnuts
the Khan Aga had delivered up a ferment of tiny souls. I quickly
put a tea towel over the bowl. It ticked like a bomb. I removed the
bowl to the warming plate for fear of cooking them.

I don't know how close to death they had been. They were
certainly torpid and apparently comatose; eyes tight shut and
little fuse-wire feet clenched tight. The one that had been in my
pocket was quite dead. Perhaps it had been the one nearest the
entrance hole, the one exposed to sharpest chill. I doubt that the
rest could have survived another frosty night. It had been too
cold for too long. At Aigas we have recorded minus eight degrees
Fahrenheit on a few numbing occasions, lasting ten days and driving frost two and a half feet into the ground. Three consecutive
winter weeks of twelve or fifteen degrees of frost is not unusual up
these glens.

Later I was to learn from the *Handbook* that the record is sixty-one wrens communally roosting in a nest box and ninety-six in a loft, both in severe weather. I learned too that they squat up to two and three layers deep, heads facing inwards, tails towards the entrance or sides. Also it seems it's not altogether a happy arrangement. They don't really like it, but it's their only hope. Mr Armstrong's 1955 observation is that 'much squabbling occurs at [the] roost, and up to four or five birds [have been] seen falling in a bunch as they tried to evict one another'.

The remarkable *Handbook* publishes seventeen and a half large pages of small print on *Troglodytes*. Six and a half of them are dedicated to its song. Someone once told me that if the human eye were as important to humans as the kestrel's eye is to the kestrel, each human eyeball would weigh four and a half pounds. By the same logic the wren's voice is 37.1 per cent of its worth. I rank it higher than that. It is, quite simply, dazzling. The *Handbook* again:

> Behaviour combines quiet skulking with frequent, noisy and irascible squabbles with other birds; actions include obvious bobbing, tail-wagging, and body-swivelling, and amazing vibrating of the whole bird during singing. A well-structured rattling warble of clear shrill notes, delivered with remarkable vehemence. A pulsing warbling phrase delivered as if the bird is trying to burst its lungs.

My twenty wrens were now a problem. I was reluctant to put them outside again. I feared that they had insufficient left in them to cope with another night of grinding cold. I transferred them to a cardboard shoebox. They made no attempt to fly, although they did scuttle around the bowl like mice, trying to evade capture. It was as if they knew that flying would expend too much vital strength, let out too much heat – that they weren't ready to go. I put the box in the boot room where it was cool but well above freezing. I placed some finely grated cheese and some water in jam-jar lids and left them alone in the dark.

I resisted the temptation to go back and look. I thought they needed peace and rest, so stayed away right through that night and until ten o'clock the following morning. I reckoned that ought to be long enough. I lifted the lid: twenty wrens looked up at me from forty shiny dots of eye. The cheese had gone. Every last curl. I had wren cheeselets in a box. Twenty light bites. I was thrilled. Not only did they look well again, but they were cheese-filled and fluffed out like canapés. I set the lid aside and gently reached inside to pick up the jam-jar lid to refill it. There was an explosion of wrens. A multiple jack-in-a-box. Cave-dwellers burst out in every direction. A whirring diffusion of winged cheeselets scattered to every corner of the boot room.

The Aigas boot room contains more footwear than an old-fashioned shoe shop. They stand in rows on shelves all round the room. There were then, and are still, boots of every size and shape from my long leather riding boots to little red wellies that briefly served the twins as toddlers and had never been given away. There were the abandoned boots of years of rangers as well as all those of a large, outdoor family. There were dozens of boots and shoes. It was a room made for wrens. Legions of dark caverns for cave-dwellers. Every time I approached a perching wren it darted off into another cave. I went from boot to boot catching nothing. In no time at all I was defeated. I gave up.

I grew cunning. If they liked cheese I would give them cheese. I would put the cheese in a box, prop the lid open with a stick tied to a long string and retire to outside the window. As soon as a few wrens entered the box I would pull the string and – *Hey Presto!* – I would have them back in hand. All I had to do was repeat the process until I had caught all twenty.

I sat outside in the cold for an hour and a half and froze. I gave up for the second time. No wren emerged from a single cave and the cheese remained untouched. In disgust I abandoned my ploy. I took the nest box back to the tree and nailed it up again. I warned everyone to be very careful when putting on a boot and I tried to forget about wrens. I succeeded, until the following morning.

The day dawned bright and frosty. I came downstairs late and hurried about my usual daily chores. The sun beamed in through the windows, flooding the house with yellow light. As I walked down the passage towards the boot room on my way to the back door, I could scarcely believe my ears. The corridor rattled with birdsong. Pulsing, warbling phrases bombarded my ears with remarkable vehemence. Crescendos of shrill melodies were bursting their lungs all round me. The air vibrated with trilling so loud that I had to hold my hands to my ears. I ran out into the bright sun. I propped the back door wide open. I left it open all day.

One by one they emerged, trickling out like guilty children, fluttering along close to the ground and away into the frosty shrubbery of the garden. What was to surprise and delight me most of all happened a few days later when I was standing outside the garage in the chill dusk, frost crisping the grass all round me. I saw two wrens come flickering through the branches to the same tree. They dived straight into the nest box as if there were no time to lose. I stood quietly and watched. In the next few minutes another eighteen wrens came whirring in, scurrying from tree to tree, chucking and chittering angrily to each other just as the book says: 'Sites often traditional. Nightly establishment of roost seems to be initiated by a leader, probably a resident male, with much agitation.'

That spring wren song split the air asunder. It cleft a vibrating wake through the dawn chorus, gilding the air, hallowing the morning. Now that I had a locus, now that they were *my* wrens, I wanted insight. The song was personal now, intimate and precious. I heard them as sparks of rage against winter, pearls of morning dew, fleeting glimpses of the Everlasting. They were demi-semi-quavers of radiant hope. I wanted to know more, I wanted them to bare their secret rustlings to me so that I could learn their skulking ways. My life became studded with wrens. I tried to imagine myself that small, shrinking myself down to a voice-box wrapped in tiny, cinnamon-flecked feathers. I wanted to know how on earth, when everything else was getting bigger, when everything was busy struggling away from the amoeba, they came to be so small. When competition seemed to dictate size, *Troglodytes* evolved alongside every other bird and then went back to Go. How does a gene for smallness not get pushed aside? How does it make itself heard? Maybe that's the clue. Perhaps if you're that wee you have to have a mega-voice, a well-structured rattling warble delivered with vehemence. Perhaps you have to vibrate amazingly with each pulsing phrase, even if you have to burst your lungs in the process.

I wanted to locate their secret lairs, watch them picking filaments of wool from the fences, find their intricate orbs of moss and horsehair, count the extra eggs that automatically arrive to compensate for heavy losses in our hard winters. I wanted to fill my head with seventeen and a half pages of pure delight.

TWELVE

The Players

Act first, this Earth, a stage so gloomed with woe
You all but sicken at the shifting scenes.
And yet be patient. Our Playwright may show
In some fifth Act what this wild Drama means.

ALFRED LORD TENNYSON, 1809–92

We are compilers of information here. It is the way we do things
and the way of the people with whom we share our days. It's our
job to look into, to find out, jot down, annotate, compare notes,
look up in books, to record for ourselves and for those who come
after us. It is what Aigas does to us. It infects us all. By this
process we become part of the place.

Those with whom we work, whether employees or guests passing through, are inquisitors: 'What's this?' 'What is going on?'
'How many are there?' 'There's one I don't know!' 'I've never seen
anything like that before!' These are everyday Aigas texts. We are
trading in detail: an ageless lichen and a tuft of bog cotton here, a

footprint and a crystalline rock there, the morning dew, a pool of dark water, an orchid, an ash tree's shadow, a butterfly, a wood wasp, an adder, a wren ... We progress in steps, one by one, piling detail on tiny detail. Form and texture mould our days. Falteringly we climb ever higher. These fragments of awareness are the stairs that lead us gropingly towards insight. Perhaps somewhere up there, somewhere behind the mountain, there is a bigger picture.

And these inquisitors and our colleagues around us are the players in our seasonal, cyclical, elemental drama – the dramatis personae of an epic which Aigas is acting out in us all whether we know it or not. So we endeavour to write the script. We keep a log. That is to say they – the players, our staff working with our endless throughput of inquisitive participants – formally record each working day. They describe every expedition into the field, every significant sighting or event, every stumbling foray into the unknown. We now have more than twenty-five years of such logs.

The years spill from one library shelf on to the next. In maroon board bindings with steel corners, the volumes are aged and tatty and look now distinctly Dickensian against the garish folders of the present day. Thousands of typed pages of apparently repetitive records of the weather, size of groups, objective, destination and a few paragraphs of text recording places explored, the species seen: the trivial, the obvious, the intriguing, the entirely predictable, the somewhat surprising and the downright unlikely.

Reading the logs is a therapy. I can raise my spirits in an instant if I dip in. Real personalities and real people are logged here. They have unwittingly snared themselves in a web of words. I chuckle as I flick through the years. As I turn the pages characters rise genie-like from the half-closed eyes of memory. Forgotten names smile back at me; words illuminating their faces, their laughter and their tears from the haze of so many people over so long a span. I recall those whose failures surprised nobody and others whose successes were easily anticipated.

Bright moments stand out. I am reading about the day a badly lost slate-coloured junco – a sparrow-like North American bird – flopped exhausted from the sky on to the path in Glen Affric almost at the feet of a young ranger who was leading – it just so happened – a group of experienced birders from Connecticut. His name was Roddy Miller. He was a teenage student and a zealous birder who had begged to be given the chance to lead an adult group in the field. I remember being doubtful, but his enthusiasm won. The westerlies and the Gulf Stream, which combine to bring us our mild climate, had streamed this poor bird three and a half thousand miles across the Atlantic and landed it like an alien in the draughty emptiness of a Highland glen. Roddy had never been to the USA, nor had he any more knowledge of American birds than one can glean by flicking through a field guide, which is what he had sensibly done in preparation for his professional debut with a group of Americans. He studied the bird carefully through his binoculars for a few seconds and turned and announced to his charges: 'Slate-coloured junco – male,' as if it were as regular on the Affric trails as a pied wagtail.

'Yeah,' responded one of his charges. 'We know. But what the heck's it doing here?'

'It heard your accents and dropped in to ask you the way home,' Roddy replied with exceptional nineteen-year-old presence of mind.

No slate-coloured junco has been recorded in Glen Affric before or since.

But the logs do far more than record such splashes of aplomb. They record change. I see that in the spring months of the 1970s and on into the eighties we regularly spent several hours a week quietly watching nesting lapwings swoop and gyrate across the rushy cattle pastures that were everywhere in the glens in those days. It was a vivid learning game for those who were unfamiliar with the antics of bird display, enjoying their wild mewing cries and marvelling at the protective camouflage of the birds nestled on their eggs. The best fields would commonly hold up to twenty pairs of lapwings and two or three pairs of curlews as well. As the young hatched into little matchstick-legged bundles of marbled fluff it became a game of testing skill to spot them pecking about the tussocky grass around their strutting, anxious parents.

In those days these were common events, adding pleasure to days of blander field studies. They were moments of living illustration, excitement-filled, vital, enriching and always fun. But the world was changing. Britain was closing ranks with the politics of Europe and the predatory process of standardisation was baring its teeth. Cattle rearing was being swept aside by the craze for hill sheep supported by subsidies based on numbers rather than quality. Agricultural development plans were busy drawing in capital funds to drain and improve pastures. The Highland glens were not permitted to remain backwaters of rural insouciance. The little grey Ferguson tractors that had epitomised the crofting landscape since before the war now rusted silently in their corrugated-iron sheds. Instead, shiny red Czechoslovakian four-wheel-drive machines were grinding across land never ploughed by machinery before. Old grass lays rich in wild flowers and many different species of grazing plant were rotovated in to be replaced by vivid green cultivars of Italian rye grass, diploid and lush.

Lapwing and curlew numbers dwindled as grazed moorland and rough pastures disappeared and chemical weedkillers and pesticides purged the vegetation and eradicated the invertebrate life so essential to the chicks of these bird species. After a few years they became so hard to find that we gave up, unable to justify the time. Now we have to drive many miles to find a pair of nesting lapwings.

Careful analysis of the logs reveals fewer and fewer species in particular sites. One such, an upland loch, tucked away a thousand feet above Loch Ness, was consistently rich. It is called Loch Laide (perversely pronounced *latch* in Gaelic, although it is actually Old Scots or English, *lade*, meaning a millrace). It rests in a sheltered pocket of moorland beneath a hill overlooking Loch Ness. In the 1960s its reedy marshes and islands of bog bean harboured the largest concentration of the rare and flamboyant Slavonian grebe (*Podiceps auritus* – the eared grebe) in Britain. A dozen pairs dived and bobbed, chittered and danced across its sixteen acres of peaty cloud.

In those days Loch Laide was a phenomenon of diversity and productivity. It was a dazzle of eutrophic wonder, a naturalist's dream. The slow deposition of nutrients into the loch through its marshes and surrounding maze of unkempt wetlands supported an astonishing array of microscopic and invertebrate life, which in turn gave sustenance to fish, amphibians and a bright collage of birds. Dragonflies and damselflies skimmed its dark rills. Caddisfly larvae trundled their twiggy cylinders across the peaty beds of a dozen tiny streams. Trout rolled languorously to the surface to mouth at dense hatches of mayflies and springtails. Frogs and toads pouted gutturally from their swamps. Palmate newts shimmered away into the weed as we stalked the mossy edges. Out on the water the grebes contended angrily with tufted duck, pochard and scaup diving for their harvest of molluscs, crustacea and insect larvae. Every year a pair of mute swans heaped their voluminous nest mound on to a mossy promontory on the edge of the reeds and, to an unforgiving raucous cacophony, several hundred black-headed gulls obliterated a whole islet of bog bean. Their unmusical grating cries corrugated the air like the churning of an aged machine. Perpetual squabbling and bickering wafted curtains of aggravation across the whole loch. Sedge warblers rasped from deep inside the jungle of *Phragmites* reeds and acrobatic reed buntings trilled prominently from shaggy fringes of the wind. The shallows were pierced by lone, stalking herons while busy cliques of redshank and oystercatchers piped their hysteria across arcs of shingly strand. In the dense runs of willow shrubbery crowding the banks, mallard, teal and little grebes probed their muddy secrets. Moorhens and coots furrowed murky canals in the reeds and clogged the marsh with their soggy nests. Drumming snipe flickered over unmapped deltas of rushy swamp.

Into this miniature Okavango of fecundity slid a procession of villains to add drama to the plot. Nowhere as rowdy and animated as Loch Laide could escape the bright eye of the otter. The black-headed gulls exploded into frenzies of outrage as the shiny slither landed on their island to plunder their nests for fledglings and eggs. So rich were the pickings at Loch Laide that for many years a pair of otters occupied a holt in a choked culvert on the far side of the loch, well away from the road. Summer after summer we could rely upon fine views of the adults and their kits nosing through the reeds and marshes.

As if this were not enough, the distress of the gulls rose to new heights when the broad shadow of a hen harrier floated across. The otters could shrug off the gulls' angry stoops and shrieks and forage virtually at will, but the hen harriers were far more exposed and may even have feared being struck by a gull. They chose to stalk the island from low behind the willows and emerge suddenly to row swiftly in and snatch a fluffy gull chick before too many adults knew what was happening. Then they winged off to a remote heathery knoll to dismember their prize. These snatch-and-run tactics were often observed by hooded crows perched on top of a birch or on fence posts not very far away. Of all the crow family, the hoodie is an opportunist *par excellence*. No sooner had the hen harrier broken free from the flight of angry gulls than the hoodies would set upon it, working as a pair, diving and mobbing to make it drop its prey. Often they succeeded and the harrier had to float off and search anew. If this mobbing failed, the hoodies would quickly return to the gull island to exploit the disarray of the scatter-brained gulls, nipping in and grabbing yet another unguarded chick.

Even while this was going on, another raptor regularly

elbowed its way across the loch. In the days when ospreys were still rare in the Highlands it was a great thrill to see these birds crash into the loch and snatch a trout. An expedition planned to witness Slavonian grebes parading their outrageous marmalade eyebrows would often be hijacked by ospreys stealing the show.

I turn the page and find myself back at the loch and laughing. There are incidents one never forgets, and some that expand their value with rediscovery after so many years. Early one spring morning I drove to the loch with a party of eight enthusiastic boys in their late teens. They were on an ornithology course. Their enthusiasm was palpable and I had saved Loch Laide until nearly the end because I knew they would enjoy its guaranteed performance. The day was idyllic, I now remember, the sun streaming in and the spring air as smooth as syllabub.

The loch throbbed with activity. The Slavonian grebes were in full prancing display, disappearing beneath the surface to grab a symbolic gift of weed and then, treading water like performing dolphins, they sped across the surface, each vertically posturing to its mate in a strange ritual ballet entrancing to behold. Others were quietly brooding on their heaped nests of floating weed.

We crept quietly into the willows to a suitable vantage-point. I busied myself with the telescope, training it on one of these nests so that everyone could have a good look at this uncommon bird. It took me some minutes to get it properly aligned. I talked quietly about the grebes as I did so. All grebes surround their breeding activities with elaborate displays, so I was taking my time explaining some of the complex machinations of the Slavonians' behaviour. When I stood up to invite the boys to look through the telescope I was surprised to find them all facing in the opposite direction, all with binoculars pressed to their brows, all watching some other ornithological drama of the loch. I raised my own and followed their line. They were certainly bird-watching.

About sixty yards away across a bay a small tent was pitched on a grassy headland. A motorbike was parked beside it. I had noticed this when we arrived and thought nothing of it. Campers often choose such alluring pitches. It was still so early that the incumbents were probably firmly cocooned in their sleeping bags. They could have had no idea we were there. But some moments after we had taken up our position a young woman in her twenties had emerged from the tent, slipped out of her night-dress and tiptoed elegantly to the water's edge. She was tall and slender with Scandinavian blonde hair falling straight to her shoulders. She waded in to the loch up to her calves and stood there in all her natural finery, pale and startling. Delicately she stooped to scoop up water in cupped hands and trickled it sensuously over her sun-washed skin. Then she closed her eyes and raised her arms, hands open-palmed in supplication to the sky. She tipped back her head so that her long hair fell clear of her arched back. Droplets of water sparkled like diamonds on her tight, perfectly formed breasts. This was no posturing pin-up girl. It was the Lady of the Lake, mystical and serene. It was Calypso tempting Odysseus into her arms, offering us immortality. It was Aganippe, nymph of the spring at Mount Helicon whose waters inspired all those who drank them. And it was every nineteen-year-old boy's wild dream of a young woman's beauty shimmering with the magic of the morning. It was also clear that Slavonian grebes had momentarily lost their appeal. We stood in silence while this goddess saluted the stark beauty of the loch. She held her pose, statuesque and shining like a Botticelli angel, for several minutes. Then she turned and waded ashore, back into her tent. Nine breathless males tiptoed back to our vehicle. We left the grebes for another day.

This arresting incident stands out among years of more scientifically orientated visits to Loch Laide. But, for all that little loch's reliability and remarkable diversity, those visits were to be short-lived. In the 1970s another fashion was ploughing its way across hundreds of thousands of acres of Highland moors: blanket afforestation, principally in lodgepole pine and sitka spruce, two species imported from North America for the commercial production of fibre, was seen to be the most productive use for the empty uplands. The land was cheap and available in vast supply across the Highlands. Whole glens were being ring-fenced for forestry. Tracked ploughs were clawing the peat into deep channels up and down the contours to drain the moors and provide planting beds for the young trees on the turned sod, high above any competition from heather and any fear of saturation from sphagnum moss. The rapid run-off, dark and acid, silt-laden and sterile, had to go somewhere. In those days overzealous foresters permitted drains to be funnelled straight into burns and watercourses. This new activity scoured its channels across the hills above Loch Laide. All winter long, black water rushed into the loch.

Year on year our logs recorded the effect. Invertebrate life was washed out or buried in silt and the Slavonians began to fail to rear their chicks. In a few years they had gone altogether. Whatever had specially appealed to the rowdy gulls disappeared and they moved on. Diving ducks sought clearer water elsewhere. The otters no longer bred there as the loch became hemmed in, surrounded by a dense palisade of dark forest surging upwards, spearing the clouds. The loch had plunged from bright eutrophy to dark oligotrophy in a few short seasons. Like our water goddess, nature had, for now, let her moment slip by. She had saluted the passing hour and moved on.

At the end of winter and when, like buds, the days begin to split open and expand, we mobilise our own resources to tidy up the place, do a little outside work after months trapped in the office and prepare for the annual intake of visitors. We turn our hands to any task the place demands. We renovate buildings inside and out, the tang of fresh paint seeming to urge the winter out of the door. These exertions are a communal activity joined by whichever staff are available as a welcome break from their normal functions. Over the years I have shared this honest toil with many of the Aigas players so that buildings, paths, garden steps, nature trails and features of our work bear their names or their associations.

Dick's Den is one of the student accommodation cabins named after our gardener and handyman, Dick Bethune, retired now and in his eighties, but who revisits every few weeks to check that we aren't letting his standards slip. He gave the last ten years of his working life to Aigas and our welfare. For much of his career he had been an estate joiner and there was nothing to which he couldn't turn his hand. Working with him was a delight. I still can't pass Dick's Den without smiling at the merry hours of mirth we spent converting it from an old potting shed and workshop into the cosy cabin it has now been for so many years.

As we erected partitions and pinned rafters into place I would often be called off to answer a telephone or attend to some tedious detail in the office. When I eventually returned I would find my work had been straightened, levelled, dismantled and reassembled with better joints, or subtly adjusted by a hand and eye far more skilled than mine. And Dick would be quietly pressing on with his own work without ever saying a word.

Where the loch trail crosses the burn there is a handsome bridge known by everyone as Duncan's Bridge. We didn't need a bridge, the stepping stones were fine, but Duncan Macdonald needed to build a bridge. That spring bridges were in his head like fish in the mind of an otter. There was no deterring him. So we sanctioned the bridge to get him off bridges and on to something else. We might even have thought he would never do it. We were wrong. For a whole weekend the birchwoods whined to a chainsaw's frantic buzz and rang with the clamour of hammer blows. Suddenly there was a handsome bridge over the burn. The path had been diverted in a broad loop away from the stepping stones. Dry-stone revetments squared the banks' shoulders to carry a plain but wholesome wooden structure with a handrail on one side. It was Duncan's bridge. Once it was built it became the obvious place for some of his school groups to engage in freshwater studies.

Put children in a burn on a sunny day and in no time you have a chain of mini-dams stemming the flow. Eddying pools swirl and fill. Debris collects and mud and stones are slapped, piled and poked into ever more ambitious structures. Water splashes wildly. Dams burst and have to be built all over again by wet feet and muddy hands. Laughter echoes through the wood. Duncan stands on the bridge and directs, nudging a little science into this happiest of country pursuits. When that school next returns to us the children rush to discover what wildlife has moved into their pool. Nets dip and dribble irresistibly. It appeals to all our deepest hunter-gatherer instincts. A whole chunk of insight came free with Duncan's Bridge.

In every season and in every cyclical intake of young staff there are events and unplanned happenings that round the reality of the Aigas experience, that lift their time here out of the humdrum and plonk them firmly into the stark chill of unromanticised nature. They are events that come like thunderstorms from behind the mountain, swamping and engulfing and suddenly making everything different from what it was before – pulling deep focus, raw and unforgiving. I have come to see it as a valuable, although unplanned, function of the field centre. It is a part of working with wildlife and with the environment, and for all of us there come moments when lessons are learned, data is permanently logged.

Last year we were working on the new garage, shovelling earth and spoil, filling in against the new wall. We were a team I had coaxed out of the office into the first March sunshine: Susan

Luurtsema, our programme manager, Sarah Kay, our head ranger, Jessica Seal, the field officer, and me. It was good work and gladly joined. At mid-morning one of our trout fishers came by and told us there was a deer caught in the wire fence just off the nature trail in the woods below the loch. We dropped our tools and hurried to check it out. The girls were cheered by the notion that we could free it and watch it return to the woods. Only I had a sinking feeling.

They sped off to locate the trapped animal and I went to get a gun. (I learned long ago that to have to return for it later only means delay and increased suffering, if not danger.)

They had found the animal easily. It was last year's red deer calf, now rising eight months old. Its right hind leg was twisted into the top wires of the stock fence, caught while hopping over, following its mother on its way back to cover from a night's grazing in the fields. It is a sad and common occurrence in the Highlands. Fences the mother hind can jump easily cause calves to hesitate and lose momentum so that they land a hoof on the top wires. If it slips between two strands, as the animal descends the wires twist and close around the hough, gripping it like a trap. Over the years I have found many such deer that have suffered this lingering, perpendicular death.

We approached to about twenty yards and had a good look. Fear danced in its wild eye as it lurched pitifully to left and to right. I decided that the best way to handle it was for three of us to rush in and, while two pinned the little deer to the fence, I would cut the wire to free it. Sarah and Susan volunteered.

The deer panicked as we closed in, leaping away and falling back each time as the trapped leg jerked angrily in the fence. The girls fell on it, expecting to be able to pin it down easily because it was no larger than a slender nanny goat. To their astonishment and distress it plunged and kicked out from beneath them, heaving them off and lashing out wildly with the one free hind hoof, catching Sarah's leg twice in quick succession so that she cried out. As they struggled I snipped through the top wire. It pinged free, curling back down the fence to the next post. Still the deer leg was trapped because the unhappy beast's struggle had twisted the wires right round the leg. The skin was stripped back to bare bone, the shredded fur in bloody strips dangling from the fence and the leg. The tendons were showing white and clear; the Achilles partly severed. We knew that even if the wounds could somehow be stitched back together infection-free, the foot was never going to work properly again. As well as this we all saw that the angle of the trapped leg stemming from the pelvis was badly wrong on that side – at best, a dislocation at the hip; at worst, torn ligaments, too.

As the girls got their breath back, now applying all their weight to the sorry animal, pinning it to the ground, the last wire snipped free. The leg fell uselessly to the ground, our worst fears confirmed. Something was very badly wrong at the hip as well as at the hoof. I made the decision. It was unfair to prolong the stress. I cocked the rifle and placed the muzzle against the domed head of the calf. Sarah, who was holding its head down, screwed her eyes tight shut and grimaced, turning away. The little rifle cracked like a snapping stick. The deer collapsed beneath them and hot blood welled up from the neat round hole in its skull.

We stood up. The corpse rolled limply away from the fence. I saw Sarah fighting back tears. She retreated to the foot of a tree a few feet away, sat down and cried. Jess looked white and drawn. Susan, still flushed from her exertions, took off her glasses and wiped her face with her hands, avoiding my eyes. None of them had witnessed an execution before. They needed time to refocus, to cope with their own tangled and abruptly roused emotions.

Death is nature's liturgy. It defines nature as prayer defines a priest. It imposes itself without discussion; it brooks no debate. It is also a sacrament. It is the vital process by which nutrients are returned to the soil and it breathes hope and a future into the great Ferris wheel of creation. One of the penalties we pay for our elevated consciousness is that death can sometimes be hard to take. We walked back to our work in silence.

The sudden death of a deer calf is noteworthy but not significant. We record it because it becomes a statistic, another minute detail in the Aigas jigsaw puzzle. It is a fact of our place and our time. Fences kill deer. It's a snippet of mildly startling information these young rangers can add to the database Aigas is building inside them all. There are plenty more deer – arguably far too many in the Highlands – and no one will miss that one, just as no one misses the roe deer that perpetually commit suicide on the road between us and Beauly. We see their corpses draining into the roadside grasses all year long. I have hit many over the years, usually at night or in the early morning. They come frolicking out of nowhere: with three hundred and fifty degrees of safety to chose from they go for the ten degrees of certain death. We stop, reverse back and see that the creature is dead; many drivers don't bother. We curse at the cracked lamp lens or the scrape and the dent, or both. Then drive on. No tears, no choked words, nothing much logged in the database. 'He'll not miss that one,' Bob used to say.

But to hold the domed skull in your hands, to feel the innocence of first soft fur, see the terror in the liquid eye; to feel the life collapse beneath you, flaccid and sudden, like switching off a pump; and to watch the bright blood pulsing – that's different. It goes in; straight in. Logged for good. We would talk about it one day soon, but not just then.

I did a count the other day, totting up names from the logs. Always three or four rangers a year, sometimes five or occasionally six, spread over twenty-five years. It reminds me that there are well over a hundred living fragments of the Aigas database out there somewhere, plying their experience and their information in pursuit of life and hope. Many keep in touch and have become family friends. We cherish their news and their Christmas messages every year. Their periodic visits brighten our lives. Others disappear apparently without trace until one day I bump into them at a conference or one of the many events that clot the environmental calendar. Or, suddenly, there they are, smiling at the door never doubting that we shall remember them as vividly as they remember us.

In the pursuit of a career in nature conservation or environmental education it is precious insight to have first-hand experience of a place. To sample its history, its rocks and its soils, to get to know its plants and animals and test the surging pulse of climate and its seasons in such a place, and to discover a little wildness can all be galvanising, even life-altering, to those who care. It can give them the spark to carry them on into the often daunting and dispiriting world of environmental politics. There can be few places better than these hills and these glens in which to cut such worthy teeth. In the course of our work Aigas delivers that experience to the rangers whether they strive for it or not. The hills and moors are their own tutor. Lessons properly learned are not forgotten.

Arriving with the buds of spring each year and with sap rising all round them, the annual crop of girl and boy rangers and the team who run the household for our guests – cooks, kitchen girls and domestics – are inevitably in their late teens and twenties. The rangers are natural science graduates just setting out on the first tentative rungs of a career and the seasonal domestics are often students and undergraduates, too, working their vacations, travelling, picking life's fruit. A gang of up to twenty bright, young, carefree boys and girls thrown together in laughter and in labour in an exquisitely beautiful Highland glen. Together they blaze a lusty trail through an Eden of warmth and plenty. Only a few weeks into the season we gradually become aware of playful pursuits through the rhododendrons, the flashed looks and blushes, furtive whispers in the stationery cupboard or a sudden and uncharacteristic interest in laundry. By throwing them together year upon year we inadvertently stir this simmering broth so that from time to time relationships gel and happy announcements allow us to congratulate the couples with ill-feigned surprise.

Other romances, of course, have failed. Sometimes the ones we have quietly watched over for many months and for which we harboured the greatest hopes suddenly collapse amid tears and bitter words. Even in this upland Arcadia the mating game is far from being all fun and roses. I have learned to stay well clear. Lucy, by contrast, from her fount of endless maternal charity, would like to tender balm to every broken heart, and succour the inconsolable sobs.

Inevitably there are some gaps.

A lovely young girl called Sarah who worked here in the eighties contracted a brain tumour and died still in the bloom of youth only a few years after leaving us. We lost our neighbour, Peggy Ross, long before her time, too. She was the Aigas postmistress until the Post Office closed her down. Then she came to keep our books and run our administration. She became a mother to our little office, ever patient, perceptive and forthright, her Highland good sense lending dignity and order to our often chaotic lives. With great courage she had fought a cruel cancer for many months. In her name we planted a rowan tree in the gardens. I pass it every day. It is tall now, well established and standing proud. A young man called Jason was killed in a motorcycle crash in Venezuela only months after being a ranger at Aigas. He engraved himself on our memories with one remarkable feat. He was shearing our ewes with hand shears. Somehow he managed to insert the sharp point of the shears through the dense wool, through his trousers and into his own thigh, and then cut himself open for six inches before the pain made him realise what he had done. He walked back to the house with blood streaming down his leg and said to me with unforgettable sang-froid, 'I'm so sorry, I seem to have cut my leg.' I still have a bone-handled sheath knife he left here. I was uncomfortable about sending it on to him lest he cut off his arm. It sits on the bookshelves in my study. I have never quite known what to do with it. He was utterly delightful, just twenty-four when he died.

A few miles up the glen, in a graveyard beyond the little village of Cannich, stands a polished grey stone. It reads:

> 24352019 Lance Corporal V. Macleod
> The Queen's Own Highlanders
> 27th August 1979 Age 23.

Victor Macleod was our handyman. He came to work with a haversack slung over his shoulder with the words 'Vic Macleod – Handyman' proudly scrawled across the front in black felt-tip marker. I think he was eighteen. He was alert and cheery and fun to work with, but he hankered after adventure. One morning he came to work on a bright and shiny motorbike. For a few weeks it was his pride and joy. And then one Monday he was back on foot, hitching the four miles to work along the winding glen road. I asked him where the bike was. He had spent too much money in the pub on Friday night and had to sell the bike to pay his debts. I was sorry; he was more phlegmatic. The Highlander's laissez-faire allowed him to shrug it off although it would be weeks before he had saved enough to replace it.

The glens could be stultifying back in those days, a dangerous trap for young men who never broke free. Work was limited to a few pursuits, and recreation, especially in the long winter months, often revolved around drink and the undeniable camaraderie of the public bar. Without transport to other places and new experiences this could become cloying – a world limited by a self-perpetuating cycle of introspection. Alcoholism is a problem in remote areas all over the globe. But Vic was having none of it. One day he suddenly asked me what I thought of the army. I told him that it offered wonderful opportunities for travel and learning new skills. Was he thinking of joining up? 'Aye,' he said to me cryptically, 'it's the only way.' A few months later he was gone, leaving his empty haversack hanging in the workshop, gone off to the Queen's Own Highlanders, one of the most prestigious Highland infantry regiments. I only saw him once more after that, at a parade in Inverness. He cut a fine figure in his swinging kilt and its long ceremonial sporran, his white spats and his Glengarry bonnet and plumes.

In the 1970s it was inevitable that he would serve in Northern Ireland. The Troubles were rampant and British forces were a constant presence to keep the peace, or at least to keep the warring factions apart. Being in the middle is always the worst place to be. To the IRA they were a legitimate enemy target. Vic had found his adventure; he was doing well. He achieved his first stripe while working with a rapid reaction force patrolling the border country. They travelled in Puma helicopters, a coveted target for the terrorist rocket launchers lurking in the border undergrowth. He died along with seven other soldiers and both pilots as the helicopter exploded in mid-air.

Vic was buried with full military honours in the Cannich graveyard, a Union Jack draped over the coffin borne on the shoulders of six of his uniformed colleagues. Generals stood among shepherds in the gentle rain that day. The whole glen turned out to salute its soldier son who wore the Queen's Own cap badge of a Highland red deer stag and its old Seaforth motto *Cuidich 'n righ* – Save the King – with such pride. In shoulder-bracing dignity these words are engraved at the foot of his stone: 'May his sacrifice help to bring the peace and freedom for which he died.'

I left his haversack hanging in the workshop for several years. It seemed to speak to me every time I passed. Vic Macleod – handyman. Then we converted the building and it disappeared. Life keeps moving on.

THIRTEEN

April

I have seen the lady April bringing the daffodils,
Bringing the springing grass and the soft, warm April rain.

JOHN MASEFIELD, 1878–1967

It is April. At Aigas April has come to mean two things to me: daffodils and ospreys. The reality is, of course, that it means many other things as well: it is when the world is freshening up again; when the field centre begins to buzz again after months of office-bound inertia; it is when the sun's first warmth is yapping at the fleeing heels of winter. But it is daffodils and ospreys that bring special resonance to my April days.

First come the daffodils. England dispenses with most of its daffs in March. By April in most years, godly English ladies are struggling to find any daffodils to freshen their altars and chancel arches; they've moved on to lilac, forsythia, cherry blossom and tulips. But here in the Highlands winter plays a game with spring, seeming to let it run and then hauling it back again as a child fools with a puppy on a string. So spring arrives late and bewildered. Some years April seems to be backward looking, belonging more to winter than March. Sleet and hail squalls go barrelling past us, down the valley, punctuated by heartening shafts of petulance from the sun. In other years the whole month is blessed and side-lit with yellow warmth that bursts sepals and sends cock chaffinches into paroxysms of ardour. The daffodils and the ospreys come whatever the weather. They are wired to arrive in sleet or shine.

But there the similarity ends. I have nervously watched the daffs for weeks as their lances pierce the snow crust when their first green inches are so vulnerable to careless feet. When the flower buds probe like praying hands I hurry out each morning to see which will show colour first, where the first gold will spill. It is a competition short-lived. Jostling hordes of yellow gold quickly throng around the winners, vulgar and loud.

Once, on an afternoon of rare April warmth, I sat down among them to read. I fell asleep. As I lay back my head nestled between their rigid stems. When I awoke some minutes later I wasn't sure where I was. Their trumpets seemed to have closed in over me so that the sky was a blur of softly flowing yellow, formless and lucent, pinning me down. I lay still and tried to focus but they were too close. Slowly I became aware of sound, as of a distant conversation, seeming to come from the daffodils all round me. I closed my eyes again and concentrated to block out the chaffinches in the rowan tree above me. There was a distinctive atmospheric murmur, like the frightening fizz of silence in a child's brain. It was almost as if the daffodils were trying to tell me something, urgent and intimate. When a breeze tugged at their bell-mouths their stems squeaked like the staves of an old ship.

The moment passed, but the image stayed, altering my view of daffodils, making them somehow personal and confiding. It is an image I can't cast off; it's locked in, private and prescient, so that when I see daffodils, even clustered in a vase, I seem to hear the squeaking stems and the gilded murmur.

Ospreys are different. Yet the knowledge of their imminent arrival has the same prescience, the same frisson of expectation each April brings. The Highland osprey was shot out as a breeding species by 1917. Victorian sporting ethics were discriminatory to a point of puritanical obsession. It is hard nowadays to comprehend the rigour with which they applied their single-mindedness. Wildlife was game or it was vermin: fair or foul, precious or base. It was desirable or despicable: priceless and worshipped or vilified and purged. There seems to have been nothing in between – no middle ground, no weighing in the balance, no benefit of the doubt.

For all his natural history skill Old Bob had been a product of this totalitarian discipline. Kill all carnivores, all hooked beaks and everything else that gets in your way. The stark image of his woodland gibbets where he hung the wrecks of the animals and birds I loved has remained with me all my life. As a boy I used to try to imagine the multifarious corpses of his life's work heaped in one vast rotting midden. Weasels, stoats, foxes, badgers, otters, hedgehogs, magpies, crows, rooks, jackdaws, jays, gulls, cormorants, mergansers, herons, all owls, buzzards, sparrowhawks, peregrines, hobbies, all harriers, rabbits, moles, rats, voles, mice, shrews, adders and grass-snakes, and even eels and pike, all perished at his hand or his heel. They were snared, shot, poisoned, trapped, gassed, smoked or burned out, ferreted, netted, dug out, flushed with dogs, bludgeoned or skewered with whatever implement came most readily to hand.

Just once, as a boy of about twelve, I shot a tawny owl with an air rifle. It was in an old yew tree, not very high, but dense and dark inside. The owl sat next to a main stem perhaps fifteen feet up the tree. I think I was looking for wood pigeons' nests, a task for which I was paid pocket money in those days. The owl opened one eye. To this day I do not know what possessed me. I had reared tawny owls from silver-white bill-clacking balls of fluff, gusted prematurely from their nests on windy nights, to the finely barred, alert and perspicacious young adults they quickly grew to be. I loyally trapped and dismembered mice for them and I wept as they floated away to freedom a few weeks later. I knew the silken intricacy of that soft plumage; I had winced at the needle-sharp talons on my hand, peered into the huge amber orbs as deep as oceans. This was a bird I knew and loved. It was Old Mr Brown whose wisdom and authority imbued the collective consciousness of millions of children.

Is it surging testosterone blinding the moment? Does some rogue gene loaded with destructive assertiveness catch unawares all twelve-year-old boys with air rifles? I pulled the trigger. For a moment the owl appeared not to move. Then it tipped slowly forward, tumbling through the branches limp and useless. It was quite dead, shot through the breast. It landed at my feet. I picked up the ragged corpse, hot and floppy in my hands. I sat down and cried the bitter tears of shame.

The English countryside of my childhood was purged of its wildlife by thousands of gamekeepers employed by every estate and shoot, every river and lake. Many farmers harried their hedges and copses with the same destructive fervour. It was the norm. It says much for the wildlife itself and even more for the diversity and extent of natural and semi-natural habitat present in the post-war countryside that anything interesting survived at all. And yet, upon the favoured few a golden glow of paternalism and protection shone above and beyond their required function as quarry. Partridges, grouse, pheasants, woodcock and snipe, curlew and plover, salmon and trout, mallard and teal, swans and wild geese were serenaded in verse and song, immortalised in art, silver, jewellery and, ultimately, the taxidermist's glass case. It was as though an unwritten chapter of Genesis had decreed: 'These shall be fair; these foul. These thou shalt worship; all others shalt thou exterminate with all thy might. And the Lord thy

God shall see that what thou doest is good and no man shall gainsay thee.'

Here in the Highlands the hate list held other exciting names: wildcats, pine martens, polecats, golden eagles, sea eagles (or the erne, as it was then commonly known), ospreys, ravens, hooded crows, hen harriers, red kites, merlins and goosanders – even seals. Of these several were to be pushed over the brink by the end of the nineteenth century. The last sea eagle went the way of the wolf in 1916.

Two mounted eagles from the Victorian era glare at each other across the Aigas hall. I bought them at a country house sale only a couple of long rifle shots away from here. One is an immature sea eagle, and the other a golden eagle. Both have broken toes, somewhat ineptly repaired by the taxidermist. What this reveals is that both were trapped at the nest – a common practice in those days. A keeper would watch to see which eyrie was occupied, wait until the pair was established there, then sneak in and lay tooth-jawed gin-traps in the detritus of the nest lining. In no time at all he would have them both. Many large houses and sporting lodges displayed whole museums of their plunder. As a historical record and a teaching aid these gaunt relics are more valued now than they ever were in life.

The polecat was virtually to disappear by 1870. Writing in 1919, the sporting naturalist Charles St John says that the polecat is 'practically extinct in Scotland'. The ease with which this wild ferret could be trapped and the fineness of its mustelid fur made it a double target. In 1829 four hundred foumarts (or 'foul-marts' because of its strong musky smell) were sold at the Dumfries fur market. In 1831 there were six hundred polecat skins sold. But by 1866 there were only twelve. None subsequently appeared at Dumfries. To this day there are no wild polecats in Scotland but, like the red kite, the species did manage to cling on in some of the remoter parts of Wales.

The red kite was extinct here by 1880 and, along with the sea eagle, has only very recently been successfully reintroduced to the Highlands. The wildcat retreated to the remotest glens and the pine marten became so rare that many observers thought it also to be extinct.

A now widely quoted extract from the *Topographical, Statistical and Historical Gazetteer of Scotland* for the year 1853 gives us a gripping insight into what was happening on the ground:

Glengarry, until recently the property of the chief of the clan of Macdonald . . . was sold in 1840 to Lord Ward for £91,000 [over £2.5 million today]. It abounds in game . . . but, like most estates . . . it has also been subject to the ravages of vermin. From the lordly eagle down to the stot [*sic*] and weasel, those destructive denizens of the wood and wild find ample room for exertion amidst the vast and unploughed recesses of the Highland glens and forests . . . Annoyed by the loss of game, this gentle-man . . . engaged numerous gamekeepe[rs] . . . and award[ed] prizes of £3 to £5 to each of those who should prove the most successful . . . The keepers pursued the slaughter with undeviating rigour and attention. The result has been the destruction, within the last three years, of above 4,000 head of vermin, and a proportional increase in the stock of game.

The published list of vermin destroyed at Glengarry from Whitsunday 1837 to Whitsunday 1840 is as follows:

11 Foxes; 108 Wildcats; 246 Martin cats; 106 Polecats; 301 Stots and Weasels; 67 Badgers; 48 Otters; 78 House cats going wild; 27 White-tailed Sea eagles; 15 Golden eagles; 18 Osprey or Fishing-eagles; 98 Blue hawks or Peregrine falcons; 7 Orange legged falcons; 11 Hobby hawks; 275

kites, commonly called Salmon-tailed Gledes; 5 Marsh harriers or Yellow-legged hawks; 63 Gos-hawks; 285 Common
buzzards; 371 Rough-legged buzzards; 3 Honey buzzards;
462 Kestrils [*sic*] or Red-hawks; 78 Merlin hawks; 83 Hen-
harriers or Ring-tailed hawks; 6 Jer-falcon or Toe-feathered
hawks; 9 Ash-coloured hawks or Long blue-tailed hawks;
1,431 Hooded or Carrion crows; 475 Ravens; 35 Horned
owls; 71 Common fern-owls; 3 Golden owls; and 3
Magpies.

That we now have ospreys is a fluke.

Scandinavia was kinder to its ospreys in the nineteenth century – or perhaps there were just larger forests, more lakes, fewer
people and less fervour. In any event, a good enough population
survived to migrate to West Africa every winter. There they min-
gled with other ospreys from other parts of Europe. The fishing
was good, the climate ideal, and the company ought to have been
OK. But in the closing days of every March *Zugunruhe* and a
genetic quirk picked them off their swamp-side perches and
began to elbow them back across the six thousand miles of coast
and wetland to the countries of their birth.

In 1955 unseasonal easterly gales gusted two Scandinavian
ospreys off course to Scotland. Whether they were travelling *à
deux* or they both just happened to be blown by the same winds
of chance, we shall never know. What we do know is that they
found each other and stuck together on the River Findhorn. Was
one of them ill perhaps, shot at over trigger-happy Italy or Malta
and carrying lead? Why didn't they push on for home, only a
day or two away across the North Sea? Maybe they were just late
because of the detour, and the nesting urge overtook them – any
port in a storm. Or is it even possible that deep in the mysterious
coding of one of those birds' genes there lurked a spark of
electro-chemical recognition waiting for the River Findhorn? Can
the osprey smell the waters of his long home-water like the

salmon? Was some vestige of that wild river's murmur stored in its avian amygdala? Had the Scottish and the Scandinavian osprey populations interbred long ago in a primeval, unpersecuted past, genes loaded with prescience like the daffodils? We can only guess.

That April, the story goes, a keeper on a Findhorn estate turned to the laird and commented: 'Those white buzzards are damn difficult to bring down wi' a shotgun.'

The laird was more enlightened. 'What white buzzards?' he demanded. 'Show me.'

In the top of a lanky Scots pine on the river bank the first pair of Scottish ospreys to attempt breeding for thirty-nine years were busy ducking the shot and the female was doing her best to lay eggs. They didn't succeed in rearing a brood for another four years, during which time the enthusiastic laird guarded his secret jealously. Fate was kind. Those birds didn't get shot over Italy or Malta and they made it to the Gambia (where we now know that most Scottish ospreys over-winter) and back again for three consecutive winters until at last their fixation with the Findhorn bore fruit. The Scottish osprey was back.

Now, nearly a half-century later, we have some one hundred and eighty pairs well established, breeding and migrating merrily. Attitudes and the law have also changed. The osprey has become a symbol of successful nature conservation and protection. It is an icon for public involvement in wildlife. Well over a million people have visited the RSPB's Loch Garten osprey hide to see the white buzzards for themselves.

Aigas is irresistible to ospreys. Several pairs nest near us. With the rich shallows of the Beauly Firth only five miles away, our river gliding by and the loch stocked with trout, we were bound to attract them. They began to appear here in small numbers when we started the field centre in 1977 and they have been a constant delight ever since. Their inward migration has been an annual climacteric for all my time here, a consciousness ever brightening our spring days. 'It's April – Oh good! The ospreys will be here soon.'

So here I am at the loch.

I wasn't the first to see the April osprey this year. Hugh Bethune, our maintenance officer, who spends his days restoring domestic harmony to the lives of our staff and guests, spied it on his rounds. When he came into the office yesterday morning he just mentioned it in passing in his laconic Highland way – no fuss, no drama: 'The ospreys're back at the loch,' said as if he were telling us the postman had been. Duncan's heart missed two beats and he knocked over his coffee. 'What!? When?' I didn't hear until later; by then several of the staff had been and seen for themselves. Hugh was right. One bird had arrived.

I am here just after dawn. It is ten to six. I have come to see the osprey or fishing-eagle, perhaps two. It *is* that predictable, and it will likely stay around all day, but I come at dawn because I want to see it alone. I am greedy. Some of Aladdin's trinkets I find hard to share. I have not seen this bird since September, and now I'm hungry for ospreys and want to hoard new images by myself. I bring no gun to greet these white buzzards. I carry no gin-trap to wire into the nest bed. I shall record their numbers, like the eighteen ragged corpses from Glengarry, but I am recording life, not death. Just me and my indispensable Zeiss binoculars and the April dew staining my shoes beside eight acres of sky. I stand in the birches. Their purple trails are also loaded with promise although green leaf is still a whole month away. I am excited. I am fifty and excited at the prospect of seeing a bird I have seen a thousand times on three continents. The Findhorn keeper would have been excited, too, as he raised his gun not quite fifty years ago. Funny how things turn around.

The still morning air splits wide open. A sharp, insistent cry repeats five – no, six – times. Then again, echoing. I turn to search the pine fringe serrating the blue sky at the far end of the loch. The unmistakable white head is held high, statuesque, heraldic, defiant. An easy shot. Then he lifts off. My binoculars follow the silhouette; all elbows and pent-up power. He circles the loch above the trees and cries shrilly as he goes, thin and echoing. I can't see another bird. I think he is checking it out. He is expecting company. Perhaps his partner hasn't arrived yet. The call is a challenge, a plea: 'Are you there? Where are you? Answer me!'

I am here, enclosed in a circle of glass. My whole being is trapped in my hands. I am being drawn around the cloud rim by this fish-eagle. Now he is all black against the sky, a shape bigger than a buzzard and without the lazy glide. This bird has to work. Wings made for fishing don't soar well. To rise from the water with a fish in his talons, he has to scoop air in bucketfuls. His wings have to rotate high over his back and churn their spread pinions downwards like plough shares turning deep furrows of bright air.

He lands on the bendy tip of a larch tree. He holds his wings aloft, archangel-like, while it steadies to his weight. Now he is heraldic again, head held high; the crest is raised and imperial eyes scour the dark water below; a continuous murder screams in his nervous centres. I pull focus. I see sharp little jerks of the head. His neck stretches as he sees fish and weighs the odds. I long for him to dive. He lifts off, launching himself forward. I hold my breath. He stretches over the loch and hovers, only for a second, almost as if he has made a mistake. Then he banks steeply and rows away again, lower now, below the tree line so that I can see the chocolate mousse and cream of his nape. He is heading round the loch towards me. I keep very still although I don't think my silent presence will deter him. He no longer expects to be shot here. I know I can't fool him. His world operates on a level far more vivid than ours; his eyesight is many times sharper than mine – an acuity I can't achieve even with the thoughtful precision of Herr Carl Zeiss. For him everything is danger, excitement and exaggeration; life is a *qui vive* far more taut than anything I can experience. Long ago he will have seen me and my twin rings of glinting optics. I am comforted by that certainty. We are sharing the shaft of fine morning air between us in a way that shores me up. This is why I came.

Without warning he tips and folds. The long oar-wings have collapsed from the shoulders and he is delta shaped, rocketing to the water, blue feet thrust forward, talons spread. With a sharp intake of breath I drop my glasses. For a moment our veins coalesce, his and mine, the hot blood seeming to run in a circuit through both of us. I need to witness the whole show, hear the loch ring with the water crash, see the sun-glinting ripples race away from him in pulsing arcs. I am not disappointed. He rests on the surface on half-spread wings for a few seconds, his yellow eye boiling with fire. He looks as if he has emerged from the depths like a mythical water griffin, fierce-beaked and angry. I know he has caught a fish. If he hadn't, he would have pulled out straight away, lifting easily and gracefully to resume his search. But these few seconds are pumping oxygen into the super-muscles of his breast, the lateral pectoralis major and pectoralis minor streaming from his sternum, summoning power for the great heave. He has to lever free from the surface drag and haul the gyrating fish with him, expelling water from his mocha plumes as he goes.

I am back inside my lens rings. I can count the water-pearls running from his back. Up come the wings until they meet high over his head and then scooping down and back they shovel up great gulps of the morning. He lifts with his legs trailing and a brownie is pierced in the crimped talons of one foot. It's not a big fish. It's a wild brown trout of 'breakfast size', as old Dunc MacRae used to say, just fitting across the plate, toothy grin at one side, tail fins fried brittle at the other. He can raise this fish easily. He is clear of the water now; droplets are still streaming back to the loch. Five feet up he shakes in mid-air, a ripple starts

in the pinions and builds backwards down to his tail and his creamy breeches. A fine mist momentarily shrouds him. Powering wings haul him out of it, banking as he goes, inscribing the edge of the loch to avoid the trees. He circles round. I see his clench on the trout shift, turning it head first and gripping it fore and aft with both feet so that it rides like an under-slung torpedo. It continues to squirm hopelessly. It is all a trout can do at the end of the world; make a few last apocalyptic contractions. My bird is black again now. Wingbeats are shallow, even and unhurried. He turns again, heading back towards me but high against bright white clouds. As he closes I can see the gold ring of his eye and the charcoal eye-stripe running back through snowy white cheeks into his chocolate mantle. He passes overhead. I shiver. For a moment I am with the fish. I can feel the flesh tug of the hooked beak, hear the snap of ripping gill.

Suddenly he is gone. April is complete. I have only been here for seven minutes but the whole month has opened itself up to me, drawing me away from winter and into the season of all our expectations. I walk quietly back down to the house inhaling the morning. Daffodils are everywhere, jostling.

FOURTEEN

Giving Back

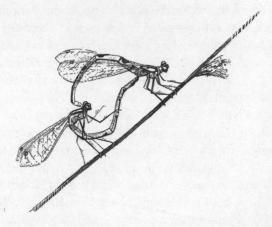

Those who contemplate the beauty of the Earth find reserves of strength that will endure as long as life lasts. There is symbolic as well as actual beauty in the migration of birds, the ebb and flow of tides, the folded bud ready for spring. There is something infinitely healing in the repeated refrains of nature – the assurance that dawn comes after the night and spring after the winter.

RACHEL CARSON, 1907–64

I have come to the birchwoods in the rain. It's the middle of July and the day is miserable. It seems to have been grey for days. Rings of Atlantic mini-lows are dawdling their sodden will across us. When the sun does manage to squeeze through in powerful explosions of wet light it reminds us that it is supposed to be summer.

Then the clouds swirl back and the rain blots us out all over again. The land is awash. The air is burdened; up and down the glen tireless burns roar like lions in the night. Midges revel and feast.

At the loch a few members of the local art club in nylon waterproofs cower beneath huge umbrellas, emitting clouds of citronella. As I pass them I sneak furtive glances at their workmanship. Out on the water the lilies fragment the dark surface like a jungle camouflage pattern; avenues of darkness wind through maps of pale verdure generously sprinkled with pure white blooms. A dab of gold glows from each pellucid core. The last easel I pass has no landscape – just the lily mosaic. Today we have our own private Monet.

The birchwood behind the loch restores my soul. Like Wordsworth, 'it disturbs me with the joy of elevated thoughts'. The wood and I are partners. We have been together for twenty-five years. We have grown up here, sharing a truth. I wanted it and it needed me to make the space to get it going. It can do fine without me now, but I keep coming back to check on it. Today I feel more like a parent than a partner – and like most parents I think I know best.

When I came here all those years ago I found this land exhausted. It had been grazed and burned; burned and grazed. When it wasn't being chewed it was on fire. Sheep picked over the charred ground searching for green. Underground, the fireproof roots of purple moor grass, mat grass and the needle-like deer grass pushed out false hope. They kept on coming. *Mollinia* and *Nardus* and *Tricophorum* – an unholy trinity, none of which is worth eating – and a few other fraudsters conspired to fool generations of crofters into thinking green meant good. The result was desolation. Desolate wet slopes, old and cynical. Bare peat glowered through meagre pasture, thin and unpalatable. Acid-loving insectivorous flowers, butterwort and sundew, broke the monotony with their delicate treachery but made the point. With insufficient nutrients available in the washed-out soils they had to rely on a diet of flies and midges.

Little stars of yellow bog asphodel crowded the waterlogged hollows – and still do, but now they garland the edges of the birchwood.

By the simple ploy of removing the close-cropping pressure of sheep and deer and stopping burning, and, for a few summers, by putting Highland cattle on to dung it well and break up the peat with their sharp cleaves, we kick-started the restoration process. Then we withdrew. Nature took over. Birch seed rained in on the wind. Fieldfares, redwings and mistle thrushes clattering through in the autumn gorged themselves on rowanberries and wild cherries from the geans up and down the glen. Then they generously fired their cloacal missiles across the hill like an air strike. All we did was stand back and watch.

Some years ago an elderly lady named Helen Foucar contacted us out of the blue. She was the daughter of an official in the Indian Civil Service of the 1920s. Helen was sent home to boarding school in Cheltenham. The Gordon-Oswalds were her guardians. Rather than suffer the long ship passage to Bombay in the summer heat she came to Aigas for her holidays. When, recently, she returned to the house after an absence of sixty years, with touching delight she proudly showed us the proof of her claim. As she inched her way towards adulthood her height was marked on the jamb of the drawing-room door: faint scratchings of history we had hitherto overlooked. When she died she left us her photograph album of Aigas before the war.

The photographs were a wonderful windfall. They and her graphic memories were a revelation. They gave us immediate and accurate insight into the Victorian estate, the Gordon-Oswalds themselves and many other details of the property. Not all of them were her own. Some large prints had been given to her by Mrs Gordon-Oswald and pre-dated Helen by many years. One in particular grips me. It is a full plate of a Victorian picnic party, taken in 1890. Three women, three men and a boy pose at the loch. Their exact position is clearly identifiable by the dry-stone dyke that still stands and by an outcrop of grey schist upon which the dam would be built only a few years after the photograph was taken. The figures are statuesque; the limitations of the shutter speed and the photosensitivity of the 1890 bromide plate required them to stand still for some seconds. (We believe the photographer to have been John William himself. In the tower he had constructed an elaborate dark room with sinks and close-fitting shutters.) Behind them a rowing boat stands off, also posing; a long painter secures it to a pine tree. The loch is as calm as glass. The women are dressed not just to the nines, but for the puritanical nineties. They wear full-length bustle dresses buttoned to the chin. Broad lace hems trail the ground and peplum overskirts hang from waisted jackets with long sleeves and lace cuffs. One lady, the oldest of the three, perhaps mother or mother-in-law to the other two, has a white shawl around her shoulders, crossed over at the front. All three wear elaborate bonnets with pale clusters of flowers crowding the brims. Their long hair is tied back in buns or French pleats. All three wear gloves: no flesh but the minimum required for breathing, seeing, hearing and a demure smile. One girl perches on the rock.

The men are more relaxed – just. They all wear tweed, but the oldest, a patriarchal-looking gent, grey-bearded and sombre in a frock coat with a broad-brimmed black hat like a Homburg without the cleft, seems to be clad in city clothes of fine worsted cloth. The others, including the boy of about twelve who sports a straw boater with a wide black band, have the coarser, baggy look of Harris tweed in well-used three-piece suits; gold watch-chains link the men's waistcoat pockets. The two adult men are in peaked 'fore and aft' caps and wear black ties and rigid wing collars – just the thing for a picnic. One man holds a cane like a music-hall compere.

The photograph reveals a great deal. When we were first given it I went to sit on the girl's rock, still clearly exposed at the modern loch's outlet. I drew grace from the knowledge of their pleasure in this place. I could share something with them, something real. But the background, the hill behind the loch, the broad expanse of hill encompassing the loch's basin and wrapping us round, astonished me. Even though it is slightly out of focus, I can see every wrinkle. I can read the land's palm. I can determine every contour of the skyline and every rock and hollow across its face. At a distance of a quarter of a mile away across the still water I can read its vegetation like a script. It certainly isn't difficult. In 1890 it was as bald as a plate. Not a single tree existed. No shrub, no juniper, no broom or gorse, no eared willow at the water's edge – nothing. It is as though it has been shaved like a wheat crop, leaving only a skim of low, stunted heather. Its impact is stark, shocking. It makes me wonder how they did it.

I don't think that red deer were the significant factor at Aigas. They were here – there is no doubt of that – and intentionally so in artificially high numbers, as they are on many sporting estates today. But numbers were probably insufficient to suppress the vegetation to such an extreme. Deer are very good at taking out young trees, especially in winter when everything edible lies beneath a snow crust for weeks on end, but trees do still manage to get away. Their seeds find gullies and crags, ravines and rocky places where the deer cannot go. They veer skywards from wet fissures, triumphant, like tiny enclaves of resistance in a war. No, it wasn't the deer. The answer lies in the closed minds of the Gordon-Oswalds and their servants. Their land management was as rigid as their pose, and entrenched. It was a class structure: black or white, either acceptable or beyond the pale. In 1890 grouse and moorland were *it*; trees were not.

You couldn't be the laird of a proper Victorian sporting estate without grouse. They belonged to the sacred trinity of social approbation: salmon, red grouse and red deer, those three; at Aigas the greatest of these was the grouse. To have grouse in shootable numbers you had to have moors – moors of purple heather, *Calluna vulgaris*. And moors had to be kept as moorland, just as they are to this day in the drier eastern hills of the red grouse range in Scotland.

In these broad shoulders of open country where the natural tree cover had been erased by man's survival needs centuries before, moorland arrived as a pseudo-climax. It arrived because the ecological cycle of restoration had been truncated, summarily cut off. The trees which carry the nutrients up from the substrate and deposit them back on the surface in leaf fall were not there, and without them nor were the humus-building bacteria. So the podsolic soils acidified and stagnated as peat. Heather loves acid and peat.

Heather has always been there as a forest component beneath the trees; freed from their limiting shade it grasps the ecological niche and expands its claim. The grouse expand with it. Thinking this is just the thing, industrial man, no longer directed by primary survival needs, applied his spare cash to keep it that way. He burned it and he weeded out anything he didn't like – virtually everything except heather. This he fired in strips to stimulate young shoots and to prevent it from becoming rank and woody. The moors became patterned and striped, put to fire and the sword as if the Duke of Cumberland's men, lacking good Highland houses to burn, had turned their wrath upon the hills.

When I first came here an elderly gamekeeper named Archie Chisholm lived in a lonely cottage at Culbernie on the other side of the river. I was told that he had worked for the Aigas estate before the war, so I went to see him. He was enthusiastic and helpful. I brought him here and walked the ground with him, nudging memories out of him like teasing sticky raisins from the bottom of a jar. One day we were up above the loch and he was telling me about the pines being felled for the war effort. As we walked we happened across a huge gorse bush. It bristled in spiky splendour. Its almond blooms were past and it stood there in a haze of green glory. Underground, its noduled roots were busy fixing nitrogen. To me it was part of a cycle, nature tentatively realigning itself after decades of abuse. To him it was a weed; an insult pock-marking a heather moorland to which he had donated part of his life. Before I knew what was happening Archie dipped into his jacket pocket and came up with a cigarette lighter. He bent down and lit the dry grass at the base of the shrub.

There is something about a gorse bush that makes it explode. Like the fronds of some conifers thrown on to a bonfire, it bursts into flame with a crackling roar and a surge of dense yellow smoke. I was horrified. It was too late. The whole bush vanished before my eyes. Seeing my astonishment Archie admonished me for allowing it to be there at all. It was, he insisted, 'ready for firing'. He shook his head gravely. 'You'll never have a moor if y' allow that kind o' weed to take a grip.'

Like every other Victorian moorland owner, the Gordon-Oswalds had issued an edict: there shall be no gorse on our moors, no broom, no willow, no trees, no argument. And it follows that as a consequence of their rigorous policies there shall be no bellowing chaffinches, no trilling willow warblers or wrens, no double-brooded dunnocks weaving through the gorse bushes. No roe fawns shall be dropped in the dappling shade, and, in the autumn, no leaves shall shower a future into replenished soils. Nor did they foresee that if such universal policies pushed native woods back too far, one of their most prized quarry species, the black grouse of the moorland edge, would eventually disappear, too. And there they all stood, imposing their lofty domination and their magniloquent, land-changing authority beside the loch. I am quite sure no alternative view impinged upon their tightly buttoned rectitude. That was the way things were done, and that was that. After all was said and done, God was on their side.

Now, more than a quarter of a century later, I am standing in a wood – my wood. I am as proud of it as Monet must have been of his water lilies or Michelangelo of his heavenly host towering above the Sistine Chapel. My wood was less work, but it took about as long. To me it is as beautiful. If I had been asked how long it would take to create a birchwood from nothing I would not have known the answer. When I came here all those years ago no one was into creating birchwoods. The Forestry Commission told me birch was a weed. There was no place for what we now call native woodlands in their regimented policies for the forced production of fibre. When, quite early on in my wood's existence, I showed off my young saplings to a visiting forester, he went silent. He looked nonplussed. He didn't know what to say to this wild youth who wanted birchwoods. At last he came clean: 'I can't think why you want these. There are no jobs in birchwoods.' From his perspective, of course, he was right. There were no grants available for native woodlands and most people wouldn't have known what to do with a birchwood if they had one. As Fraser Darling had found twenty years before, ecology was still shrouded in suspicion. Conservation fared no better. Within its murky ethos lurked the connotations of long hair and beads, beards and sandals.

In twenty-five years you get a proper wood. The trees are bigger than one might imagine. It has been a long time since I could link my hands around their trunks. Nor can I see the clouds overhead. The canopy is full and fat. But half a dozen swallows don't make a summer. I don't just come here to measure or count trees. In fact, I almost don't notice them any more, I have become so used to their gentle presence. I come to share in the woodland's softly rolling cycles, to breathe the warm, sweet scents of fertility. I come to applaud its fungal introit to the shortening summer days and to honour the leaf galls that brush my face. Spittlebugs blot my trousers and common blue damselfly males quiver their startlingly electric blue abdomens in front of their dull mates. So taken are they with one another that if you sit still they will land on your arm. Beside the burn bulging palms of male fern, *Dryopteris*, lean their dripping fronds over frothing pools. Wild foxgloves line the path in arrays of blowsy extravagance. Their lolling mouths and speckled under-lips beckon seductively to the industrious bumble-bee, *Bombus magnus*, with her natty white tail. On the moorland edge the other two Highland heathers loiter in dry corners: cross-leaved heath, *Erica tetralix*, and bell heather, *Erica cinerea*, the first as pink as sun-blasted eye-lids and the bell heather as decadent as burgundy wine. I come for the aura of the woodland, to glory unashamed in the thronging orchestration of the living earth.

By July the crescendo of birdsong has died back. Mating and rearing are over but for a few double broods such as the thicket-loving dunnocks; the need for shouting is past. But the chaffinches are still there, in almost every tree, cheeping now as if it's the best they can manage. Willow warblers have become furtive and monosyllabic. Gone are the shrill arpeggios tumbling from high places; now they pick aphids from secret larders in the willow tangle.

In rain like this the wood closes in on me. Birches are poor pro-tection. Their neat leaves shed the water in fat droplets more wetting than the rain itself. The burn prattles excitedly. The air seems to take on the gleam of water, effulgent and new, so that when the sun breaks through the whole wood is trussed with lances of brilliant gold. Then the long grass steams and a cock chaffinch, forgetting himself, bursts into exuberant song.

In the 1980s I bought some patchy Forestry Commission plantations that they considered too small to be economic. They were of tightly packed Sitka and Norway spruce with a few larches and Scots pines sprinkled in like seasoning. They were sterile and gloomy. No light struck the needle-littered floor and nothing grew there. The scent of mould hung on stale air. Up in the sunlight tits and goldcrests combed the tight crowns and occasional flocks of crossbills trooped through, plucking cones. By day red deer stags lay up in their cool caverns, but the plan-tations didn't fit with what we were doing at Aigas. I longed to clear them and start again. I applied for a felling licence. To my delight, times were a-changing and the notion of native woodland was no longer so alien to the authorities. 'Why don't you just restructure them?' suggested an enlightened official. This encouragement uplifted me, urged me on. That I wanted to use them for educational purposes met with an unexpected rash of enthusiasm. I could scarcely believe it.

Now, after the passage of more years than I can immediately recall, we have achieved just that. As you trail up the path from the house to the loch we have kept a slender strip of spruce plantation on the right and restructured the woods to the left. It's a demonstration. On the same walk Duncan (who came to us nine years ago complete with pony-tail, beard, earrings and beads, if not sandals) can show his boisterous schoolchildren the difference between a plantation man-made for a crop of pulpwood and a reconstituted woodland infiltrated by nature. You can stand and soak up the forceful distinction. A few paces into the plantation the darkness closes around you and you think you are the only living thing for miles. A few steps in the other direction and you stand in a woodland mosaic with a lofty coniferous presence of Scots pine and a few spruces mixed all about with birches, rowans, geans, one or two oaks, hazel, goat willows – even a holly has found a niche. The air is vibrant with birdsong and the ground beneath your feet is a constantly changing quilt of grasses and sedges, wildflowers, heathers and ferns, rushes and mosses in the wet hollows. Willow and juniper scrub, broom and clumps of glossy woodrush bar your way. Life throngs around you. Sunlight fools with the spectrum. Spiders string their silver nets across your vision. Flies drone and wasps hum in the now stretching pine fronds. Gnats dance before your eyes. If you return at dusk or the early morning, roe deer browse in the dewy clearings. Red squirrels play hide-and-seek with you, overlooking the give-away of their scratchy claws on the rough pine bark. You can see where the badgers have nosed their grubby snouts for bugs and bulbs, turning up dark, fibrous soil, heaving with life. Everything is giving back. Every scrape is preparing the ground for yet more seeds and opportunities. Cycles are spinning like the earth itself. If you are lucky, a woodcock will spring from under your feet and twist away through the birches on silent, looping wings. I keep hoping that one day the theatrical black grouse with gorged red wattles and its curling tail feathers will return its preposterous lekking dance and its hissing, wobbling call to the Aigas woods. (They appear regularly in the Victorian gamebooks from this glen, but they are now very rare.) All we have done is handed back to nature the chance to rebuild some natural capital. We have quit fighting it and let it flood back in. We have made spaces and given honest labour to the sun and the rain.

In April 1996 I found myself sitting in a meeting of the Royal Society of Edinburgh attending a lecture by Sir Martin Holdgate, the President of the Zoological Society of London and former Director-General of the World Conservation Union, among other global achievements. The lecture was entitled *What Future for*

Nature? Far from being doom and gloom, it was everything I had hoped for and quite a lot more. Sir Martin outlined the four great waves of human impact upon the natural world. The first was direct hunting and killing; forest clearance and the use of fire by hunter-gatherers resulting in the extinction of the ancient worlds of *Smilodon* and the woolly mammoth. The second was the loss of wild habitat to the proliferation of agriculture. The third is the current one of industrial and urban man and the devastating pollution we produce. The fourth is the rarely considered accidental and intentional translocation of species by man's travels around the globe – everything from tobacco to tomatoes, rats to goats, house sparrows to elm-bark beetles, all busy invading and displacing other local species. Then, to my particular delight and excitement, he suggested a fifth, new and exciting wave of incipient human activity. He called it restoration ecology. By this he means 'environmental protection measures, pollution control, sustainable development and programmes of conservation' – conscious human effort to maintain the beauty and diversity of the landscape and such species of the world as we have left.

I drove back to the Highlands through the great whispering mountain passes where the red deer dotted the snowfields like raisins on a bun. As I crossed the Kessock Bridge over the Beauly Firth, I could see far below me the skimming wake of a pod of bottlenose dolphins, *Tursiops*, their arched elephant-grey backs undulating their way up the flooding tide. My good friend Dr Paul Thompson of the Cromarty Lighthouse Research Station tells me they are a species thought to be clinging on here by the slender breadth of a flipper, struggling against the presence of man, pollution and climate change. Their symbolism ripples a huge question mark across the surface of man's grand ambitions. Every time I see them I have to stop and watch in case suddenly one day they're not there any more.

I wound my way back up the glen until I topped the rise at the Crask of Aigas; rounding the bend, the valley opened up before

me and the woods of home glowed brightly in the frosty sunshine. The phrase restoration ecology had stuck. A name had
been pinned to our work. When I stopped at the house I went
straight to the woods. They were winter woods. April knows no
birch leaf – the 57th Parallel sees to that. But *Zugunruhe* and the
long scriptures of genes were already at work. The redwings and
fieldfares were with us in chattering hordes, lingering for a few
days before heading on up to the north. High skeins of geese
were driving wedges across the sky. Great tits were sawing like
yellow-waistcoated carpenters from the tops of pines and robins
persistently tinkled like wind-chimes. They couldn't wait for
spring; they needed to get going right then. Life was erupting all
round me. On the goat willows yellow catkins were bursting
incandescent firecrackers. I saw a pile of fresh spruce logs Hugh
and the rangers had piled beside the track in my absence. We are
still making new spaces for the ever-expanding birches and
rowans, letting the native Scots pines fatten like marrows.

From the old plantations I pushed on up past the loch. My
birches stood in a purple haze of buds waiting to break. Toads
croaked their guttural messages from the marsh. Sir Martin
would be pleased with this, I thought. From a Victorian heather
desert to a wood bulging with what Professor E.O. Wilson has
termed biodiversity, all in the space of twenty-five years. That's
what it is all about – living diversity. Perhaps Old Bob's era of
destruction, oil slicks and Margam's senile marshes of industry
can be yesterday's impacts after all. Perhaps the next generation,
my children's generation and the Aigas generation of Duncan,
Susan, Jess and Sarah, will make other choices for their future –
are already making those choices, are pulling back from the
abyss. Perhaps that's where we're headed if we don't lose our
nerve – if we can only keep our eye on the ball.

As I stand here in the rain, allowing whirling optimism to flood
endorphins into my brain, I hear the sound of someone approaching

through the wood. It is Duncan. He is smiling. He is also covered in wispy green lichen, and the powdery smears of algae stain his jeans. 'What *have* you been doing?' I ask.

'I've been up to the osprey platform, checking it out. They're due back any day now and I thought I'd better get up there quick.'

The artificial nest is perched in the top of an old Scots pine high on a rocky outcrop above the loch. My old friend and colleague Roy Dennis (Mr Scottish Osprey himself) erected it for us years ago. The ospreys dutifully come and check it out every year, but we are still waiting for a successful breeding pair to settle in. 'But you'll never guess what I've just seen!' Duncan is beaming all across his face.

'No,' I admit. 'What?'

'I have just seen a *black grouse*!'

FIFTEEN

The River

... this sleek, sinuous, full-bodied animal, chasing and chuckling, gripping things with a gurgle and leaving them with a laugh, to fling itself on fresh playmates that shook themselves free, and were caught and held again. All was a-shake and a-shiver – glints and gleams and sparkles, rustle and swirl, chatter and bubble.

KENNETH GRAHAME, 1859–1932

Hermione helps me to ease the boat through the bluebells and down the grassy bank. Thank God for plastic boats. It bumps and grinds over stones and stumps. In the end, where it gets steep, we let it go. It hits the water with a dull splash. We nearly forget to hang on to the rope. I haul it back in.

This is almost an annual event. I have done it many times, but this is Hermione's first. I have waited until she is old enough to take the early start, the long day, the portage over the shallows and the stealth we need to do it properly. We have cushions and Thermos flasks of hot drinks, sandwiches and rolls, chocolate biscuits and apples. It is an adventure. Like all good adventures, it starts early. It is 4 a.m. We were up at three-thirty – the witching hour. I read that it's easier to wake up properly at three-thirty than at any other time of the night. We took the boat upriver last night and secured it on the bank before turning in early. Now we're back at the river and the sun is well up. Mist is drifting off the damp fields like smoke. Our plan is to ride the current all the way down to Aigas. We have come eighteen miles upstream to Cannich (twelve miles by road) to a convenient launching place. We have loaded our gear, checked the spare rowlocks and oars, and we're off. Cosied in her fleece, Hermione nestles into the bows in a heap of cushions. Out on the water it is chilly.

I have chosen the day carefully: the second full moon in June. A full moon because, inexplicably, the weather always seems to be clear. (*Encyclopaedia Britannica* admits that there is no scientific explanation for the happy correlation of anticyclonic weather and the full moon.) And June because I want the maximum daylight. It has come good. The morning is as smooth as silk.

We spend our lives looking at the river. The house was built there because of the river. The underlying soils and gravels of the Aigas fields were terraced and deposited by the river. Our wildlife throbs to the river's pulse. Together with the red deer and the grouse, the Atlantic salmon powering upstream to spawn afforded the house its Victorian pomp. Every once in a while it is good to be on the river and look back at ourselves.

We are about halfway down its course to the sea. The source is high in the Affric Hills. It streams off the rock of the high tops, trickles out of snows packed into the north-facing corries, slips by the glacier-scoured rim of an ice-capped pool, drops over sheer, broken ledges, gathers itself, and plunges headlong into a roaring pothole. When it emerges again lower down it flushes across rocky sills in ripples, finds another pool, foams and bridles and spills again. All the time it reinforces itself, gathering authority and the complexion of old sherry. Through high, gentle meadows it glides a tranquil reach before plunging again into the deep, frothing burns of the heather moors. The peat holds it fast like a sponge. It is the peaty moors that keep the rivers alive in high summer. The moorland burns are swollen by a thousand feeders. Merrily they join the amontillado throng. Our river tumbles through high banks and sharp rock grooves. It sucks, spouts, gurgles and hustles its way down. Down, down, down. Through boulder-strewn gullies and deep runnels, across shingly fans and between wet rock walls, it cuts and crashes through its cream-flecked youth. It grows and grows. It ripples and falls in musical cascades. Its eddies curdle under tree roots. It rattles its stones and clunks boulders along its rocky bottom after the rains. It cuts rock. Grey sills of gneiss and schist striate its hustling bed. It rushes from pool to pool. The hen dipper in her waiter's tails and red waistcoat bobs and skims over freshets of aeration. She dives beneath the shimmering curtain and emerges again to flicker off downstream to her mossy nest. She crams yet more caddis-fly larvae into the ravening gape of her impatient young bulging from a crack in a rocky wall. Our river joins and breaks free, joins again, merges and surges, like Highlanders marching out of the glens to war.

By the time it arrives at open country and the sleepy village of Cannich it is a proper river, fit for the blue of any map, despite its name: the Glass – *glas*, the grey-green river – unimaginative perhaps, but certainly accurate. It is wide and swift over the shallows, green in sunlight and grey in cloud, cutting broad sweeps as it veers drunkenly from one side of its valley to the other. Undercut banks hang waiting to fall. Sand bars smile in pale crescents and then bleed away to nothing. In the slack water foam-flecked pools swirl with eddies and load their peaty silt into long ribs of chocolate mud where sedges take root in the summer only to be ripped out again by the winter floods.

We ease out into the current. The bows snatch and we're off. I need the oars only for steerage. I can face forwards and dab. We are flotsam in green plastic, like the bottles tossed over the bridge by Cannich youths idling on their bikes. We bob along generating no sound. We are a green bottle stalking the morning lost in the chuckle of the stream, 'all sparkle, rustle and swirl, chatter and bubble'.

The spring has been dry. May and June are our driest months. The river is down. We can see the bottom everywhere except in the narrow channel where the current runs. Hermione has already seen trout that have ventured out into the shingly shallows to feed, darting back into the dark pools beneath the alders. She is excited. We shall have to keep to the current if we are to say afloat. Even this little rowing boat, thirteen feet long, draws seven inches.

I last came here in March when the snows were melting in the high hills. A melt and the rains came together this year. The west wind ripped back the snowfields like a dog towing a rug off a bed. Overnight the mountains turned brown and then black and sinister, carrying a burdensome sky. The air smelled of rain. It was mild for March and the wind said rain. Nervous crofters nudged their cattle and sheep up the hill. The wide eyes of my horses were rimmed with white. I brought them in. The river was urgent and swollen with meltwater. It had already consumed its banks. It was level with the sodden meadows. It just spread itself angrily, a wide brown thong snaking between fields. High up the wind rattled the bare ash branches in petulant bursts. The looming sky filled itself in with darkness. Then it rained. Just when there was nowhere for the river to go it rained. It rained and it rained. It seemed that the gap between the flooding fields and the clouds was going to fill with water – was filling up with rain as I watched. The hills vanished. They had been washed away. They were rushing by in solution, thick, brown and swirling.

It rained for eleven days. The river broadened by the minute, like a snake that has swallowed a horse. Whole trees whirled past. It spread to meet the valley walls, a frothy brown lake, like a fjord, long and curving. Lucy and I drove down the valley just to look. The power of the river draws you out to gawp. It came right to the road, lapping at it in the usual two low spots at Struy and Creleven. A triangle saying 'Flood' slowed us down. We laughed. It brought a smile to an otherwise unfunny day. For ten miles the whole valley was raging with angry water and beside a puddle they placed a sign saying 'Flood'.

When the valley could take no more the Hydro boys opened the flood gates on the dams at Aigas, Kilmorack and Fasnakyle. They call it 'spilling' round here. When you see it you laugh out loud. It's a nervous laugh. It spills like Niagara, with unspeakable, gut-gripping violence. Zillions of tons of angry cappuccino hurl down the concrete chutes the size of dual carriageways at the sides of the dam and smash into the river bed. It surges against huge rocks with a deafening thunder. The air fills with roaring, choking mist. 'A bit late,' the crofters said. They always do. The Aigas Gorge – half a mile away – raged so that I could hear it in the night, like a train that never passes. The rain stopped. The clouds turned white and edged with satin. Then the sun came out and the mountains were there after all. We all looked surprised. In two days the flood went away, draining like a bath. But the debris still hangs from the alder branches far above us. A one-legged plastic doll, naked and headless, is suspended like some ghastly reminder of the Culloden aftermath. Hermione can't believe it. I have to insist that it *was* that deep. I stand up in the boat and still I can't touch the flood line. The flood had spread its brown scum right across Bella's fields and flights of mallard revelled in the brimming marshes.

As floods go this year wasn't bad. I've known far worse. Before Hermione was born, in the days when I dabbled at farming on the flood plain, we ran seventy pedigree Highland cows and a bull called Tearlach (Charlie) at Carnoch, six miles upstream from Aigas. They were ideally suited to the rushy fields where they lay in the meadows strewn with wild flowers, contentedly chewing the cud. Travelling up and down every day to check their calving was a happy chore I came to relish. Late one summer a sequence of violent cloudbursts struck high in the hills. The thunder awoke us and we lay in bed watching the sheet lightning spread the pallor of a sickly child across the sky. The police in Inverness phoned in the small hours to say that a flash flood was expected. Carnoch floods quickly and among the first of the valley farms. At first light Lucy and I hurried down to see how bad it was. We were too late. The river had burst and spread across all the low-lying meadows. Only a few islands and the tops of the fences stood out. Most of the cattle had moved to the high ground beside the road and stood there with Tearlach huddled in the rain, but a few – nine, I think – were stranded among some alders on a long, thin strip of dry land down where the river bank normally was. The water was still rising and it was still raining hard. There was nothing for it but to go for a boat.

When we returned an hour later the islands had all disappeared and the stranded cows stood up to their bellies in swirling water, belling loudly. They were perilously close to the real river, which was thundering through like a stampede. If they attempted to swim in that direction we should lose them for certain. Nothing could survive in that torrent of uprooted trees and debris surging past. I rowed as hard as I could across the flooded field but the current was too strong; it swept us away so that I had to retreat to slack water and try again upstream. Lucy sat in the bows with a rope. Eight times we rowed in to those cattle and seven times we were swept past before Lucy could secure a cow. I was nearly exhausted. On the seventh attempt she managed to get a rope noose on to the wide horns of an old cow called Mairi Pollock. Lucy transferred to the stern and as I pulled gently away into deeper water Mairi reluctantly followed. She waded tentatively forward until only her head, chin held high, was above the water. With a loud, heaving moan she struck out. Her nostrils flared and fear pranced in her bulging eyes. Her breath came in short, snorting surges. She was sixteen years old and I could not imagine that she had ever had to swim before. None of them had. But mercifully they began to follow. One by one they gingerly waded into the current and launched out behind us. We had one shaggy head in tow and eight swimming and snorting loudly beside us, spreading themselves in an arc of horns and noses behind the boat. Sixteen upturned horns, sixteen heaving nostrils and sixteen staring eyes pursued us across that angry swirl. I was astonished how quickly they swam. I had to row as hard as I could to prevent them from overhauling us and tangling with the oars. There was no question of going against the current; we could only edge slowly across it in a long diagonal, heading for the side of the valley.

I could no longer tell where we were. Everything looked the same. The trees were half-drowned and unrecognisable; the fences were now fully submerged. I was frightened that we would cross one without knowing it and the cows' flailing legs would catch in the wires. I rowed and Lucy urged them on, calling to them by name and encouraging them every yard of the way. At last the road was in sight and there was slack water ahead. Then the boat lurched and snagged on a fallen tree under the water. The torrent was pushing us further into it. I couldn't row back out again against the current and the cattle were coming up on us fast. I only had twenty yards to go to the roadside fence.

Just at that moment a police car came along. To my huge relief the driver saw us, stopped and came to the roadside fence. It was Archie, the local bobby, whom we knew well. I called out, waved frantically and shouted, 'Archie, I need a rope to pull me ashore. Have you got a rope?' He smiled broadly and waved back, shouting, 'Aye, I have a rope but y' canna have it in case I need it for an emergency!' To our disbelief he got back into the car and drove away, still waving cheerfully.

There was nothing for it but to jump overboard and heave the boat off the tree by hand. The water was up to my chest and the branches snatched at my feet, but somehow I managed to free it with the cows milling round me so close that I could feel their hot breath on my face. I was scared stiff that their sharp, flailing hooves would accidentally catch me under water. Taking the rope from Lucy, I waded old Mairi to safety until she arose from the water, huge and dripping like a horned serpent. Lucy rowed in behind me, trailing her flotilla of flaring nostrils and sweeping horns. We were safe.

It is three months since this year's little flood; the river must now be almost at its lowest of the year unless we get a really dry summer. The mallard are wondering where their marshes have gone. The salmon fishers are eyeing up the clouds, fingering their beads for rain. No fish will run in these lows. We need a good spawning because the salmon are in trouble. Yet the river never dries up entirely because of the blanket peat on the moors and mountains. It is a vast sponge that only slowly lets its waters drain. There's enough peat up there in the hills to keep it running all year. And, of course, it gets replenished; the rain keeps coming. We are surrounded by ocean. The mountains mix the oceanic air, burdened with cloud 'unspeakably troubled', as Kathleen Raine says, more efficiently than any humidifier. They force it upwards to cool.

For a child the river is a world of wonder. For me it is the re-enactment of a childhood long ago. It is wild and real. We are running the wild river in a little green boat. We are Swallows and Amazons, Ratty and Mole. We are Tom Sawyer and Huck Finn rafting on the river. There is no sound of motor, no rush of cars; we see no houses or fields. We are drifting between banks of wild nature. We are in nature's last great stronghold in this valley. The sheets of bluebells and brilliant clots of marsh marigolds in the wet flushes are stabs of bright colour in the long green lines that hold us close. The fresh leaves of alders and birches lean and trail, and grey willows straggle beside us. It should be night but it's day.

The sun is up and the water beside us is dancing with silver light. We are running through wild wet woods and rushy marshes where people rarely go. We are voyeurs; invaders in the private world of herons and ducks and otters, deer sipping the morning, owls and foxes forced to hunt in the daylight and ospreys eyeing up the shallows for salmon parr and brown trout. To them we hope to be just another green bottle. We're bobbing flotsam dabbing an oar here and there to keep us right. We have all day and eighteen miles of chances to discover the river.

It is not long before we meet a roe deer at the stream's edge. It is a handsome buck. He is brand new. His short antlers are new and clean: waxy with knobbly shafts – pearling, they call it – and three shining points, just polished by thrashing in bushes and fraying the bark of young trees. His fresh summer coat glows a brilliant foxy red, sleek and glossy. He has a wet black nose and a circular band of black around his muzzle with a white flash at the tip of his chin. He sees us and is not alarmed. He stares straight at us, expressionless and intense. He is as graceful and beautiful as a gazelle – he *is* the Highlands' gazelle. I press my finger to my lips. Hermione shrinks down in the bows. We drift closer. He stands on a sandy strand, head erect, ears straining and a pale throat patch glowing under his chin. He is utterly motionless. He emits an aura. Like Narcissus, it is as though he knows how beautiful he is; that he was, only seconds before, adoring his own reflection in the shallows. He's not the slightest bit embarrassed at being caught at the mirror. Not even his nose twitches. As we pass we shall be fifteen feet from him. If our scent stays with the current and wafts past undetected I think he will stand. He doesn't know what we are. He has no image of boat and man logged in his memory bank. He is incapable of splitting us apart. Fear runs on electricity; it has to connect.

I am so lost in the deer that I forget to navigate. I fail to see the stump lodged in the river bed up ahead. My coxswain isn't on duty either, she's absorbing pure roebuck through her binoculars

at minimum focal range. We hit with a lurching bump. Hermione
lets out a little cry. The binos are jerked out of her hands; but
she's well taught – they *are* round her neck. The buck springs
away, sand spurting from his slot marks in the bar. In a bound he
has gone, up the bank and away into the unfurling bracken and
the alder woods. Then we hear him bark: brisk and staccato. One,
two, three, sharp echoing barks ringing from the wood like a man
clearing his throat with a harsh cough, monosyllabic and cross.
So he didn't get our scent. He still doesn't know what we are.

Roe deer do not bark in alarm, although it sounds to us as
though they do. A frightened or alarmed deer will disappear in
silence. Often you don't even get to see a frightened deer. They
slink off fast. The bark is a sign of excitement or puzzlement. It is
most commonly brought on by the presence of another roebuck
that has ventured into the barking deer's territory. It says, 'I am
here but who the hell are you?' He is in there somewhere, our
buck, looking back, wondering what in the name of God's breakfast we think we are doing on the river at four-fifteen in the
morning.

As we round a bend a mile or two on, Hermione asks, 'What's
that noise?'

'What d'you think?' I tease.

She listens intently, head first on one side, then on the other.
Slowly the realisation dawns. Her eyes widen. 'It's not?'

'Oh, yes it is,' I insist.

She tightens the tapes on her life-jacket.

It's louder now, a dull roar, not like a proper waterfall – the
Glass has had none of those since the dams were built in the
1950s – but rapids nevertheless. The sound is industrial, like
some ancient mill grinding away, its machinery making the same
continuous tuneless drone. The water is rippling beneath us. The
shallows are rattling shingle. The deep current where we are
gathering speed is whispering darkly, urgent and pressing, like
frightened people hurrying out of a building after a bomb-scare.

Up ahead I can see white water. One or two large boulders lie in our path and I steer between them where the current swells and dips. Green weed beards the rocks and cream eddies spin off into slack shallows at the sides. I can see Hermione's knuckles whiten on the gunnel. She is staring dead ahead. The river is roaring now. I have to shout, 'Hang on!'

The bows plunge suddenly, dipping down fast water, and I hear a little shriek from Hermione. We lurch to the right and I have to haul on an oar to choose a path through the next boulders. These are under the water and the current mounts them like a stallion, rearing and pawing. I think we could go over them but I don't want to risk it. I try to go for the gaps. We spin and rock; I haul again but not enough. We strike a submerged boulder with a loud thud and the boat bounces away and swirls on down. I haul frantically to bring the bows round. Two more lurches and a hard pull to the right and suddenly we're through. We're cruising along on choppy water the colour of brandy. I can see the bottom again to one side, only a few feet deep.

At lunchtime (actually ten o'clock, but we have to pretend it is lunchtime because we've been up for so long) we land on an island. It's a bit of my old farm that the river has decided to claim for itself. A flood channel has cut through a slip of meadow and stranded it and its bankside alders and willows between two running prongs of the stream. The island is going back to nature. Ungrazed and left to its own it is treeing up. It is a tangle of shrubbery and saplings all fighting for precious soils and the daylight. We tie the boat to a fallen log and carry our basket to a grassy spot at the water's edge. We explore the thin slip – about an acre – of island.

A dead ewe is hanging from a tree, jammed there by the flood, three feet above the matted grass. Her scrappy fleece has shrunk on to the skeleton like plastic wrapping on a frame. Her putrid body has drained out of her gaping mouth and a wide rent in her side, opened, I suspect, by hoodie crows. Other forces have been in there, too. We peer inside. Whatever she once had has gone. She is as hollow as a box. No guts, no liver or lungs, no heart, no udders – nothing but a backbone and ribs like the staves of a wrecked boat. Her eye hollows leer at us from bare bone. A blue-bottle crawls out of a shrivelled ear and careers off, buzzing. Her tongueless mouth yawns a perpetual boredom of teeth and parched skull. Hermione can't resist giving it a prod with a stick. A sexton beetle, *Nicrophorus*, tumbles out of the ewe's throat; its carapace is red and black in mottled contrast like a Roman tile. Hermione catches it in her hands and it scurries frantically out between her fingers and falls to the ground. This happens three times before she is content and lets it go. As we walk away we glance back. The ewe seems to be laughing.

We find where an otter has habitually left the water and entered it again, sliding down the bank on his tummy. We see his prints in the mud – recent, too. A stained patch of sick grass and woodrush tells us he urinates there – a liquid signpost to any lutrine callers. I think he was here this morning.

The sun is already hot. We sit on the bank and eat our soggy sandwiches, the rolls Lucy lovingly made for us last night, and we munch our biscuits. I lie back. The couch grass smells like cricket pitches years ago. I close my eyes and the sun is still too strong. I turn sideways. Hermione has found some red ants in the sandy soil; she is fending them off with a grass stem. I wonder how ants get off an island.

'Daddy, you're snoring.' I struggle back to the surface. I didn't mean to drop off. I raise myself up on to one elbow, blinking. Hermione is still quietly prodding ants beside me. Past her, over her hip, just there, not eight feet away the sleep-blur focuses on a face. It is wet and shiny. It sparkles. It is round like an old tomcat's. It has ears like aspen leaves, neat and curved. It has whiskers, stiff and hard, arrayed in a downward fan. Beads of water hang from them, catching the sun. Its fur is spiky, as though it has just been rubbed with a towel. Eyes like black pearls peer. It is transfixed. It stands square on; slightly pigeon-toed on short legs, broad-fronted like a strong dog. Its body rises behind it to a curved hump and a long, sleek tail curls down to the river. From its tip a trickle of water is running back to the river.

It is looking straight at us.

Thank God we are lying down. We don't look human. 'Don't move,' I growl at Hermione through my teeth so quietly and so sternly that she freezes. 'Otter. Turn *very* slowly.' Her eyes pass through mine like a cloud crossing a puddle and they keep going, slowly, gently, down the length of my body and out across the river, still panning, slowly ... slowly ... over her own legs and back into the bank behind her. Her head stops. I know she has connected.

The otter has not moved. He is astonished; he can't quite believe his eyes. Never before has he met a human on this island. He thought it was his: a place where he can slide in and out without a care. Somewhere to crunch his fish with needle teeth and roll in the spring grass. Perhaps he brings his mate here – perhaps *she* is the mate and she has a holt here, under the alder roots? I shall never know. I know that any second now he or she is going to turn and slip back into the river with scarcely a ripple. He will re-enter the river by melting. He will vanish in a ripple-thong. He will leave only the mark of his five spread toes in the sand and his liquid image seared into the quick of our singing amygdalae. I know that this is one of those million-to-one chance encounters that gild the lucky. Hermione may not see an otter like this again for years. I hold my breath.

I have often seen otters at Carnoch before. For many years I treated the farm as a nature reserve and we built an artificial holt in the bank to encourage them. One day my old friend Brian Jackman, who was then the wildlife correspondent for *The Sunday Times*, came to stay. He was writing a book on wildlife. More than anything else he wanted to see a wild British otter. I said I would give it a go. It was 13 March 1984. We rose early and left Aigas in a snow flurry. This was a man who was experienced and knowledgeable; a man who had stalked elephants in Amboseli, camped among lions in the Masai Mara and trekked for snow leopard in the Himalayas. I desperately wanted success for him. It was a long shot. In 1985 he published his account of our morning in *The Countryside in Winter*, illustrated by Bruce Pearson's delicate watercolours.

I had scouted the ground the night before. There was a fresh salmon kill on the bank and fresh prints in the mud. I was hopeful. We left before dawn and headed straight for the salmon. As we examined it I became aware of two otters staring at us from across the river. Brian's diary reads as follows:

They were swimming just under the bank: two fierce whiskered heads raised inquisitively in our direction. One dived almost at once. The other remained for at least a minute, as if intrigued by our presence; then it, too, submerged.

Moments later it reappeared and ran up the bank, whistling loudly as if looking for its companion . . . On land it romped along with a sinuous porpoise roll, displacing its thick fur so that it was no longer sleek and glistening but bristled with sharp points.

Back in the water it swam directly towards us, still piping anxiously and pushing a bow wave along with its blunt nose . . . this was a youngster which had not yet learned to fear man. Only when it was within 20 yards of us did it turn and dive.

All my life I have wanted to see a wild British otter. Now I had seen two in a morning. I looked at my watch. It was fifteen minutes since the otters had first appeared.

I am glad that my daughter has seen an otter in the wild. For me, after all these years at Aigas, it is a symbolic moment, like passing an exam. A musician must wish for his child to know music; must gladden when he or she makes each grade. Nature and wildness have been at the core of my work for so long. I have lived it by night and by day. I have striven to know its ways. That some shaft of deeper Aigas consciousness might colour the lives of my children always thrills me.

The otter is also a shadow of my past. I came to the Highlands of Scotland to work with Gavin Maxwell in 1968. His name is inextricably linked with otters after his brilliant and deeply personal exposition *Ring of Bright Water*, the book about his West Highland home, Camusfeàrna, and his ill-fated pet otters, Mij, Edal and Teko. It was published in 1960. In 1969 Gavin died suddenly of lung cancer. He was only fifty-five. I was out of a job and six hundred miles from home. At the time I thought I should have gone back. The chances of finding anything other than manual work in the Highlands at that time were very slim. But the words of the foreword to *Ring* haunted me:

> I am convinced that man has suffered in his separation from the soil and the other creatures of the world; the evolution of his intellect has outrun his needs as an animal, and yet he must still, for security, look long at some portion of the earth as it was before he tampered with it.

A year later we took those words and wrote them into the very foundations of what we were trying to achieve by creating a field centre, first at Guisachan, my former Highland home, and then in 1977 at Aigas. We wanted people who came here to see a swift and a wren and a golden eagle and to know them all. We wanted them to share the ash tree with us, and the rowan and the birch and the Scots pine. We wanted to show them a roe deer shining in the morning sun, and to understand a little of the pipistrelle bat and the otter as well. The long history of this place and the people who have lived their lives here with their stone circles and their black houses and crofts were essential elements, too, but above all we wanted people to see a bigger picture. We wanted them to locate themselves and perhaps the whole of humanity reflected in the sweeping, all-embracing cycles of this wild upland.

I don't know how long Hermione and I stared at that motionless otter, Maxwell's 'friendly daemon ... [who] ... put vetoes upon my reason and sent me to look for berries in the proper season'. It cannot have been much more than a minute. We saw his nose rise and his nostrils widen a fraction as he pulled us in, sucked in our shedding molecules and dragged them over his fizzing sensors. Without any hint of panic or alarm he turned and slid into the river. The last we saw was his wet, humped back disappearing below the rippling surface and a thin line of bubbles heading away downstream. In a whole minute you can absorb a lot of otter; an otter can absorb all it is ever likely to want of man. Neither Hermione nor I will ever forget that otter. He will never venture to the island in such happy innocence again.

There was nothing to say. We returned to our boat and set off down the river once more. We had many miles of the long, still pools of the river's maturity to explore.

SIXTEEN

The Awesome Winter

I, singularly moved
To love the lovely that are not beloved,
Of all the seasons, most
Love winter.

COVENTRY PATMORE, 1823–96

Here we live two lives, each utterly distinct from the other, like light and dark, war and peace, then and now. We have a winter presence and a summer one, almost as though we occupy two lands, shifting between them like migrating birds. If we meet strangers and they ask, 'What do you do?' I want to counter it with, 'Do you mean in summer or in winter?' It's as though in winter we think opposites, feel extremes, breathe another air, speak with another tongue. The two take on different meanings so that in summer there is the Aigas place and, quite apart, another Aigas winter place to which we are magic-carpeted on the winds of the turning year.

Outsiders find it hard to understand this division. City-dwellers whose worlds follow unseasoned cycles have scrolled their lives across such boundaries; they are no longer forced to metamorphose with the tilt of the earth. Central heating has blurred their perceptions and hauled in their sensations. No so here in the Highlands. Winter fires us up. It fuels our emotions, adjusts our routines, keens our edges, raids our houses and gift-wraps our vehicles. It causes us to take stock and reflect on the earth's spontaneous yield. It recharges our ambitions and locks us safely away like the trout beneath the ice until, in its own good time, it decides to hand us back our lives.

'What on earth do you do all winter?' folk sometimes ask us as if, like the swifts, we should have cleared off to Africa. But it isn't like that. Winter in the Highlands delivers up compensations as precious to us as the dawn chorus and the darkless nights of the summer solstice. It is a haven to which we slink off after the long season, a space for contemplation and spiritual renewal – a chance to think again. We also have a deal of work to do.

The field centre ploughs on until the very end of October; sometimes it spills into November if an Indian summer has fired the leaves on the geans and gilded those last glowing weeks of autumn. When our last guests depart we hurl our hats into the air as much with relief that we have survived intact as with smiling anticipation of the calm the close season brings. November immediately founders and sinks. We have denied time off to our dedicated staff all summer long; in November they try to catch up. December is a rush of office work to tie down the loose ends of the season just gone and to count the cost of being ready for the one just around the corner. Then Christmas and Hogmanay – two weeks of hopeless Scottish distraction. We give up and close down. Some things you cannot defeat – better to join the fray than rail against it. Suddenly it is mid-January; the new season is only six weeks away. We have seasonal helpers to find, interview and train, new expeditions and programmes to plan, facilities and equipment to repair and fresh paint to splash around. And they ask us what we do all winter! To a man we count down the days to the return of our students. Hats well thrown in November are eagerly donned in March.

For me *Zugunruhe* works in reverse. The shifting season settles me back with the calm of a prophecy I know will fulfil. It brings grace and a little poetry into my whirling days. I watch the high chevrons of greylag and pink-footed geese straggle into the Beauly Firth with growing peace and pleasure. Almost everything else has gone long since. The summer migrant birds are as fickle as the northern marsh orchids that so recently lent their episcopal splendour to the moors. Their moment has come and gone. By September I can't even find their spotted leaf whorls. They have shrunk back into the sphagnum, belying their eye-fixing panache of a month before. The furtive cuckoo has dealt its parasitic eggs about the hill and is long gone. One per nest, their fat, murderous chicks have been slavishly fed in programmed oblivion by meadow pipits and sedge warblers whose own hatchlings were ruthlessly evicted long ago by the cuckoo squab. As soon as the willow warbler has bred it moves out, leaving its adolescent young to pick aphids from the aspen leaves for a few weeks longer. The summer hangs in suspense as July gives way to August. The great green stain is everywhere and nature seems to take a breather. Bracken fronds, so delicate when they emerged, are now coarse and hard-edged. Life dawdles, uncertain what to do next. All subtlety coagulates in a moment of dull flatness, almost of stagnation. The clouds idle, seeming disinterested; the empty moors and corries whisper low conspiracy. In the woods only the song thrush gilds the shortening evenings.

Suddenly one morning I hear the robin's song falter. Gone is the melodious carillon that has graced the dawn chorus for many weeks. For reasons known only to itself and its genes, a staccato autumnal solo now tinkles in the still air. Screaming to be fed, young buzzards harass their parents from tree to tree. Red kites quarter the freshly cut stubble fields for dismembered mice and voles. At dusk rooks and jackdaws throng the avenue in huge flocks before settling to roost, raucous and persistent. Chittering nervously, the swallows and house martins gather and linger, waiting for their second broods of young to strengthen. But in late August the swifts just go – there one minute, knifing the air into vibrant wafers, a hollow emptiness the next. They've skimmed south. The longer cool nights have weakened the bug throng and the stars have had their say. Irresistible forces older than rock are drawing life out of the Highlands as surely as warmth drains from a corpse.

The whinchats that chinked from every broom bush are nowhere to be seen. Wheatears no longer pose on boulders and fence posts. Redstarts have abandoned the oaks on the drive and the spotted flycatchers have spotted flies elsewhere. The shadow of the osprey no longer strikes fear into the loch's trout and the wagtails, grey and pied, have deserted the dam. Common sandpipers whose thin cries echoed from the river banks all summer have dipped and flickered back to the coast for the long migration to the southern hemisphere. On the high moors the curlews have pulled out and the golden plover have ganged into robotic coveys, jinking this way and that, sometimes a hundred strong, heading down and away to the mud flats and across the North Sea to the Low Countries. The high corries whisper deliciously as if they are trying to tell you something, like a shell pressed to the ear. Only the ravens and hoodies are left to mob the golden eagle as he floats across empty moors. By the time the red deer stags have roared their last rutting challenges a dusting of snow has starched the high tops.

Our cheerful public have caught the mood. They have firesides of their own awaiting them across the many countries from which they come. For a few days, perhaps a week, we wonder what has hit us. The woods are silent and the shrieks of children have vanished from the avenue. The common-room door no longer bangs. The dinner gong is still. The clatter of cutlery and plates is missing from the kitchens and, like the osprey, our South African cook has taken flight to Cape Town. Her young kitchen helpers have lugged their laden backpacks down the staff stairs, hugged each other and promised to keep in touch. The hens in the paddock still parade the fence waiting for cook's ringing call and the scraps that now won't return until March. Seasonal rangers have honed their CVs on the office computers and handed in their maps, compasses and first-aid kits. The lawn-mowers are silent. A deafening hush descends.

Hugh Bethune is putting finishing touches to the log stack he has been quietly building all year long. Oh, the joys of a log pile! A good log pile is to winter as ice cream is to a sandcastle. Wrens have started to roost in its dry caves. *Uroceros* has drilled its future beneath the bark and the wood mice have invested in its dark interstices. They should be OK. We operate a three-year rotation to ensure the firewood is properly dry; wet wood clogs the chimneys with tar. If they have chosen their site well, deep in the heart of the eight-foot stack, there will be time enough for the mice to come though the winter in their moss and grass nests and for the horn-tail grubs to pupate safely in their powdery burrows.

Ground frost clinches the dew. Chloroplasts falter and fail. Sap slows and thickens. Xylem stagnates like a canal. The green stain of summer seems to read the stars, too; it leaches away in the night so that the leaves blush and pale. Early morning mists now shroud the river. Stinging nettles crumple and wilt. A gilded haze settles across the birchwoods. Rowanberries flare. Fieldfares and redwings, just in from Scandinavia on an east wind, bicker and heckle among the rowan's crimson clusters. Up in the pinewood fungi are shouldering the needle litter aside. Fly agarics, *Amanita muscaria*, in abrupt and forceful intrusion, are everywhere. Their seductive caps are loaded with hallucinogenic muscarine. Don't try them: their hallucinations can be permanent. They line the forest roads and the nature trails, prettily ramming their scarlet, white-scabbed domes into the light. Several delicate species of *Russula* toadstools stipple the woodland glades: one, sickly red with pallid gills, seems to deserve its name *emetica*, but still almost everything eats its crisp white flesh – slugs, voles, mice, squirrels, even the badgers have a go. It's hard to find one intact. Huge shaggy parasols, *Lepiota*, silently erect themselves under the western red cedars – the last place you need any shade. Stony paths are scattered with cupped *Peziza*, twists of orange-peel lying exactly as if they had been tossed aside by a child. The sky clears and the sun skirts the loch like Mars, low and red. Rust canters through the bracken. *Tricophorum*, the rod-bladed deer grass that shrouds the wet hollows on the hill, is suddenly touched so that a Tuscan glow of terracotta spreads across the whole moor in the slanting light, sharp and cool.

The gradual retreat since the year turned is now a rout. Life is diving for cover. Midges have done their worst and perished

under the moon. Golden-ringed dragonflies have stabbed their last ovipositors into the mud of the marsh, depositing one egg at a time; the abdomens of Highland darters have dipped among the browned lilies in a crimson curl. The green pads are sinking fast. Every day the red squirrels in the pinewood venture further afield. Last week it was blackberries they raided along the bank of the burn, now it is the hazel hedge behind the stables they're pillaging for nuts to bury frantically in the leaf litter. Their incisors are incising the clean flesh of the last saffron-fluted chanterelles under the birches, too. They seem to be hurrying, a deadline to meet. They filch loops of bacon rind from the bird tables at the house. They must put on fat and hoard their spoils away for the long dark days ahead. Far less rushed, and with agricultural aplomb, the badgers in the Tomich Wood are harvesting ripe bilberries and rolling bundles of grass and bracken bedding into their deep setts.

Lucy claims this is her high spot. It is the moment in the year she loves most – and she lives out a private harvest festival of her own for as long as she can make it last. I see her out foraging with a tartan scarf round her neck and a trug on her arm, now with a feast of chanterelles or the brown *Boletus* ceps shining like penny buns. Sometimes it's a hoard of rowanberries for the bitter jelly that glazes her venison roasts, or glossy blackberries she and Hermione have heaped in their wicker baskets.

Laced with cinnamon, the last apples and plums stew richly in huge aluminium pans on the Aga. Trays loaded with lidless jars of chutney stand cooling in the larders. The air is tart and steamy. She rummages among the last tortoiseshells and red admirals languishing through the herbaceous borders. Her secateurs snip and click. Always too late, the Jack Russells leap and snap at the butterflies that throng the buddleias sagging with riotous bloom. She sweeps into the hall with armfuls of Michaelmas daisies and sheaves of bronze dahlias, hurrying before the frosts get them, stacking them into extravagant, blowsy arrangements bursting with colour – static pyrotechnics in every room. The house takes on that autumnal aroma of heavy productivity, like new-mown hay but with the richer confusion of scents of a Parisian *parfumerie*. Not content with the wild palette of her garden and the woods, for the last groups of the year she scatters the scarlet and gold leaves of sugar maples across the white linen tablecloths on the dinner table. At night we lie awake and listen to the red deer stags roaring their throaty challenges in the woods all round us.

The year is exciting again, coming alive with new arrivals. The geese bridge the skies in long echelons and the rowans are strident with heckling redwings. Winter is coming. We're heading off. The sun, ninety-three million miles away, is doing its best. It just keeps on going, pumping out the nuclear radiation that has given us life, searing and soothing, invigorating and free. It's us who drift away as though we've lost interest. We're tilting and spinning into our long ellipse; it will take us further and further away.

One morning Hugh arrives for work looking more than usually grave and shaking his head. 'Have y' seen the Ben this morning?' He knows perfectly well that I haven't because Aigas is tucked in a hollow and you have to go a few miles up the road to see Ben Wyvis – literally, 'the awesome mountain' – simply known round here as the Ben. Awesome is right. All summer its three thousand four hundred feet loom above us to the north like a dead brontosaurus lying lumpily all on its own on the moors. It has a long, humped back and a fat tail called Little Wyvis stuck on like a child's plasticine model of a monster that has lost its head. The locals, virtually none of whom has trodden its tundra summit (nor would most of them ever consider doing so), eye it suspiciously, expecting it to bring bad news. It usually does.

Had I seen the Ben, I would have noticed it was white. You can hardly miss it. In the night somebody thoughtful had placed a pure white shroud over the poor dead beast. It happens every

November. It must be something to do with the way the easterly air circles the mountain, chilling its cloud into the first snows, layering them round like a bandage. It stands stark against the burnt umber of the heather moors all round it, glowing and slightly sinister. There's a fair chance that snow will now lie all winter long, locked in its subtle gullies until May. Winter has arrived on the Ben. I hope its ptarmigan are dressed for the party. If they're not, the golden eagles that nest on a crag on the north of Glen Glass most years will have high sport until their prey, the grouse of the high tops, have completed their moult to startling white. The fat wattles of summer are trimmed down to a thin red crescent above the eye. It doesn't do to be caught out. The Ben's first snow is a forerunner, a message writ plain – awesome. Ignore it at your peril.

There is no guarantee of a white winter, even here above the 57th Parallel. Looking back down the years I have lived here, I fancy they were more frequent back then than now. 'That'll be the global warming then,' say the locals with a tone of total resignation that suggests the apocalypse might also not be far away. But there is a guarantee of *some* snow, and always of bitter cold. I have never known a winter without a smattering of white weeks even if it has been flushed away almost as quickly as it arrives by slicing wind and rain. But every now and again, like last year, we have the real thing, the proper climate everyone else on our latitude gets – no nonsense.

The warm westerly air stream that awards us our gentle climate in summer and permits palm trees to survive on the west coast of the Highlands is our prevailing wind. It is the one we expect. We count on it. It keeps us lush and green in summer, the moorland peat boggy and the burns tinkling. But every so often a high-pressure zone circles round us like a soaring buzzard, bringing cold, dry air from the north and east – from Franz Joseph Land. If those two clash, like Zeus and Kronos, they feud mightily. They wage war. If the chill Arctic air wins, we have a blizzard on our hands – and our feet, and in our eyes and ears, and stinging into our cheeks as we scuttle from the car to the house. It clogs the Victorian parapets; it loads the trees so that they bow and break, and immaculately feathers itself across the lawns like an eiderdown. Then comes the frost. Silent, hard, clear and cutting, it crusts the eiderdown and sugars the trees. Pearls hang from the telegraph wires. The bushes and fences grow crystals like salt. Ear rims tingle and burn. Noses glow. Ghost-like, every breath hangs in the air. Feet give away hard intelligence.

At first light I am out. I want to see the evidence for myself before the dogs and cars churn it up and Hermione bundles the eiderdown up into a snowman. I want to see who has been calling in the ever-growing night. The first snow is a precious page in the book of Aigas. The suspicions of the summer can be confounded or confirmed in a few minutes. Lucy thinks a fox has been staking out the hen house for some weeks. Occasionally we have caught his uric pungence on the morning air. The Jack Russells have quivered excitedly and piddled against the hen-run posts, having their say. Now we know. There he is. Not even his legendary cunning can hide this vivid incrimination.

The oval spoor of a big dog fox is plain to see, his single file weaves in and out of the bushes, skirts the pond and crosses the lawn we call the Tear Drop. Nor is he alone. A smaller, lighter trail stitches around him almost as if they are working together, harrying the shrubbery for whatever they can flush out; slightly apart, the vixen lurks in ambush. They have circled the hen house twice, once in each direction. I can see where he has stood stock still for several seconds; his front pads are only a foot from the locked hatch. Their warmth has melted deeper – listening. He has heard the hens shuffle uncomfortably, the nearest only two inches of board and wire away from his tingling nose. Five faint dimples pock-mark the snow crust. Saliva. He turns away, walking slowly, looking back.

A few yards out into the paddock the vixen has squatted while she waits. A yellow stain has seeped between her spread pads. Then they have taken off together across the moonlit whiteness; a few yards apart, loping an even, gently winding pace up the hill towards the loch. I let the hens out and stand back to watch. They seem wholly oblivious of their visitor. God was not kind to the hen. She has so little brain that she is condemned to the lower ranks of the creator's pyramid. She is fair game for anything with teeth or claws. Daily her eggs are filched from beneath her bottom and she never seems to notice. When a predator strikes she doesn't seem to carry a gene for preservation at all.

We can't keep hens. Note the verb – *can't*, not don't. We do, about twenty mixed reds and a few Aberdeen rangers, and some Scot's dumpies and a bantam cockerel thrown in for Hermione who adores their fluffy chicks. But they're ephemeral. They pass through Aigas like passage migrants, transmogrifying involuntarily from witless but happy free-range worm-peckers to something's next meal. The first we know is when the Jack Russells find a broken hand of mangled pinions beneath a rhododendron bush. Foxes, wildcats, pine martens – especially pine martens – passing otters, toothless and grumpy old badgers, all have a go, especially in the short nights of high summer when the stupid birds are fooled by the light and think they don't have to return to the hen house to roost. Lucy sighs and replaces them – her resignation an acceptance as much of being married to a naturalist as of the reality of living up a Highland glen. At least this time the foxes went hungry.

Tracking is like reading. Once learned it willingly delivers up its secrets. The alphabet is short and simple, but the languages, one for each species, are many and varied. In the long winter nights when there is no other way of monitoring the movements of wildlife, the snow reads like a thriller. Hermione and I take off into the woods and fields, small gloved hand in large, feet crunching and breath clouding our faces as we toil up the hill. As we pass the kitchen garden we stop to marvel at the chicken wire honeycombed in sparkling white. She can't resist pinging it and watching the snow fall away like icing sugar. Fat, fleshy flakes have awarded each fence post a four-inch hat, cuboid and slightly domed. We pass through the wicket gate and into the Garden Field, following the snowshoe scamper of a brown hare.

To a naturalist, a virgin snowfield is like turning back to an older, pristine age. For as long as it lasts, and until one sets foot upon its perfection, the presence of man is subordinated to a few dulled wrinkles beneath the skin. The land is purged as though the glacier has come again in the night, wiping it clean. One embarks upon a new journey, an expedition into a purer nature where man is not acknowledged, has not visibly interfered. I tell Hermione not to look back. Behind us our footprints lead back to the imperfections of knowledge and the frailties of our human world. Ahead lies an Edenesque freshness of dazzling beauty and pure adventure.

Out in the field we find that the red deer have been down in the night; the shining pasture is criss-crossed with their slots and bald scrapes where they have pawed the snow to reach the grass beneath. Khaki droppings have burned their way through the ice crust and lurk, shining like green ingots, two inches down.

As we approach the wood on the far side we find a drama written out for us on the pristine parchment. Thin trails from tiny feet thread from hole to hole. Wood mice, *Apodemus*, have surfaced and skipped daringly over the crust. They make a skiff, barely an indentation, five inches between bounds, and then they're down again, tunnelling under the snow in relative safety. We count them: 'There's one! There's another, and another.' Excited, Hermione runs from one lacework trail to the next. Vole tracks are smaller and closer together. We get a feel for just how many mice and voles this rough old pasture must support. There's activity every few yards. Hermione shouts, 'Daddy!' I hurry over. She is crouched over an imprint so complete, so immaculately created and with such starkly engraved emotion that it rivals Edvard Munch's *The Scream*. A mouse trail like all the others skitters along the surface. It is even, measured and tells only of pulsating life. Then the trail ends. Night talons have snatched from nowhere and the thread is abruptly consumed in a skirmish of shining crystals. To either side, etched with exquisite precision and symmetry, are the whole flowing wings of the tawny owl, spreading and drawn softly across the page. There is each soft pinion, each leading edge, every filament delicately inscribed, fixed for a moment in time by the sealing frost. At the heart of the skirmish glows a tiny garnet of ice-blood. We skirt round it in silence.

In the wood the snow has only made it to the forest floor where there are clearings. Here the trees are weighted and bowed, looking troubled. Hermione runs from one to another with a cry of delight, tugging at branches that shed their load in a glistening shower; she laughs as they spring back into the bright air. The badgers are about. It's not yet cold enough for them to have holed up in their bracken beds. Their sturdy, five-toed pads and long claws are easy to read and we find their rootlings every few yards where they have dug and tugged, snuffled out some tuber or luckless beetle. We see where they have dunged in shallow pits with all the careful presence of a house cat in a litter tray.

When we reach the loch the sun is so bright that we have to squint at the brilliant ice sheet that greets us. We have a rule. A full week of continuous frost lower than twenty-three degrees Fahrenheit, night and day, must elapse before anyone tries to walk on the loch. Even then we test it carefully by cutting holes with an axe. Five inches is the minimum for walking: no skating or fun and games until there are eight inches of ice in several different test holes. I learned the hard way many years ago.

It was very cold. The ice was very thick. I had stamped on it, jumped up and down, and hurled a rock at it as hard as I could. But I knew that at the far end of the eight acres, where the burn enters from the birchwood, there was said to be a deep spring, now flooded by the dam the Victorians built to create a water supply for the house. Springs don't freeze. Moving water only freezes in extreme conditions. Underground water never freezes. So, with my daughter Melanie, then five years old, following a safe distance behind, I set out across the loch to mark where it wasn't safe. I carried a can of orange aerosol paint to inscribe an arc across the dangerous corner so that the children could skate and play in safety. I found it.

The ice collapsed beneath me like a trapdoor. I plunged vertically to my armpits, supporting my weight on spread arms. There was no warning, no boom, no cracking or tipping of floes – just a sudden plunge. The ice had formed. It was several inches thick, but it was soft. Only the top inch was hard. The movement of slightly warmer water rising beneath had kept it from clinching through in that final concrete grip. At less than a quarter of my weight, Melanie, only three feet away, was fine.

I tried to haul myself out but the edge kept breaking away under my weight. I urged Melanie away, retracing our steps across the loch, back to the dam so that she could run down to the house for help. I was alone in the loch for about fifteen minutes before they arrived with a ladder and a rope and hauled me clear. It was a revealing experience. I have concluded that the *Titanic* was rough luck, and a grievous loss of life, but I no longer feel sorry for those who died in the freezing sea. I do not believe they suffered. As I waited I remember thinking of Gino Watkins, the brilliant young explorer whose reputation at twenty-five already rivalled that of Scott and Shackleton. He died on 20 August 1932 when a calving glacier separated him from his kayak while out seal hunting in the Arctic Ocean off Greenland. With colossal bravery and knowing it was his last slender chance of survival, he shed his clothes and swam after his boat. He caught it but was unable to climb aboard. He clung helplessly to the stern until the freezing sea overcame him and he slid finally and tragically away.

It is cold – of course it is – and one fears for one's life as in any severely threatening situation, but the cold and the anxiety are quickly quelled. A warm glow infuses the freezing limbs as the blood withdraws from the capillaries to protect the vital organs. Nerves rapidly chill to numbness. I was in up to my chest. My thrashings had thoroughly wetted my arms, which were pinned to the ice to support me. I could no longer feel anything with my hands. My body ended at my breast bone. Whatever was below had gone, sloughed off like a lizard's tail. When they put a rope round my chest and hauled me out – I was unable to hold the rope – and dragged me on to firm ice, they asked, 'Can you get up?' My brain heard and understood the words, but no longer had any authority. I am told that I smiled. It was all I could do. No other muscles would respond. They might as well not have been there. Worse, I was in no pain or distress. I was glowing and a cosy well-being was spreading through me. I was happy. There was no question of getting up. I just wanted them to leave me lying on the ice so that I could drift, like Gino, gently into permanent sleep.

But, of course, Peter and Rob and the other rangers were far too professional to allow anything of the sort. I was hauled off and rudely bundled into a vehicle. At the house I was dumped in a lukewarm bath and my temperature was slowly brought back to normal. Now that *was* painful. It passed through in waves searing like toothache. I lay groaning in its long, slow torment. My white toes were unable to tell whether the incoming water was hot or cold as I lay out the agony of refilling flesh.

Today the loch is magnificent. The snow-covered ice shines and sparkles. I recount the tale of fifteen years before to Hermione. 'Are you *sure* it's safe?' she demands. We go to the Illicit Still and get an axe. I hack a hole. Five inches: enough to hold, but not enough to risk it. We decide to skirt round the edge and explore the marsh where we can't normally go. Here, almost invisible in the snow, a slight mound crusted with frost turns out not to be snow. It is a dead swan. It's a whooper, named for its whooping call, the wild swan of the Arctic just in on the north wind. It has come to our loch to die. It waded out into the marsh and sank on to the ice to die. We brush off the sparkling crystals from its yellow nares, as bright as the wild flags that bloom here in May. Its eyes are shut, the neck as graceless as a stick. We prise its stiffness from the ice. I am still carrying the axe and I have to chip away to release its feet. Hermione spreads a black foot, which creaks like an old leather purse. The tough webs uncrease and splay, revealing the powerful paddle. The black leg is strong, the bones short and stout. She folds it away again. She is sad. There is no clue why it died, but there are many possibilities. I ease my fingers up the feathers to its breast bone, which is hard and sharp. The bird is emaciated.

I explain that many swans carry lead from gunshot wounds; that irresponsible sportsmen get bored and take a pot shot at swans for the hell of it. Or that it has taken in lead shot with its food from the bottom of a loch or pond where wildfowlers have shot duck for generations. This poisons swans and geese. They sicken; they don't feed, so they die. Or, again, careless fishermen abandon their nylon cast and hooks in the water and these get eaten or stuck in the bird's gullet or innards so that it starves. We extract a pinion – a long, rigid quill for her feather collection – and leave the corpse on the marsh. The foxes at least will be pleased.

The whoopers are like the Ben. They are a climacteric from which there is no turning back. During the long green summer we forget them, put them out of mind and concentrate on swifts and ospreys. We never see them go. In April they're there on Finlay MacRae's river fields in their dozens, whiter than surf, standing about in wet patches softly fluting to each other like a wind quartet warming up. When they're disturbed their necks erect and stiffen like yellow-handled walking sticks. They strut nervously, priming themselves for flight. They carry the tautness of the true wild, quite different from the posed, voluptuous ogees of the mute swan. These are finer and purer than the mutes. Mutes belong to lakes and city park ponds, boating resorts and May calendar pages. They are the clichés of the wildfowl world, not to be taken seriously, there for snapshots and sandwich crusts. One day in late April, sometimes just into May, the whoopers are gone. Finlay is pleased to see the back of them. Now his muddy patches can green up. They've left in the night – a moonlight flit – tugged away by the stars and the lengthening days, heading north by north-east to an Arctic wilderness still locked in winter.

It's not Finlay's winter barley that keeps them on the river fields, although he could be forgiven for thinking it is, but the deep knowledge that if they go too early, when they arrive in Iceland or Finno-Scandian Lapland, to whichever of these two populations our whoopers belong (I don't know), there will be nothing to eat and no water to land on. Their breeding grounds are only three or four days' flying away – give or take a few rest stops on southern Scandinavian lakes on the way. May can be a winter month in the Arctic. The whoopers need a sharp rise in temperature to thaw the tundra bogs and lakes and to rouse the first green lances for feed. Once they're gone, for six whole months, we never give them a thought.

But their return, their late October arrival to the strath, bugling their wild, haunting, blood-tingling voices across the night sky, is one of the most stirring moments of the incipient Highland winter. They seem to be dragging winter with them from the far north where I went as a young man to try to discover the true meaning of wilderness for myself.

Polar wastes have always drawn me. Avidly I read Scott and Shackleton and Cherry-Garrard, Amundsen and Nansen. I was astounded by the ineptitude of Franklin. By the age of twenty I was determined to go. First I went to the far north of Scandinavia, to Varangerfjorden where Norway curls around Finland and Russia. I was anxious to see what Scotland might have looked like soon after the ice cap retreated. I was intrigued by the notion that Scandinavia was still recovering from the release from the great ice burden that had depressed the landmass by as much as two thousand feet at the height of the last Ice Age. Right now, isostatic rebound is still lifting the land out of the sea by up to a third of an inch a year. I discovered the horror of the Arctic summer. I met black fly for the first time.

In subsequent years, accompanied by a team of friends, I

took modest winter expeditions to Lapland. This, almost more than any other, was an experience that was to help me to understand the Highlands and the Aigas place. We ploughed our Land-Rovers up the Arctic Highway, trekked with our Sami guide across the frozen wastes of Sarek and tramped through the silent primeval forests of Muddus and Padjelanta. We found the trails of lynx and wolverine, fingered the scored bark where a brown bear had gouged its territorial markings, deep and terrific. We met huge bull moose in the willow scrub and stalked the clicking hooves of reindeer herds through virgin spruce forest. We found the old Scots pine forests of five thousand years ago, the bountiful Highland forests for which our Neolithic men and women broke rock, where they raised their thatched rondavels and for which they lugged their boulders up to the Iron Age fort.

One searingly cold January day in a wild corner of Lapland we emerged from a spruce forest into a vast clearing of snow waste. In the low sunlight it looked like a desert of pink and white oyster-shell ridges and humps stretching as far as the eye could see. It was a bog. Far north of the Arctic Circle the permafrost prevents ground drainage and the summer thaw fills pools of swamp where, among other delights, the black fly breed. Now, in midwinter, it was locked in ice. We set out to cross it.

Every fifty yards or so we came across humps that were raised higher than the surrounding bog. They were circular and artificial in a way that defied the wild asymmetry of the swamp. I climbed on to one. It seemed soft despite its frozen rigour. I pulled away the powdery snow with my mittened hands and dug into its matted interior. There I found a frozen egg. It was large and white, as smooth and heavy as a large pebble from a shingle beach. It was unmistakably a swan's egg, addled and dead. The realisation dawned that we had happened upon a whooper nesting ground. In the middle of this great swamp where they would be relatively safe from predators like Arctic foxes and wolves, surrounded by open water and quaking sphagnum, and among a patchwork of sedge pools, the swans had come to heap their soggy mounds. As I looked around me I could see them in every direction. There were dozens of them, like the systematically repeating relief pattern on a huge counterpane of icy crêpe de Chine.

I stood holding that egg for some minutes, allowing the image to fill. I pictured the swans picturesquely dotted across the landscape atop their mounds. Nearby the cobs lazily dabbled and preened. I thought of them arriving in long undulating skeins, bugling softly to those already down as they circled and planed in on the peeling water. I imagined them with their little flotillas of grey cygnets sifting through the sedge tangle, grubbing their ochre faces across scummy pans for the rich animal and vegetable vichyssoise that will grow them quickly through the short summer. I visualised them gathering into flocks hundreds strong as the September days shortened, thrashing the water into foam as they tested their newly grown pinions and their strength for the long haul ahead.

When they arrive at Aigas they come up the river in the night. They have landed somewhere out on the firth and broken up into small wintering flocks of ten or fifteen. They have favourite feeding grounds to revisit; habitual river fields must be checked out. For the last few years a flock has arrived here in October and stayed until the frosts become too keen when they move back to the mud flats of the estuary. That sound summons me from my bed as surely as the dawn chorus. I lean from the window to hear their haunting bugles echoing across the valley, hoping to see the moonlight flash on their broad silver wings.

And here we are on the frozen marsh standing over this silent corpse. Perhaps it was weak when it started and the long migration was too much for it. No insight here. Hermione clutches her quill. There won't be much on it for the foxes, but in winter scavengers can't be fussy. We move on. It doesn't do to stand about on cold days.

This brief foray is one we shall repeat many times over the coming months. The daylight will shorten and fail. By Christmas it will close down to a twilit six hours between ten and three. We shall wake to the hoarse barking of foxes etching the January nights when they are pairing off and mating. There will be thaws and floods and days of interminable rain and sleet so grim that the dogs refuse to leave their basket by the Aga. Hugh and Duncan will work in the woods until the heavy snow comes. They are thinning and brashing the plantations we are returning to native woodland.

Then comes the cold. Outside work ceases. Every night the land hardens with frost. Unable to work on the nature trails, Sarah Kay, our head ranger, tends the stable-bound horses. Their hot, sweet breath plumes from impatient nostrils, heads tossing with frustration at not being able to go out, as wheelbarrows and pitch forks clatter around them. Emma, my step-daughter home from university for Christmas, spends her days strapping their glowing coats, combing out manes and tails and repairing and oiling their tack. The manure pile steams its sweet odours into air as clear as gin and the friendly reek of hoof oil and Stockholm tar loiters in the yard.

We eye the thermometer nervously. It takes just five days of continuous frost to get into buildings. We drain all water we can. We check the lagging everywhere else. We turn up the heating. Every once in a while the temperature plummets so sharply that we experience continental cold like Canada or Russia. Minus eight degrees Fahrenheit is the coldest we have ever recorded at Aigas. Forty degrees of frost: a cold so severe that metal burns your hands; skin freezes to it instantly so that when you pull away the skin tears. A felling axe left carelessly on the ground freezes so that it appears to be set in concrete. The handle snaps off at the head if you try to lever it free. Oil thickens to gel. Diesel coagulates so that engines won't run. Agricultural implements weld to the mud beneath them and can't be moved. Wrens clot in their communal roosts like a ball of bees. Icicles hang from the shaggy coats of the Highland cattle so that they jingle as they walk. Trees die of thirst; their root hairs become so locked in frozen ground that they cannot take in water at all. The ice on the loch is now many inches thick. As it expands it cracks and booms like a Howitzer, eerily hollow and resonant so that we stop work and look up, alarmed. Fracture lines have shot across the middle, splitting it from end to end like forked lightning. A tectonic pressure ridge rises along it, emulating the mountains.

The locals say that such winters are good: they clean the ground, killing off bugs and pests, somehow rendering the world cleaner and fresher in the spring. Frankly, I doubt it. I don't believe that nature so readily fools itself. Besides, life has been clearing out for weeks. What do we imagine sent the swifts to Africa and the golden plover to the Dutch polders? Those species that stay *have* thought it through. They have ideas of their own. *Uroceros* pupae are smugly insulated in their woody tunnels and the aquatic dragonfly larvae have crept into the mud way below the loch's ice. The adder has gone to ground in deep hibernation, coiled in her borrowed burrow beneath the heather. The badgers are curled into the foetal position and snoring ponderously in their musky sets. The pipistrelle bats have crept far into crevices in stone walls and roofs. They have deserted their summer roosts at the Illicit Still to find safer sanctuary from the worst cold. They have become torpid; their hearts slow down, their breathing rate dwindles and their body temperature falls away until they are barely ticking over. Energy stored as fat in the last moth-filled days of autumn can be eked out for weeks by the secret of hetero-thermic torpor. They can stay like this for up to three months. It's not necessarily a full hibernation – if a warm spell occurs they will awaken, warm up and fly out to feed – but it does allow them to sleep out the frost without expending much energy when, anyway, the moonlit nights are void of winged insects. If a warm-blooded mammal like the pip can produce a trick like that, just as the wren lays hyper-clutches of eggs to recover from her winter losses, I don't believe that the infinitely specialised and imaginative world of insects and other invertebrates, which have the added advantage of being cold-blooded, can't manage the same.

Now is the winter of our utter contentment. We have done all we can to protect our property and our animals. Our short days become a brief sally into the knife-edged air to feed the cattle and horses, the sheep and the hens, and then a rapid retreat to the Aga-warm kitchen for hot broth and rich lunchtime stews. Then to the fireside. I call it 'caveman's telly'. Birch and gean logs as dry as biscuits are piled one on another and stacked round with our own peat from the hill. The combination creates a fire with the heart of a lion; the unforgettable sweet fragrance of peat smoke permeates the whole house. Blue smoke plumes vertically into the fine air, as it has done here at Aigas since man first arrived all those thousands of years ago. It is a time to tackle the pile of books that have accumulated during the long summer. As Christmas approaches Hermione and Lucy play games such as snakes and ladders and Monopoly on the hearthrug. The floor is littered with shards of bright paper like a galaxy. This year Hermione is making all her own cards.

Tea is a feast of Scotch pancakes and blackberry jam, rich fruitcake and griddle scones glistening with butter. Puccini plays softly and laughter rings us round. The children are all home for Christmas, all seven of them – James, Hamish and Emma, my step-children, as well as my four – and the house is full of whispering and rustlings and secrets badly kept. There are rituals to perform: clad in scarves and mufflers the girls collect barrowloads of holly bright with scarlet berries – if the hysterical Scandinavian thrushes have left us any. The boys choose a Norway spruce from the conifer woods and erect it in the hall. The field centre season seems far away but every day the postman brings us word of those new friends we have made; colourful cards tell of other winter joys far away. The days are short and the nights are dark and long, but never so dark nor long that the pine marten rests. In the morning I know that his tracks will be there, all round the house, checking us out for anything with which to stave off the winter chill.

SEVENTEEN

A Place Called Aigas

The earth does not argue,
Is not pathetic, has no arrangements,
Does not scream, haste, persuade, threaten, promise,
Makes no discriminations, has no conceivable failures,
Closes nothing, refuses nothing, shuts none out.

WALT WHITMAN, 1819–92

Last night was humid. I was restless. It is late July and we have had warm weather – some would say hot – for a month. At the end of every day the young staff head off to the loch to swim. Yesterday I swam, too, Hermione insisting that I witness her latest achievement: a running jump and a mighty splash, ringing the loch with laughter. The cooling water restored my humidity-dulled senses; it sent me to bed in a drift of calm and contemplation.

When my mother was six years old she contracted rheumatic fever and was nursed by nuns in a French convent. Thinking she was about to die, a wise old nurse told her to live every minute of every day to the full and then, at bedtime, before she fell asleep, she should make a habit of leafing back over the whole day in minute detail in her mind's eye, reassessing her words and actions, pondering her judgements, smiling again at bright moments of happiness. My mother passed it on to me at an early age. I have tried, not very successfully, to do it all my life.

Too often I don't get very far; sleep tugs me off despite my keenness to commit to memory the special events of the moment. But last night was good. The loch had salved my weariness and allowed me to freewheel into one of those half-dreams that load the space between full consciousness and the deeps of first, welcome sleep. At such times I find that I can see things with an extra clarity; that words come fluently, and that long-running conflicts miraculously resolve themselves with transparently rational solutions, suddenly so blatantly obvious that I wonder why on earth I hadn't thought of them before. In this all-revealing lucidity I imagined myself taking off on my old horse, up the hill into the night as we have done hundreds of times by day. We passed the loch as black as glass under the trees. The moon had spilled her cup and a pale stream of silver chastened the shadows of the far shore. The old pinewood, God's best thought hereabouts, was silent. On the edge of the moor the bracken spread before us like an ocean. It is in full canopy now and its pressing fronds polish my boots as we pass through. I don't know where I am going but I have a sense of being drawn there by an unseen hand. It's not alarming, but familiar and safe, like going home. We follow the neat trail Duncan and his rangers have just strimmed clear through the broom. No sabre-toothed tigers here. Barney ploughs on, the solid rhythm of his pace swaying me back and forward so that the saddle softly creaks and sighs. We pass the hut circles without a pause. At the old peat banks the bog cotton, *Eriphorum*, is in full white tuft, glowing like stars as we skirt round on the firm edge. We turn on to the old peat cutters' road across the heather; snorting like a navvy, Barney throws himself into the steep haul up the slope to the Iron Age fort. At the top there is nowhere else to go. We stand like a military bronze surmounting some grand palace gate. At that moment the moon slides free from cloud and the valley looms up at me in hard-edged monochrome. I can see the glinting river and the shiny tanks of the Lovat fish farm far below. I see no movement except the rise and fall of light as veils of cloud wisp across the moon, almost full, like whirling dancers.

My half-dreamed imaginings have brought me here to rewind the past. They deal in pure imagery; working up pictures from the fragments of truth Aigas has delivered up to me across the years. It is as though I have been brought here to stand and watch my life passing by, and the lives of the hundreds of others who have touched this place in joy and in laughter, in pain and in grief. Lives heading backwards down the centuries like water tumbling over rapids, every boulder an exclamation, a sensation – a quickening presence spent in this beautiful land.

Night passes into day. The sun is hot and flies buzz round us so that Barney throws his head and lashes his tail. I have to keep an eye open for clegs – horse flies – which land surreptitiously and you only feel them after their blade-like mandibles have made the incision and delivered their egregious fix of anti-coagulant. Out over the valley a red kite, so recently reintroduced to the Highlands, wheels and banks. It wears a pale blue wing tag, clearly visible as it spirals nonchalantly past. I watch its forked tail twist and veer; it seems to be winnowed by the hazy air like wafting chaff. As I look around I see that the Aigas I know is no longer there. I don't recognise any of the woods, most of which are birch and pine, and the gardens have gone. Instead, the level land is all cultivated; women and children are working rigs, tiny strip fields, with crude hand tools and carrying heavy loads of compost in creels on their backs. The dancing heads of oats, nearly ready for harvest, wave and ripple in the afternoon sun. There are no roads, only pony tracks. As I pan around the valley I am astonished to see how many folk live here. I can see scores of them dotted about all over the land; even high into the moors they are tending goats and black cattle. Black houses are scattered about the land in places where I never knew they had existed, some well into

high ground I have only ever known as heather and planted forests. Instead of the lonely crofts at Craigdhu, Tomich and Oldtown, there are heather-thatched cottages in little clusters lining the flood plain every few hundred yards. Fresh peat banks scar the hill behind me with black incisions; rows of drying peat stacks wall the view like ramparts. Threads of musky peat smoke lace the summer air. Two young boys, younger than Hermione, perhaps only eight or nine, are herding seventeen black cows and calves past me, on up the broad, well-used track to the green slopes of Bad a' Chlamhain.

I turn to the quarry and find it is not there, nor, of course, is the fish farm on the other side. Gone, too, is the little church at Eskadale, although many graves still stand inside the dry-stone wall – this was a clan graveyard for MacRaes and Frasers long before the neat little church was built. At the ferry there are three houses crowding the river bank and three rowing boats are moored with young boys and an old man in attendance. A fourth boat is crossing the swift stream carrying two women; a youth tugs at the oars, heading obliquely upcurrent. A dog barks hysterically from the landing.

In the distance, both upriver to the mountains and downstream to Kilmorack, I am struck by the absence of trees. A few small pockets of birchwood fringe the steep ground, and straggly clumps of pines caress occasional high knolls. But above the Crask and rimming the skyline right round to the loch is a pinewood of dark, rounded crowns. I cannot see the extent of this wood, but a twist of smoke tells me that men are at work up there – making charcoal perhaps, or felling timber for their building needs.

This, I lie and think, is as close to the golden age of Gaeldom as I can imagine – if ever there was one. But for all its gilded images, the trees here are in decline. The forest is being forced back like an ageing adversary. It is a sure signal that the ecosystem is overloaded. If times were golden they could not remain so for very long. Ultimately, we are all dependent upon nature's munificence. Here the restoration cycle was too ponderous, too slow in these northern, sliding climes. Natural capital was being consumed at a rate accelerated by a deteriorating climate. With the inevitability of rain from a leaden sky on a dreich day, sooner or later it would drag the Highlanders down. Too many people; too many needs. The result was always bound to be poverty and despair. In the words of my old friend Dr John Morton Boyd, 'the Highlands simply did not have the resources to give'. If ever there was a lesson for the planet it was here in the Highlands in the seventeenth and eighteenth centuries.

Yet my image depicts country folk at peace with themselves, if not entirely so with their neighbours over the mountain and further south. I see a tribal people deeply and emotionally involved with their land. Their increasing numbers and their omnipresence, using every corner of soil, every birch glade and piny spur, all make me comprehend that for all its loneliness, for all its stark beauty and its wild and mysterious aura, nothing in the Aigas place I have known all these years is pristine. Nothing is untouched, no sense of frontier exists, no hint of the wilderness for which my soul craved.

This stark truth banished any idea of sleep. I slipped out of bed. At the window, flung wide, I stood and listened to the soft breathing of the night. Nothing moved. Somewhere deep in the dark, resinous dens of the huge, one-hundred-year-old *Thuja* clumps, long-eared owlets creaked like an unoiled gate swinging in a wind. Down on the river a heron coughed its bucolic curse. I drank a glass of our sweet cold water and returned to bed. I lay pondering images. The percipience of the floating hours was still with me, still running clear, like our water, soft and pure, piped straight from the loch.

The rush of excitement I had experienced as a young man when I first came to live here had much to do with my preconceived notion of the wildness of these hills and this glen. The Highlands and Islands were fresh and new and different. They sparked a frisson of separateness; they glistened and shone like wet rock in their exciting distinction from the rural idyll of my English childhood. As the years have slipped by that first rush has matured into a much deeper awareness of the land and its people, past and present. Its mysteries have slowly unravelled and the wildness of its nature has drawn closer to hand – become intimate and personal. I saw vividly that my own perceptions back then mirrored those of so many of our guests, especially those from overseas. I could now see, stark and clear like moonlight cutting across the polished water of the loch, that the ongoing challenge of our task was to retain that first buzz and to diffuse it gently throughout the purifying processes of truth and reality.

Images began to swirl again. Clouds raced across my vision. I was back on Barney at the fort, just like before, but the journey was far from over. The ancient storytellers of the Gaelic clans, the *seanchadh* (pronounced *shennuchy*), the official recorders of legends and tales in every glen, had much yet to reveal. Barney, tolerant as ever, is bored. He plucks at the broom and champs. He doesn't really like its tart, leguminous taste. The sun is hot on my face, so I nudge his great rump round to the south. On scarcely flickering wings a kestrel hovers a hundred yards out in front of me at my eye level; I can see his head angling as his powerful predatory orbs scour the rocky slope below us. He shifts effortlessly from level to level, inscribing his shrill notes into staves of thickening air. His back and wings are exactly the Tuscan hue that glows from the pink sandstone of the house when it is fired by the evening sun. I know he nests on the sheer face of the quarry. I turn to look. The quarry is not there. Below me I now find a new Aigas I have never seen before. There are no moors, as I have known them in my time. The heather has withdrawn to a few dark caps topping the high slopes; instead, a sea of green grass and birch woodland laps around me. The black houses are gone, as is the peat cutter's road. The hut circles are now full rondavels with built-up walls and high, cone-shaped roofs of reed thatch. Wood smoke loiters through fine air. The scene is pitched somewhere in the late Bronze or early Iron Age of about three to four thousand years ago. The people living here are thought to be the predecessors of the Picts. Stone and earth walls divide the land into small crop-filled enclosures. Around the perimeter goats and cattle and a few sheep idly graze. Men and women are working in tiny walled fields, and up on Luncheon Rock small children are playing a game. They are wearing rough homespun clothes and sleeveless leather jerkins. Jewellery adorns the women: bracelets, anklets and bead necklets. The children run barefoot. A bobbery pack of dogs chase one another round a large, heaped midden. The day is hot and the land is dry – drier than I have seen it before. It tells of a different climate, temperate and benign. Women are carrying water from the spring-fed burn beside the loch. Yokes span their shoulders and leather buckets hang on either side. I see more huts up in that direction. Other women are returning from the woods bowed beneath huge bundles of sticks strapped to their backs.

Looking round, I see that the land is densely wooded. Right across the valley the slopes are quilted with the broad green crowns of sessile oak and tall, spreading wych elms. Hazel thickets surround the little loch. A few pines crowd the skyline in a long, dark fringe. The green clearings are small and these tidy people have planted crops and built hazel and dry-stone enclosures for their animals. The sky is cloudless. The river is shallow and quiet; no spume rises from the falls. A number of skin-clad coracles are hauled out on the bank and one or two more lie in the water. Boys with three-pronged fish spears are lined across the shallow river in a barricade. They are spearing salmon in the first run upriver to spawn. In the settlements there is a sense of order and industry; all around the land is wild.

At my feet I see that the fort is no longer a ruin. Stout whinstone walls enclose me to what would be chest height if I were standing, and at the east, overlooking the village below, it is higher still with narrow openings through which one might shoot arrows or hurl a spear. Behind me is an entrance through which only one man could pass at a time. It doesn't look as though it has been used for a while. I get the feeling that times are good.

There is a commotion in the village. People are dropping their implements and running to Luncheon Rock. From the woods blanketing the slopes up to Bad a' Chlamhain three men are approaching. One carries a long spear and is limping. Drying blood stains his bare leg. Two of them are carrying on their shoulders a dead animal on a pole. It looks heavy. I see that it is a wild boar. Its head hangs down. Its mouth is open and long bright tushes curve from its jaw. The villagers are excited and run to meet the trio. Salmon and boar. Tonight there will be feasting.

As I watch the night fires die and the people, happy with ale brewed from *bere*, their wild barley, drift into their huts. A single sentry with his spear and his dogs is left standing alone on Luncheon Rock. Times may be good, but not so good that they can sleep unguarded. When harvests fail, starving raiders will come from over the mountain to loot and pillage. The sentry also has a fire and he stokes it with a pine branch so that a crackle of sparks fills the air. Night encloses the land. To my surprise, crickets grate loudly from the undergrowth. The wild fluting of common cranes rises from the broad marsh where Bella's fields should be. I am in a strange land; a land I have never known. A bloodshot moon rises serenely from the forest like a hot-air balloon. As she clears the trees (surely the moon is feminine?), ascending majestically from the wispy cloud, calm and cool, she polishes the trees and the river with her old, bewitching patina.

Quite suddenly a chill runs through my whole body. Goose pimples rise like a mayfly hatch. Barney throws up his head. He shifts his weight uneasily from one rear quarter to the other. I feel a shudder pass through his flanks like the wind over the loch. What we have both heard has set our neocortexes singing. It is a sound instantly burned into our amygdalae, there for good – if Barney has an amygdala, that is. It comes again. This time not one but a whole pack of wolves are pointing their muzzles to the moon and howling that primordial utterance of the forest. The dogs in the Bronze Age village bark frantically. And then, one by one, they howl, too, their long genes tugging at the leashes of domestication. An incongruous cacophony of wild stirrings, rising and falling, answering one another like some primeval fugue, echoes throughout the whole glen. It is the song of wilderness.

This is the wild Aigas of long, long ago. The forest around me is the Great Wood of Caledon. As the climate dampens and cools, pine and birch will come to dominate; wide glades of sessile oak will close in. With axe and fire people will systematically clear it away. It is a passing image, but one that fired the imagination of Fraser Darling as surely as it has my own. I know that out there in these mixed forests of oak, gean, holly, aspen, birch, rowan and pine, along with the wolves and wild boar, there are also brown bears and lynxes. *Alces*, the towering moose with his prehistoric humped shoulders and massive antlers, is stalking the willow scrub that spreads high into the hills. Far upstream, beavers are damming the minor tributaries of the river. And there are a few scattered groups of red deer – not, as I have known them, grazing the open heather hills in artificially large herds, but strong forest deer carrying the heavily pointed antlers of mineral-rich feed and ample winter browse and shelter. Constantly alert to the presence of wolves, the elegant roe deer are there, too. In the high mountains reindeer furrow the last winter snowfields for moss. So strange to me is this ancient wilderness that I almost expect *Smilodon* to lunge his sabres at us from the willows at any moment, or the woolly mammoth or rhinoceros of the Lascaux cave paintings to come lumbering past.

Like Thoreau on Mount Katahdin, I feel out of place. It is a world as beautiful as it is strange and savage; a world to which, for all my yearning and my years of watching and listening, I do not belong. In the wolf's howl and the fluting of the cranes I can locate the wildness my soul has craved ever since Old Bob first took me to a fox's earth deep in an English wood, and made me kneel at the damp entrance to breathe its rank pungence. But it is a private fantasy more appropriate to a dream than anything I have ever experienced here at Aigas, just as it was an intellectual experiment for Thoreau, who ultimately returned to 'civilised' Concorde and to manufacturing pencils.

I came too late to these hills. The Great Wood of Caledon was gone aeons before I, with my Vibrum soles and Zeiss binoculars, arrived to prise relict truths from the acidity of its vanquished soils. But I cannot be denied the reality of the sensation. It is personal and private and precious, like a passion for music or art. It is a random association of genes touched with the long history of our species, ever present, but, for most people, denied by the realities of our daily lives. It is an echo, dim, distant and alluring. It is Whitman's 'song of the rolling earth', Gavin Maxwell's 'look long at the earth as it was before we tampered with it'.

When I next looked out over the valley I seemed to be back in Muddus or Padjelanta. A sub-arctic tundra surrounded me. The Iron Age fort was gone and Barney and I stood upon a bare rock promontory. The air was chill and damp. The earth, I concluded, had ellipsed away from the sun on its long cycle. There were no men or women here. No houses, no settlements, no wood smoke, no clearings. No livestock grazed the empty moor. The forest was thin and low, mostly scrub birch. Bog and lichen heath spread back up the hill behind me and large patches of snow lay in the hollows. Wild geese circled over a river as yet unrecognisable. Gone were the alder swamps and the flood plain was raw and swept with long bars of shingle and gravel. The geese landed here and stood clamouring quietly to themselves, unsettled and nervous. At the gorge, narrow now, the river surged rowdily through huge boulders and slabs of rock split and levered from the wet walls by frost. The plaintive cries of golden plovers pierced the air as they passed overhead. A mountain hare, as white as the snow patch it had just left, scampered down through the rocks. A buzzard's shrill cry scythed through my brain.

What I am witnessing in this immediately post-glacial landscape is the gradual building of an ecosystem, called succession by biologists. The glacier has gone. It has melted its last green floodwaters from the high corries of the Affric Hills. It has shifted mountains into the sea. Its crushing and grinding authority has freed up a billion opportunities. I have arrived in an era of frantic colonisation. Wildlife is walking, flying and crawling in from further south. Niches are filling. Systems are loading. Plants are creating soil and building carbohydrate to feed the future. Fertility is expanding by the hour. But I can see no real climax. The pinewoods of the future are only very slowly spilling outwards, sowing the wind with their grand ambitions. The geese will nest here, as will the cranes and the wild whooper swans, in the rushy swamps and bogs of sedge and cotton grass. In the fullness of time – and there is plenty of that – they will depart northwards for land at this moment still locked in ice.

On the bare rock beneath Barney's hooves I can see the terrible striations of the glacier's wings, like a tawny owl's imprint in the snow. Hundreds of feet thick, the trailing ice cap scoured over this high spur carting great schist boulders from higher up the valley. Its colossal mass ground into this bedrock as it dragged its debris through and down, pulverising and polishing. As it melted and washed out, so the fine deposits of sand and gravel streamed down the hill and spread across the flood plain in broad fans. All of this will go. Nature has begun its tireless processes of filling in and covering up. The river will flood and recede and flood again a hundred thousand times. It will gift its silt to wide marshes; bright meadows will photosynthesise beneath the splendid, silent sun. Ravening clouds will surge and churn. The seasons will dance to the earth's old tunes. The inexorable cycles of decay and the invisible mystery of bacteria churning through the mucus of everything that chews and excretes will roll out the timeless spell of creation. 'Teach the children about the cycles,' said Gary Snyder in *Axe Handles*. 'The life cycles. All the other cycles. That's what it's all about, and it's all forgot.' We do, we do. We do our very best.

In the lumpy process of waking I suddenly remember my half-sleep of the broken night. I lie and clutch at fragmenting images, reluctant to let them go. It is ten to six – that's late for me. I stagger downstairs and slide the kettle on to the Aga. While it boils I tip Ruff and Tumble, the two rumbustious Jack Russells, out into the bright morning. They rush to sign their presence on the same old corner of the hen run. I smile and shake my head. Why, when they are busting to empty their bladders, must it be done there, just so? They know nothing of genes or the ramifications of their long journey from the wolf. It's the insight conundrum all over again. We are all, as Darwin came so close to fathoming and as Fraser Darling so eloquently insisted, 'born with our complement of genes and grow with the accidents of our environment'.

Somewhere high above the forest a raven croaks his guttural oath and from an ornamental cherry tree beside the newly mown lawn a song thrush is warbling its genetic heritage as rich as plum duff. Together they represent the perpetual paradox of this beautiful place, the wild and the tamed, which has framed my life for so long. A gang of swifts whirls round the tower in a mindless tornado of rushing wings. They rocket away over the valley, their metallic screams rending the morning air. I see that yesterday we had had a delivery of fencing rails from the sawmill. I love the tangy scent of freshly sawn larch. The rangers will be pleased. They are keen to build some steps into one of the woodland trails. Today I must go up to the pinewood and see how they are getting on. There is so much to be done.

EPILOGUE

I do not know what I may appear to the world, but to myself
I seem to have been only a boy playing on the sea's shore,
and diverting myself in finding now and then a smoother
pebble or a prettier shell than ordinary, whilst the great
ocean of truth lay all undiscovered before me.

SIR ISAAC NEWTON, 1642–1727

It's Saturday again. Meeting and greeting. I enjoy this. A coach-load
of surprises, just in. I look around the room. It's exciting, like getting
a new hand at poker – you never know what's going to turn up. The
field centre staff are busy checking lists and rooms and sorting
luggage. I move quietly around glancing at name badges: a name, a
city and an abbreviation. There are thirty of them, mostly from
Georgia and Texas, one or two from Mississippi: GA, TX and MI. All
from the Deep South. And an LA. I struggle for a moment. What's
LA? I should know them all, of course, but I don't see LA too often.

'Well, hallo,' drawls the LA lady with an eager handshake. 'I am so pleased to be here.' She drags the 'am' to 'ay-am' and the 'here' to 'hey-er', somehow finding an extra syllable to tack on to each. I smile. It attracts me. I find myself wondering how it ever started. Which English dialect swept off to the humid South two hundred years ago and sprouted extra syllables like the elk growing bigger antlers than the red deer left in Europe? Of course, I think to myself – Louisiana.

It's Ark and Anth this week. We have our own codes at Aigas. Archaeology and Anthropology in the Highlands and Islands. I long to talk to them about Machu Picchu. Many will have been there. I have never made it – one day perhaps. Highland archaeology is draughtier than Peru's, but just as good, especially in Orkney, where we take them next week. Skara Brae might not have quite the same ring as Machu Picchu, but it's every bit as real, a whole village abandoned by its people for no known reason and slowly filled in by sand, five thousand years ago. There it lay, like Pompeii, until a savage storm exposed it in 1925. Every room intact, furniture in place, beds, stone dressers, even the drains. And, a few miles up the island, Maes Howe, the domed Bronze Age tomb the Vikings called Orkahaug (Orkney house). The Vikings broke into it in 1153 and signed their theft in ribald runes on the walls. 'Ingibiorg the fair widow – many a woman walked stooping in here.' 'Orkis son says in the runes he carves treasure is here hidden very well.'

I feel a warm glow of pride. This Aigas programme has been successful for many years. I know they will love it.

A big man in a denim jacket grips my hand. His name badge says Jim McColl from Houston. He doesn't let go. I feel as though I have been press-ganged, just taken the king's shilling by mistake and that he's about to haul me off somewhere. He's well over six feet and, I reckon, twice the weight of his wife. The truth is I'm just not very good at being tied down. I wish Lucy were here to rescue me. 'Hi, Jarn.' He rolls out his words like laying a carpet. 'Good t' meet-cher. Now tell me, what are y' selling here, Jarn?'

'Selling?' I reply cautiously, feeling a bit like a street vendor caught stuffing something through his letterbox. I wasn't ready for that question. 'I'm not sure we're really *selling* anything much. We certainly offer ourselves to the wide world. Aigas is just an opportunity to stay in a special place and learn about the Highlands.'

'OK. So what's your product?' he demands with an impatient wave of a hand. He lets go of me at last.

'Well, we haven't really got a product as such . . .' I begin.

He cuts me off. 'Y' *have* to have a product. Everybody in business has a product.' He sounds exasperated. He insists, 'Y' have to have a *market* and a *brand* and a *product*,' adding with final gusto, 'and if you ain't got 'em you ain't gonna survive.'

'Oh dear,' I murmur, thinking back over a quarter of a century of happy survival.

He comes closer, fixing me with steely eyes from behind rimless glasses and invading my critical distance so that I lean back on to my heels. 'I'm your market and your brand is Aigas. That'll do fine. Now all y' have to do is sell me your product. I need to know what your product is.'

'Hmmm. I'll tell you what. Wait until the end of your programme and then you let me know what our product is. How's that?'

'That's the durndest way of doing business I ever knew.' He laughs loudly. 'D' y' hear that, hun?' He beams at his wife. His whole frame ripples with wavelets from his cheeks down to his belt, where they come ashore and fizzle out against the braided leather and the big brass buckle with longhorn steers on it.

The programme goes well. God is kind and the July weather is bountiful. As we fly in to Orkney the islands are laid out below us like lily leaves on a pond of brilliant tropical blue. Big Jim McColl turns out to be a real trouper, full of fun and genuine concern for the others. He helps them on and off the old Orkney bus; he rounds them up and laughs and jokes with them all day. Everyone likes him. He's an asset. I discover that his company makes air conditioners – much needed in Houston – and that he is a highly successful businessman. With crushing pathos I also discover from another Texan in the group that Jim and Ella McColl lost their only son and his wife in a light aircraft crash only six years before. I fancy I can see it now, behind the rimless glasses, a haunting sadness like a shadow, there one minute and then swept away by the rippling laugh. His wife had told my informant that their way of coping with it was to live every day as though it were their last.

We return to Aigas. As the days ticked by I forgot about their arrival and all that product business. Orkney was a resounding success. They have all become real people, living real lives, right here, right now. They have touched the Aigas place and it has opened up to them in its inimitable, revealing way, which has framed our days and our lives for so long. We hold a farewell dinner for them, and Hamish, home from school for a weekend, pipes them in to the great hall to 'Cock o' the North'.

After dinner we assemble in the drawing room to say our farewells. They are off early in the morning. The whole pro-gramme has gone well. We are sad to see them leave. In the space of just two weeks they have ceased to be guests and become friends. Suddenly big Jim is right there. He looms over me, shak-ing my hand again like a physiotherapy session for a stiff wrist. This time I know it's real. 'Jarn, I've got your *product*!' he exclaims triumphantly as though he has just found my mother's gold watch.

'Oh good!' I smile, only just remembering what he's talking about. 'What is it?' He's got me interested now.

'Insight! That's what it is, Jarn. It's Insight.'

'So it is,' I say, still smiling.